Chicken Coop Pinky Swear

The Impossible Promise of a Century

By Peter Andrew Meerwarth

ISBN: 979-8-89109-086-6 - paperback

ISBN: 979-8-89109-085-9 - ebook

This book is dedicated to Nora and Samuel Telford to celebrate their 100th wedding anniversary. It was my privilege growing up in White Creek on the farm they purchased.

Acknowledgments

I owe a debt of gratitude…

To my family, Jan, Isaac, and Sam, the ones who have heard me ramble on and on for 20 years about writing this book. I love you all so much.

To Andrew Biernat at Selfpublishing.com for guiding me through the writing and publishing process and entertaining my every question

To Wayne Purdin-my detailed editor and Phylis Benoit-my beta editor.

To David Weeks-a writer who has supported me with his guidance and undying friendship. I truly appreciate you.

To Samuel Dewey Telford for keeping his diaries so faithfully and to Nora for preserving them and taking such wonderful photos that captured the early 1920's… and for safely storing such personal material for so many years!

To Elizabeth Howard for finding your essay book from 1923 when you were Nora's student and giving it to her on her 80th birthday.

Julia Rae Niles for being such a good niece and friend to Grandma Nora and for writing out your life story for us.

To all the good folks back in beautiful White Creek, start keeping a diary, it may be part of a beautiful story someday.

Table of Contents

Prologue

Award winning Steve Hartman, CBS Correspondent, brought a childlike sense of wonder to his feature stories about ordinary Americans in *Everybody Has a Story.* Each week, he would throw a dart at a map of the United States, pick a random name out of the phone book, and then transform a cold call to that person into a heart-warming parable for all of us. I see the same potential for striking a deep emotional chord in the untold stories of those we acknowledge with cemetery headstones. This book unearthed a love story from just one headstone with two names on it. I can't imagine what stories lie beneath the other millions of headstones across the United States. This book is one such wonderful story that Grandma took to her grave but left behind for us to find.

If there was one person I admired on this planet, it was my good-natured, hardworking, unassuming grandmother, Nora Andrew. We always called her "Grandma," as did almost everyone else who knew her. Born in 1902, I can't imagine all the things that she experienced in her lifetime: medical breakthroughs, pandemics, wars, inventions, and sweeping advances in technology. She rode on horses and trolleys, then automobiles and airplanes and eventually she saw rockets landing on the moon guided by computers. During the first five years of her life, tea bags, corn flakes, instant coffee, and Lifesaver candy were all invented; Susan B. Anthony died; and Oklahoma became a state. By the time she left this earth, Grandma had lived through 16 presidents.

Grandma was a Greatest Generation, Teetotaling, hard worker. She was wise, generous when she didn't have to be, and quite thrifty the rest of the time. She baked everything from scratch, washed her tin foil, reused glass jars, and fed all of her kitchen scraps to the cows. She certainly knew how to make do. She even mowed her huge lawn with a push mower until the grandkids were old enough to mow it for her. She loved to dress up to go out. Every time she got in her car, she made a point to look her best. She was only 4'11" and drove her car everywhere she went with the seat all the way forward, propped up on pillows and still looked through the steering wheel.

People always spoke well of Grandma and had a lot of respect for her. Faithful in attending her White Creek Church, Grandma was often found baking pies for fundraisers and helping plan events held at Jermain Hall just over the Little White Creek and around the corner from the church. She also loved baking treats and entertaining guests at her dining room table featuring a vase of her homegrown gladiolas and delicious treasures from her garden.

As a very young boy, I remember playing at her house often and doing my best not to be a nuisance. A very tall "old" lady with thick "coke bottle" glasses, named Julia, stopped by as she often did. On this particular day, they took out two large maroon photo albums from the cherry cabinet in the living room. They had them spread out across the entire dining room table and were labeling the very old photos with names and dates and places to the best of their ability. The curled and cracked black and white and sepia photos smelled dry and musty and were of no interest to my young eyes. They were laughing and talking and digging deep into their memories all morning. I slowly approached the table and watched for a while.

"What are you two doing?" I asked.

Grandma replied, "Writing things down so we don't forget because our memories aren't what they used to be! Are they, Julia?" The two laughed.

"But why?" I pushed. "Who's it for?"

"Aunt Nora, I'll let you answer that one," said Julia.

"It's for posterity," she told me after searching for the right words. Silence.

"Who's Posperity?" I asked, and the ladies laughed together some more.

***

Sometimes, I visited and browsed through the color photos in her beige photo album that sat on a side table for all to enjoy; just one photo album that documented most of her life. We weren't allowed to look in the drawers of the cherry cabinet unless it was to get the dominos out. Sadly, she passed in 1995. About 5 years later my parents gave me a box of items that had been hidden away in that cabinet for all those years.

I admired Grandma so much that I sat right down with that box and took an inventory of what was there; a student's composition book from 1923, 5 dairies from 1921-1925 that belonged to someone named Samuel D. Telford, those 2 maroon photo albums that I only ever saw that one time as a kid, a number of newspaper clippings and several old, framed photos. One hundred years have passed since those diaries were written and this book is the story that was unearthed from the items in that box; a love story from the Roaring Twenties, which, over the decades, had been forgotten until now.

1

Five Foot Two, Eyes of Blue

Nora Andrew wasn't one to drift off, but she was hot and sticking to her chair in history class on this first day of her senior year in the small northeast town of Hoosick Falls, New York. She had no reason to pay attention, which was good because all she could do was think about leaving for Normal School in Oneonta, New York the next day. In place of their senior year, Nora and her best friend, Leah Harrington, were selected to receive teacher training in Oneonta, New York with the plan return and teach at one of their hometown White Creek one-room school houses after their High School/Normal School graduation. They both knew that they had to be academically qualified to teach, but the school board chose them based on their conservative morals.

It was early September of 1920 and the sun shone brightly this humid Thursday afternoon and the rolling countryside of sprawling corn and hay fields looked as though a Grandma Moses painting had come to life. And it was here, in White Creek, that Nora's hopes and dreams would come to fruition: to become a teacher in her own school house, marry a strong, handsome farmer, raise their children, and make a good name for themselves. Farming was quite lucrative in those days, and she was feeling empowered, as women had just earned the right to vote. Although, some of the influential local ladies viewed her as being a liberated woman, as she would be working outside of the home. Nora and everyone else called this group the Biddie Bunch.

Nora was enjoying her view from the 4th floor window but as much as she loved school, she missed being able to go to the "White Crikk" swimming hole with Leah and her friend, Verna, on hot humid days like today. She gazed south out the large window at the vast mountains, toward the Berkshires, beyond the charming town with its brick main street buildings and Victorian homes. She imagined the freedom of walking in the cooler forested hillsides whose canopy blocked out the sun. *Anywhere would be better than being stuck inside on a sticky day like today.*

She had butterflies in her stomach thinking about all that had to happen before she left for Oneonta. She and Leah would be boarding at Mrs. Hovey's House, a grand old Victorian, with several other female students. She and Leah would leave on the 6:30 am train to Troy, and then another to Albany, and then onward westwardly to Oneonta. The trip was over 100 miles, and she couldn't wait. *Why must I endure a mandated first day at the high school?* She and Leah were both frustrated and sighing heavily all during what seemed to be the longest final period in the history of school days ever recorded.

Her mind wandered until the final bell when she could catch the trolley to North Hoosick to be collected by her older brother, Henry, who would be driving the buckboard for the ride home. Henry was a loveable, gentle giant but quite loud and not the sharpest nail in the bucket, but he was strong and silent, protective, and worked harder than anyone she knew. He was definitely born with issues that affected his mind. Nora wondered what was happening back home on the farm, nestled in the beautiful foothills of the Green Mountains of Vermont.

The Andrew farm, just like all the other White Creek family farms from Dr. Post's Corners to Black Hole Hollow, kept the family busy with everyday chores and projects. Seth Andrew, Nora's father, was standing at the woodfired stove stirring a large boiling pot.

"Henry, sift me another 10 cups. I'm going to start another batch." Henry's face remained rather deadpan, but he did as he was told and deliberately placed the tin measuring cup and the flour sifter into his bucket and headed toward the fireplace. As he began to sift the ashes in the fireplace, Mother, Ida, walked through the living room taking a break to stretch her back from the turning the wash all afternoon,

"Henry, you best hurry along with that. Nora will be done with school soon; is that my flour sifter?" asked Ida. Henry simply kept scooping and sifting and measuring. "Seth, do you know he's using my flour sifter?"

"Who do you think gave it to him?" replied Seth.

"You'll have to go to the Creek to buy me a new one if it gets ruined," said Ida matter-of-factly.

"Come here and look at this batch," beckoned Seth.

Ida peered intently into the pot Seth was stirring and said, "Looks like it'll be a fine batch if you don't gum it up."

"Mother! Well, aren't you your usual bright ray of sunshine today?" This batch is from that willow tree we burned last winter. Never tried making soap from willow tree ashes. It threw good heat last winter. I'm glad we have poor housekeeping around here and we never cleaned out the fireplace."

"I do miss that tree," said Ida ignoring Seth.

"It was kind of perfect on the corner there." Henry chimed in loudly, "One hundred fitty-two."

"Yep. Henry counted 152 rings on that tree," said Seth.

Ida chimed in, "152 years that tree stood there, and what gave you the right to cut it down? Hmmm?"

"It was either chop it down or it'd fall down over the road," countered Seth.

Ida ignored him, took an egg from the windowsill, and handed it to him. "Here, make sure this floats before you take it off the heat and not a minute sooner. You took it off too soon the last time."

Seth, grinned and said loud enough for Henry to hear, "I'm certain that willow tree wood is hard enough to make good soap ashes, cuz we certainly had a tough enough time splitting it, right Henry?"

Henry didn't say anything but remembered that he and Ray split all of the wood, hauled it, and tossed it into the basement through the opening in the foundation all by themselves with no father in sight. And just to rub salt in their wound, Seth was taking a nap in the middle of the afternoon while they were tossing the wood into the basement. He and Ray worked themselves up into a lather regarding the unfairness of having to cut and split the wood by themselves and Henry "accidentally" tossed a chunk of wood right through Seth's first floor bedroom window, which was located right above the foundation opening. Seth yelled at Henry, who just shrugged his shoulders.

Now, as Henry scooped the ashes out of the fireplace, he remembered how mad his father was and was relieved to know Seth could make a joke about it. Seth was a good father, but suffered from insomnia and could often take to his bed when he was depressed and couldn't sleep at night. You never really knew how Seth was going to show up from day to day, depending on how well or poorly he slept. When he got sleep, he was just fine.

Ida wiped her hands on her apron and stepped into the living room, "I'll take over here," she told Henry.

"You go fetch Nora," Seth added. "We got that load of apples on the buckboard so go easy. We don't want 'em all bruised up before we barrel 'em up to sell." Henry left obligingly. "Damnit!" exclaimed Seth. "I took it off the heat too soon."

Ida piously replied, "If you had done it the way I do it, you wouldn't a gummed it up."

There was a bunch of banging pots and swearing, and Ida heard him angrily say under his breath, "Few things are harder to put up with than the annoyance of a good example." Seth was fond of Mark Twain and frequently quoted him.

It was just about that time that Ray entered the house dripping with sweat, poured himself a large mason jar full of water, and guzzled it.

"Good Lord!" said Ida to Ray. "Look at how red your cheeks are!"

"Do you think you picked a hot enough day to make soap? It's hot in here!" He guzzled some more water. "I finished picking the first row of trees on the hill."

Seth said, "With all the rain we had last month, apples won't fetch a great price this year."

They won't be tasty," Ida called from the fireplace.

"Just go slow when you barrel 'em up," Seth continued. "Here, Ray, fetch me 2 gallons more of rainwater, would ya? And don't drag your feet. It's almost chore time."

As Ray headed out to the rain barrel, Henry, reins in hand, made his giddyap, double click noise in his right check to get Maude to start forward and they pulled out of the yard to the clomp, clomp, clomp of Maude's hooves and down the gravel road that Maude knew so well. The animals from the side yard came running to watch Maude proudly trot past them. Without any command, Maude knew to navigate gently over the deep gullies at the bottom of the hill where the road had been washed out. If she went too fast, she'd toss Henry right off the buckboard. She knew to stop at the double 3-way and then proceed carefully on to North Hoosick past the White Crikk swimmin' hole to collect Nora at the end of the trolley line. Maude was the family favorite. She most likely could trot to North Hoosick and pick up Nora all on her own.

Henry had arrived at Hathaway's Hotel early so he could say hello to the stable manager, Mr. Dunfey, and water Maude at the trough, as it was such a hot day. He then pulled around and parked near the front and try to eavesdrop on the conversations of the hotel guests while he was waiting for Nora to get off the trolley which ran from North Hoosick all the way down to the 4-story high school in the middle of Hoosick Falls and back several times a day. Nora was well-liked, shy, quiet and barely 5 feet tall; quite a contrast to Henry's loud, large, strapping 6' frame. Henry kept a close eye on Maude who disliked the Model T's that invaded her space as they raced past. Autos were becoming more and more a regular sight in this part of the world and the horses didn't like it one bit.

Henry sat and watched the hotel guests enjoying the bustle of the town from their second-floor porch and often wondered what it would be like to be a traveler. To Henry, the Hathaway Hotel was as close as he'd get to a highfalutin lifestyle. He had heard that there was a stage and dance hall on the top floor but had never been invited to any dances there. He could hardly speak in the presence of a girl. As usual, Mr. Hathaway had pulled his magazine rack out onto the front porch with the latest popular editions. Henry gave the covers a once over from his buckboard and couldn't decide which he liked more; the covers featuring the latest Model T's or the covers featuring Flappers and Gibson girls.

The trolley announced itself with a familiar ding-ding, which stopped Henry from gawking at the magazine rack. Soon, it stopped, and students were hopping off and headed in all directions; some walked home in small groups, most went toward the Hotel where they could buy candy and then go to their parents who were waiting to collect them from the long day at school.

Nora stepped off the trolley with her books and smiled at Henry. On her way to join him, Nora eyed the magazine rack as well. Magazines seemed to connect her to the world beyond White Creek and intrigued her so. She knew that during the war, many women left their homes to work outside of the home, which had been unheard of. But with their husbands gone, who else was going to take over their jobs? The war was over now, and many women still wanted to work. Teaching was just about the only respectable job for a single woman in White Creek, which was exactly what Nora planned to do. She wanted to be viewed as a mildly liberated woman but wasn't sure that she liked all the trimmings that came with that term.

Many of the magazines appeared to be risqué to Nora's tastes, but she did love some of the clothes and hair styles. It was just a year ago that the 19th Amendment passed, giving women the right to vote, which Nora embraced wholeheartedly. And then, along with that, came all kinds of talk about birth control sparked by the work of Margaret Sanger. Nora could see the benefits of female birth control but wasn't sure what she actually thought about it. All she knew was that it would not go over well with the conservative views of her upbringing…at least not without a challenge!

"Hello, Henry," said Nora with a smile as she climbed aboard. He lifted his head and smiled back and sadly realized that this would probably be the last time he would collect Nora from school, as she was heading off to Oneonta. He had been carrying her to and from high school each day for 3 years. "So, give me a full report on everything that's going on at home today."

Henry preferred silence over conversation, but Nora encouraged him to speak nonetheless, even though he could be very loud at times. She was patient and knew that his speaking would never improve unless he learned to get comfortable doing so. She knew that he understood what was being said, but he couldn't make his mouth work fast enough to get his words out, and when he did speak, it was often too loud for some reason. So, he often just listened. He told her about Ray picking apples and Father making soap.

"Soap! On a hot day like today!? My lands, there are some things better left 'til January. The candles in the cupboard will melt!" They both shook their heads.

After they passed the cornfields on the flat, and then the piece of road that followed the Crikk, they came upon the double 3-way. Maude stopped automatically but waited for Henry's signal to move forward. "Henry? Let's go. I've got to pack my things for my trip tomorrow. I don't think we have time for you to head over to see Elizabeth!" said Nora nodding her head to the right. Henry's face turned red. He moved Maude forward to the second 3-way.

Henry pointed up the hill to the west. "Sammie told me that they had 3 calves born yesterday."

"That's a lot for one day," said Nora.

"Should we go see? Sammie might be there."

Nora gave Henry a slanted look. "And why do you think I would want to see Sammie Telford?" Her face turned a little red, for she was stuck on him.

"To say goodbye. You two are always talking after church." Henry was trying to embarrass her, but Nora would have none of it.

"Well, since we seem to have so much time on our hands, maybe we should head over and visit Elizabeth Cottrell?"

Henry's eyes got big. He and Elizabeth both had cognitive challenges. They didn't do well conversationally, but they enjoyed being together; meaning, they skipped the small talk and moved directly into hugging and kissing whenever they were together. They needed to be watched every minute.

"Or how about we just go straight up the road ta home?" Nora didn't wait for his reaction, took the reins from him, made the giddyap double click sound in her cheek and faithful Maude clomp-clomp-clomped up the road toward home. Of course, Maude needed no reminding to slow down as she came to the spot where the rainwater regularly washed over the road and left dangerously deep ruts. Nora always knew that she was in good hands with Maude.

Nora had kept a distant eye on Sammie for about a year now. She was organized and had her life planned out. He was one of the few who met her qualifications and checked a lot of her boxes: he was a hard worker, he went through school, he was from a successful farm family, his family went to church, his parents were the type of farmers who took care of their farm ground and were wise and friendly enough, plus he was tall, dark, and devilishly handsome. But girls her age weren't "allowed" to court older men just yet. Sammie was 4 years older than her. She had to wait until her high school graduation before dating was acceptable. Even in this emerging age of working women and female independence, she didn't want to go against the grain too much and risk earning herself a reputation that was less than respectable. Nothing like that was about to happen. On the down side, he was a whole foot taller than her, his older brother Will was to take over the family farm, so there was no secure future for Sammie, which was a major concern for her. She was all about making a good name for herself and was certainly not ready to be the center of the Biddie Bunch gossip. She knew she was idealistic, but she was quite happy enough with that.

As Nora and Henry pulled into the yard, Ray was already out in the field, calling in the cows for milking,

"C'mbossy! C'mbossy!...C'mbossy! C'mbossy!" Henry called in the cows just like Seth had taught him, and Seth's father passed down how he learned to call cows. All proper White Crikkers had their own unique way of calling their cows. In the country of Sweden, farmers call their cows with a song passed down from the Middle Ages. It's called kulning. Cows like being milked, and they listen for their owners to call them in when it's time.

Nora shifted gears in her head toward feeding her animals. She jumped off the buckboard and caught her dress on that old side bolt that she'd gotten hung up on many times. *RRRippp!*

"Oh, heavens me! That's the third time that's happened. Mother will have my hide!" Nora skulked into the house to show Mother. "Why do men have to build things in such a way that they tear my clothes?" Ida pouted.

"Now, Nora, I've explained this to you before. Farms are not necessarily built with women and skirts in mind. You have to keep your knees tight together, gather up your skirt and tuck it up underneath and use that foot rest to *step* off the wagon; don't jump or that side bolt will catch your skirt every time. You're lucky it didn't tear the hide right off ya." Nora listened to the instructions, knowing every word of what was being said. "Now, take that off and I'll sew it up for ya tonight."

Nora trudged up the back stairs to her room and got her barn clothes on. She peered out her window briefly and took note that off in the distance, past the side yard, the dry cow pasture and the crop fields lined with stone, and just past the woods, she could see the roof of Sammie Telford's house. Then she popped back downstairs and put on her boots. She grabbed the kitchen scraps, thankful that it would be her last day of chores for a while and left them on the old stump for later. She then headed across the road to the barn where she took her two slop buckets off the shelf and whipped up a concoction of grain, soured milk, and a bit of corn into the pig buckets. She let that set for a bit.

"Here Kitty Kitty...Here Kitty Kitty," her voice swooped up high as she poured her feline friends a pan of milk. Once she saw that all 12 barn cats were accounted for, it was time to put her intricate feeding plan into action.

She lugged the two buckets of slop past the side yard and over to the hog house. Like clockwork, as soon as those 4 hogs heard their familiar pails clinking together, they started running from the side yard toward the hog house causing the geese and ducks to scatter noisily. At this time, the goats that had managed to get themselves inside the empty hay rack eyed Nora and started making their way toward the fence line. They knew that their treat would be coming over the fence soon enough. Ronna, a cow that gave a lot of milk, had fallen on the concrete and bruised her hip. She was going to calve any day now. She was glad to see Nora and started limping slowly to her section of the fence where she knew she would be fed. All the animals came a-running when it was feeding time. For the pig's sake, Nora chattered in her high voice, "Supper! Supper!"

Once Nora knew that the hogs were inside the shed and impatiently waiting at their trough, Nora put down the burdensome slop buckets, grabbed the tin of kitchen scraps off the stump and dumped it over the fence for the goats. Had the pigs known that there were kitchen scraps for the goats, the goats wouldn't stand a chance eating any supper at all. Nora talked to the hogs the entire time, telling them that she was coming in soon, and they believed her! They noisily paced around their trough inside their run-in hog shed. She then carefully fed the hogs in the hog house by pouring the first slop bucket into the trough and then the second. She watched the slop travel down the full length of the trough. She had to be careful because hogs can knock a grown-up right over if they're not careful. She told them to be nice to one another and not be so rude as they each tried to devour more slop than the others. She watched them for a while, scratched their backs a little with the great scratching stick she found. She didn't stay too long with them; even a well-seasoned farmer can't stand the smell of pig manure.

Once the pigs had started making their noise over their food, that seemed to set off a bevy of animal sounds all over the farm. The horses started whinnying and trotted into their run-in shed and stomped at the ground demanding to be fed. Nora talked to them softly as she grabbed their grain pails off the hooks and dumped 2 scoops of grain in each. "Now, now, just wait a moment. Mind your manners, please. Don't push so much. What's the matter with ya? Here, Maude, you take yours over here." And soon Maude and the Bay Team and the colts were all fed. When they were finished, Nora gathered up the empty buckets strewn all about. Maude came up to nuzzle her. "Hey there, Maude. What a good girl!" She scratched behind her ears and patted her nose.

Her last chore was to visit Momma Ronna back in the barnyard with some grain. Not only was Momma Ronna limping due to her fall, but, since she was freshening, her udder was engorged with milk and almost dragging on the ground which didn't make walking any easier. Momma Ronna was waiting as Nora slowly lowered the pail of grain down over the fence talking sweetly to the momma-to-be. With all of the other animals fed and satisfied, Nora knew that they'd leave Momma Ronna alone, and she would be able to eat her supper in peace. The barnyard had plenty of water from the spring, but Nora like to pump water into the water trough, so Momma Ronna didn't have to walk so far for a cool drink. Nora knew that it was appreciated. It was getting a bit cooler as the sun was setting behind the woods on the hill. Nora watched Momma Ronna dip her nose in the water and drink. Momma Ronna was appreciative.

Nora was always in a good mood after her chores. Fresh air was her cure for just about everything. She went inside and turned a load of laundry before washing the potatoes for dinner. Her Mother told her to leave the rest for her. She had ironed all of her dresses for her trip. There was still a half an hour before the men came in from the evening milking, Momma sent Nora to pack as much as she could before dinner.

Ida had prepared a special "last supper" with Nora in mind. She felt uneasy about sending off such a young girl into the "big city." Nora did love baked potatoes and especially the way her Mama cooked them a long time, and the bigger the better so, of course, those were already baking. The regular fare at the Andrew dinner table was completely produced by the farm except for the spices, sugar, and flour. Tonight's dinner was all of Nora's favorites: a tenderloin roast, biscuits, mashed onions, carrots, parsnips, baked potatoes, homemade apple pie with cinnamon or tapioca pudding for dessert, ice cold milk and cider from the cider mill in Post Corners, and plenty of homemade butter on everything.

Everyone was at the table and magically knew when it was time to hold hands for grace that Seth always said. "Bless us, O Lord, and these thy gifts, which we are about to receive, from thy bounty, through Christ, our Lord. Amen."

"Amen," they all said with a burst of energy reaching for the food.

"Take what's before you and pass it clockwise," was Ida's mantra. Henry always said it along with her.

As usual, Nora spoke up with the news that she heard that the Johnson's barn burned down the night before and they lost all of their horses. Henry's face saddened.

"Poor family," said Ida. "It's near impossible to come back after somethin' like that when yer just starting out."

Seth asked Nora, "Did they have fire insurance?" Nora shrugged. It was silent for a while.

Ray smirked, "Wouldn't have happened if they had lightning rods."

"Nonsense!" barked Seth. "You're telling me that tiny little rods atop my barn is gonna stand up against an all-powerful lightning bolt? Hogwash!" he said indignantly. "There will be a snake oil salesman coming along soon looking for you."

Nora had hoped that her topic of conversation would result in a leisurely debate about the taming of electricity, with her as the one with all the answers, but she bit her lip and remained silent at this point.

Ida changed the subject, "Old Man Chase finally passed last night... Mrs. Tuttle had a girl this mornin'."

Seth laughed, "Out with the old bastard and in with the new bastard!" The boys laughed.

Ida slapped Seth's arm, "Father!"

Nora said, "That poor Tuttle girl will be eating liver in no time." This time, they all laughed.

"Big day in White Creek!" added Ray.

"It's one thing when you've lived a full life, but White Creek has lost too many young ones," said Ida shaking her head. "First, scarlet fever, then the flu then consumption, pneumonia...then a war! What's gonna take us next?" It was silent for a bit. Ida continued, "Oh, I saw Mrs. Philpot at the Crikk Store earlier. She's got her hands full with the 3 boys who don't like their stepfather. She told me that things have not been going well at the farm since Fremont returned from France. The plan all along was to have Fremont take over the farm but it looks like Mr. Philpot is having an auction and selling the farm to someone else now." Everyone was incredulous.

"Now there's a nice 'thank you for your service,'" added Ray.

"Now this is not for advertisement, but Mrs. Philpot said that if her husband had given Fremont half the deal that he gave the Bennington buyers, Fremont would have bought it from him," Seth added,

"I'll have to look into giving Fremont some extra work. His father was a good man.

"It's terrible that we have nothing to fight against disease," said Ida angrily.

"The human race has one really effective weapon and that's laughter," quoted Seth from his favorite author. "So, try to find some humor in every situation."

Ida continued with a story she often told.

"I'll never forget that night when those three young Crikk boys had the fever. It was Fremont Meerwarth, Sears Reid, and Hank Bailey up in Pumpkinhook—"

"Cobb Town," inserted Henry.

Ida continued with the story she'd told so often before. "All three sick on the same night; they were just 13 or 14. You kids were all about the same age. They were the first to get scarlet fever. None of us knew what to expect. We were afraid we'd lose all three that night. What a horrible thing to go through—

"And in the morning, it was Fremont, the only one who survived the night," Seth added. "That shows he's got a good constitution to survive something like that,"

Ida said, "Those poor mothers. All good families. They were just wrong for such a tragedy. Horrible night. Who would be next?"

Seth added, "Well apparently, he's like a cat... he's got 9 lives! He survived the fever, got through the war, and survived his stepfather. And I know it's bad luck to speak ill of the dead, but Old Mr. Chase was an ass."

Ida didn't chastise Seth this time.

"So...," said Ida changing the subject, "in honor of Nora's last night with us, before she heads off to school, who wants apple pie?" All raised their hands. "Then you'd all better finish up those potatoes first! You know how much I dislike storing left-overs."

Seth turned to Henry and Ray, "After supper, how 'bout you boys help me barrel up the rest of those apples so I can take them down to the Falls tonight?" Henry nodded. "I hate to see my good apples turn into cider apples," added Seth.

"What do you think he'll end up doing?" asked Ray.

"Fremont's a good enough worker and has a good reputation in town. I'm sure he'll find a business endeavor to take on even after... all this, whether it be in White Creek or elsewhere. Times are good, I suppose he'll do just fine," said Seth.

As Ida served up the pie, she said, "Thank goodness we can buy sugar again. I don't have to go all the way to George Curtis's store. Apple pie was just not the same during the war with the sugar rations. He would always surprise me with a little bit extra. Nora, would you get the cheese from the ice box?"

As if on cue, Seth said, "Apple pie without cheese is like a hug without a squeeze. Right, Mother?"

"If you say so. That cheddar makes my jaw set up. It is not for me," said Ida.

***

Early Friday morning, Henry prepared Maude and loaded Nora's things onto the buckboard. Everyone said their goodbyes and they headed out down the Falls to catch the train. Only this morning, they just happened to meet up with Sammie Telford at the double 3-way. He was carrying cream from the morning milking on the back of the farm truck. Sammie was careful not to beep because the automobiles scared the horse. He pulled off to the side and put down the window to chat. Henry played it cool and pulled the buckboard up next to the truck.

"Why hello there. Where are you two headed?" Sammie asked, knowing full well that Nora was headed off to Oneonta Normal for the next few months.

"Gotta catch the train," blurted Henry.

"What's the news from your place?" asked Nora.

"Nothing much. Three heifer calves on Wednesday." Sammie answered with a bit of a smile, grateful to have an excuse to talk directly to Nora. "The Creamery price is good right now so I'm expecting to make my fortune with these 4 cans of milk!"

Nora laughed more than she should have. "You'll have to make quite a fortune if you're going to split it with your parents and your brothers."

"Who says I'm going to split it with anyone?" They all smiled. Sammie continued, "I'd offer to take you to the train myself but—"

Nora graciously jumped in, "Oh how the neighbors would talk to see me getting out of your truck so early in the morning!" They all got a chuckle out of that.

Sammie said, "I don't want you to miss your train. You better get going."

Nora added, "Good luck making your fortune!" And with that, Henry gave a gentle tap of the reins and Maude trotted down the road toward the Falls. Sammie headed up the lane past the Andrew farm toward the Creamery. Henry noticed that Nora was lost in thought for the rest of the ride. Upon arrival, they could see Leah already waiting at the station with her mother and father. As they pulled up, Nora protectively tucked her dress between her legs and gracefully *stepped* off the buckboard.

"Be glad you never have to wear a dress, Henry."

They smiled at each other.

"Behave!" he shouted and headed back toward home.

2

Mrs. Hovey's House

Once on the train, Nora and Leah's excitement could not be contained. They were both boarding at Mrs. Hovey's House located at 2 East Street.

"I can't imagine 14 girls in one house! Do you think they'll like us?" asked Nora.

"I don't see why not. They're no different than you or me," noted Leah as she pulled out her letter from the Oneonta Normal School and read, "As one of the northernmost cities of the Appalachian Region, Oneonta's nickname is 'City of the Hills.' The word 'oneonta' is believed to mean 'place of open rocks' in the Mohawk language"

Nora interjected, "I think there were Mohawk Indians in White Creek also."

Leah continued, "This refers to a prominent geological formation known as 'Table Rock' at the western end of the city not far from the Susquehanna River."

The girls were excited for their long trip and knew their parents would be relieved to hear word from them when they finally arrived. They made all their connections just fine and at 8:00 pm, they finally were collected by Mrs. Hovey at the Oneonta Station.

Upon arrival, they were escorted to their rooms and stayed up just about all night talking with their new roommates. Nora's roommate introduced herself with her heavy French accent, "Hello. I am Bernadette from Paris, France. It is nice to meet you."

"Paris? Nice to meet you. I am Nora from a farm in White Creek, New York."

"A farm?" And instantly, the country mouse and city mouse became fast friends with a million questions for the other." Mrs. Hovey was none too pleased with how late they stayed up chatting and chastised them insisting that they go to sleep. Nora whispered to Bernadette,

"We better do as she says."

Bernadette responded, "Bah! You walk this earth but once. We will never have a first night as roommates again!" Nora thought about that for a while.

Late the next morning, the house was buzzing with girls getting ready for their weekend, even though they had all stayed up much too late. Mrs. Hovey laid down her expectations for the kitchen, what the girls' duties were, and how clean everything was to be kept. At breakfast, Bernadette introduced herself to the group and humorously gave a brief history lesson.

"Ladies, perhaps you did not know that "normal school" from the French 'école normale' provides a model school with model classrooms to teach model teaching practices to its student teachers who look like models." All the girls laughed and thought that she did look like a model with clothes that were much more fashion forward than they had ever seen about town. She continued with her thick French accent, "We will all be learning in what some call a laboratory. So, if it's a laboratory, clearly the professors are the scientists and the children are the students, then who, pray tell, are considered to be the laboratory rats?" All the girls laughed even louder this time. Nora so admired Bernadette's courage to speak impromptu and make all the girls feel at ease. Mrs. Hovey thought, This crew is going to be a challenge! The girls all started asking Bernadette about her clothing.

Mrs. Hovey commented, "Every generation laughs at the old fashions but follows religiously the new!" but none of the girls paid any attention.

Once again, on Sunday night, the girls were all talking late into the evening even after lights out. Mrs. Hovey came through the upstairs listening for whispers.

Bernadette said, "I think that Mrs. Hovey takes her job much too seriously."

Nora thought for a bit, "True, but tomorrow we head to Old Main, and meet Principal Bugbee and get our schedules and find our way through 160 rooms. I'm sure we'd like to be rested for that."

Bernadette whispered, "You are the yin to my yang." Nora had no idea what that meant and assumed it was French for 'good night my new friend.'"

In White Creek, the fall went on with farmers helping each other harvest their corn. The Cottrells, the Dundases, and the Andrews combined forces covering the Telford corn ground quickly and then rotated farms until all was complete. The farms split the cost when the wagon broke down. That's just the way it was done, and harvest time was as much a social event as it was a commercial necessity to feed their animals or to sell and turn a profit.

As the fall progressed and left the trees bare, Nora worked hard at her studies, tried to learn French from Bernadette, and was required to speak up in class more than she was accustomed. Henry and Ray moved from helping Seth sell loads of apples and pumpkins to a thorough cleaning of all the pens, spreading manure, planting winter wheat, and cutting wood by hiring men who were down on their luck. Sammie missed talking to Nora at church to the sideways glances of the Biddie Bunch.

Nora invited Bernadette to come back to the farm for a much-needed Thanksgiving break. Leah and Nora and Bernadette had quite a day on the train back to the farm talking about boys, some of the ladies at church, and how carefree things seemed to be in Paris. Both Henry and Ray were google-eyed over Bernadette and could barely string together a coherent sentence around her. Nora had fun showing Bernadette how to feed the animals. Bernadette loved every minute of it after she got used to the smell of manure.

The day after Thanksgiving, Reverend Manning invited families to help decorate the Little White Creek Baptist Church, as the first Sunday of Advent was imminent. He knew his congregation was made up of busy farmers, so he always beckoned the congregation with, "many hands make light work." He reminded them that he was busy with a small farm also. As usual, those who could showed up to help, which included the Allens, Barbers, Boots, Mrs. Philpott and Reimer Meerwarth, Perrys, Telfords, Tuttles, and the Andrews with Bernadette in tow. Henry, Ray, and Fremont Meerwarth gathered running ground pine up in the woods on State Line Road after their Thanksgiving meal and now the women and Reimer Meerwarth were busy winding it together. Reimer had polio and for many years walked with two crutches, but now he needed a wheelchair and never made any bones about working with the women. He always did what he could. He loved feeling useful. He had the strongest arms in White Creek, or *Crikk*, as the locals pronounced it. Any job he could do seated, he would do it, whether it was sewing, milking, or husking corn.

The Meerwarth boys often helped out at the church but rarely attended services with their mother. Fremont, in particular, didn't care for preaching. It didn't matter any that in the1850s his grandfather paid $20 for a deed to a pew at the very same White Creek Baptist Church and he fell upon hard times and couldn't keep up with the taxes and the church took the pew back.

Fremont would say, "That's not church; that's business. Besides, Grandpa wasn't one to mince words. If the pastor went too long, he'd always tell him afterwards, 'No sinner is ever saved after the first 20 minutes of a sermon.'" Fremont connected with God in nature and thought that the true church was on its feet and not on its ass. He'd rather be out doing something and that's what he did. Both he and Reimer were born to be farmers.

On this decorating day after Thanksgiving, the older always paired up with the younger to give them experience for the next year. Little Rachel Boot always seemed to gravitate toward Nora, especially with Bernadette by Nora's side, Rachel felt like she was seated with royalty.

Nora explained how it usually took three to four vines wound together to satisfy Ida, who oversaw the garland each year. "And if there's a bare spot, just weave a short piece of ground pine in and *tada,* it's perfect!" Her explanations were as much for Bernadette as they were for Rachel.

Bernadette was in love with country life in White Creek. "I feel like I'm in a Currier and Ives card that has come to life," she said.

In addition to the garland-making group, one group was making wreaths, another was setting up the tree that was a little too large this year, so they had to cut a few of the branches off the back so that Marilyn Robinson had room enough to slide onto the bench to play the organ. And anyone who was left over was asked to decorate the tree. Though it was quite noisy, everyone seemed to be having a grand time when Ida asked Nora to run up to the attic to find a box of ribbons and ornaments that seemed to be missing from the decorations that came down earlier. Nora handed off her duties to Rachel and Bernadette, who were eager to show they could wind the ground pine and pass inspection on their own merits.

Up the narrow creaky stairs went Nora on her mission to find the box no one else had been able to find. She had thoroughly looked through the freezing attic with her candle lantern and had almost given up when she remembered that sometimes items were stored in the stair well up by the bell tower. So up another, even narrower, rickety staircase to the landing, and there was the box. She heard a cough up above. She had to investigate to see who was up in the bell tower. Much to her surprise, she found Sammie sitting on a bench looking to see who had discovered his hiding place.

"Sammie! What are you doing up here? You're going to catch your death of cold." Sammie smiled.

"Sometimes, the hubbub gets a little too crazy for me."

"I hear," said Nora laughing, "but I thought you would enjoy all that. You're not a stranger to being the center of attention."

They both chuckled and she joined him on the bench.

"Your mother wouldn't be happy knowing we were up here alone," warned Sammie.

"Well, what she doesn't know won't hurt her," Nora replied with a smile and her new sense of independence.

"So, you'll be heading off to Oneonta Normal again on Monday? You're always on the go!

"Well, I have my exams and then I'll be home for Christmas and most of January." Sammie took her hand. It was the first time he had touched her. His heart was pounding in his ears.

"I think it would be swell if you would be my squeeze." He had rehearsed that line so many times in his head. It sounded completely stupid out loud. Nora appreciated his effort and desperately wanted to oblige. But reason took hold, even though her heart was pounding. She put her tiny hand on his.

"You know, we've known each other ever since the beginning of time. You're busy with the farm, and I've got school. How about we don't ruffle any feathers and wait until I graduate in June before we move in that direction? I don't want to give the Biddie Bunch any reason to gossip about us!"

Sammie pondered for a moment. "I think that sounds like a good idea… but face it, we'll always get looks from those old biddies!" They both chuckled. She patted his knee.

"Would you like to help me carry that box down the stairs?" As they stood up, Nora paused and looked up into his big brown eyes. He leaned in, took her in his arms, and gave her a nice long kiss. She knew that they would make a great team no matter what they decided to do in the future. Nora patted his broad shoulders and sighed. Another kiss. "Let's get those decorations downstairs before Mother sends up a search party." Sammie picked up the box of decorations and down the rickety stairs they went to rejoin the bustling crowd below without any notice.

Nora couldn't wait to tell Bernadette about her first kiss. They told Leah all about what had happened in the bell tower on their trip back to Oneonta. Both Leah and Bernadette could tell that Nora had told Sammie to "wait" but that she had already fallen for him. The three wondered how many first kisses happened up in the church bell tower after Leah explained that Mason kissed her up there as well and how romantic the view was until she passed gas. The girls roared with laughter on the train. In the lunch car, the girls grilled Bernadette about what life in Paris was like and pictured themselves there. She then explained her voyage on the steam ship and why she came to the states.

"After the war, your president passed the Emergency Immigration Act allowing student-learners like me into your great country. My parents jumped at the chance to provide me with an American education." The girls were starting to gain a bit of understanding of how big, yet connected, the world was.

The girls' discussions went on and on. Leah and Nora were cut from the same cloth and understood the meaning of back-breaking farm work and housework, how the Biddie Bunch would not approve of young Nora cavorting with an older gentleman, and they shared the very conservative views of the Violet Club, which staunchly supported Prohibition. After Nora's sister Sarah's shotgun wedding, it fell to her to show the world that an Andrew could do things the "right" way. Bernadette just listened. During quieter moments, they gazed out the window and remarked at how beautiful the sprawling mountains central New York were, though they didn't quite live up to that of White Creek.

Bernadette had a worldlier perspective on things. She'd been drinking wine with her dinner and kissing boys since she was 13. She had quite a different perspective on boys and dating and wine that wasn't so restrictive. Her wish was that the girls wouldn't just follow rules but would live life with *zest*. Nora and Leah knew her views would not work in White Creek, however, they found Bernadette's outlook on life quite refreshing and less constraining. For the first, they understood a different culture and Bernadette felt like White Creek life was a fairytale where you literally spoke to the animals to the backdrop of beautiful sunsets over the mountains and rolling fields. Bernadette admired the satisfaction completing so much of the hard work that farm life presented.

The girls arrived back in beautiful Oneonta for their last two weeks of classes and then finals. Though Mrs. Hovey religiously locked the doors at 10:00 pm, Bernadette was often breaking curfew and either had to find someone to let her in or she climbed in through a window. Nora did her best to keep track of her. During their final week of testing, Bernadette convinced all of the girls from Mrs. Hovey's house to go to a speakeasy to dance to the new jazz music. At first, most of the girls objected, especially Nora who thought that they should be studying. But Bernadette convinced them that music was music. Dancing was dancing.

"For goodness' sake, the more things are forbidden, the more popular they become! Dancing is like taking the most fun exercise you've ever had. We walk this earth but once!" The girls bought it and off they went. They so desperately needed a break from their studying. And even Nora and Leah tangoed and Charlestoned the night away. They were too shy to dance with other boys, so they danced together as did others from the Hovey House, much to the enjoyment of the onlookers. It was the first "best night" of Nora's life. She so wished Sammie was there with her, although she doubted she could ever get him to dance. When they finally got back to the Hovey House, it was 3:00 am. Mrs. Hovey had started locking Bernadette's usual "sneak-in" window so the girls hoisted Bernadette into the front parlor window.

Bernadette snuck around to the front door to let her giggling housemates in. Mrs. Hovey watched the whole thing from the kitchen, trying to contain her laughter.

After finals, Bernadette joined her parents in Manhattan for the six-week break. Back in White Creek, Nora couldn't wait to see Sammie at church, even though they would barely be able to say hello without feeling the scrutinizing glances. After Sarah's situation, Nora had taken it upon herself to make sure she married appropriately, at the right age and to a man who met her parents' approval. Seth and Ida were still feeling the sting of Sarah's shotgun marriage. Though they received much understanding in private, they often felt a palpable disapproval when out and about in town. They felt as though they had done something wrong in raising Sarah and they were hellbent on making sure Nora didn't make the same mistake. Nora and Sammie were fully aware of everyone's thoughts on the situation and acted accordingly. Nora kept her grades up and Sammie worked hard to save money from his farm work. They wrote to each other at least once per week.

At church, Nora noticed that Sammie was clearing his throat during the sermon, so she passed him a life saver. He then continued with a cough. Afterwards she reminded him that a good hot cup of tea with honey would do the trick, knowing full well that Ma Telford was most likely on the task of making sure he had the correct remedy.

"Why did you come to church if you had such a cough?" asked Nora.

"I wouldn't have been able to see you," replied Sammie.

Ida and Seth loved Sammie so terribly much that they wholeheartedly approved of both Sammie and the Telford family, so Ida invited him over for Sunday dinner. They sat for hours chatting and comparing farm work stories and when it came to chore time, the Andrew boys went out to the barn, and Nora and Sammie moved the big comfy chairs to the fireplace and sat drinking hot tea with honey and lemon enjoying each other's company until Nora sent Sammie home to go to bed because he clearly was coming down with something.

No follow-up kiss tonight, thought Sammie.

The following Sunday, as Christmas Day approached and Seth was to sacrifice his prized tom turkey for the feast, Sammie wasn't at church for the Christmas Eve service. Nora had heard through the grapevine that his cough had gotten the best of him, and he was lying low until it passed. Everyone kept up a good face when it came to anyone who was down with a cough, but it was known that if it persisted past three weeks, it could very well be consumption, but you weren't to let yourself think that far down the road.

White Creek had had enough experience with consumption, as most called it, to know that it was improper to speak of it, as it could full well just be a bad cold. But Nora was concerned, nonetheless. Ida could tell that Nora was preoccupied with Sammie's illness.

"Nora, dear, you know we all love Sammie. Don't live in fear today of what could be nothing tomorrow. He's a strong young man. We all know you fancy Sammie… but today, he's just got a bad cough."

Nora listened and appreciated the reminder but didn't respond. Mother didn't realize just how much she fancied Sammie.

"The best remedy for you is to look for ways to make somebody else's day better, get your chores done, and keep saying your prayers. Take something that's a mess and make it pretty. Way back, when my baby passed, I took my pantry apart and painted it three times." That truly connected with Nora's heart. Mother almost never spoke of the time her baby died.

"And you can always help make my day better by helping me with the baking," added Ida.

Nora appreciated her mother's words and headed upstairs to change out of her Sunday dress and into her work clothes. It felt good to be back into her farm chore routine. She enjoyed helping out the boys by doing her part. As she slopped the hogs, she spoke gently to them. She took a stick and scratched the big mama behind the ears.

Nora had such plans for her winter break, but Sammie's cough wasn't cooperating with her vision! He was missing from church and all she heard was that he still had a bad cough. She sent him a card or two in the post, which everyone thought was silly, since they were next-door neighbors. In White Creek, your "next-door neighbor" could still be several miles away. Just before Nora was to return to Oneonta, she and Ray saw Dr. Shaw's buggy drive past their farm on the way to Telfords. She knew that Sammie must still be in a decline. "Dr. Shaw gives everyone a shot of whiskey," Ray remarked. "That'll help Sammie feel better." Nora wrote a final note, placed it in her gift basket to Sammie, and asked Ray to deliver it.

Dear Sammie,

So much for our sort of "first Christmas." I do hope you feel better soon. There are so many things that can cause such a bad cough. Be sure to do what Dr. Shaw says. I am headed back to Oneonta Normal until Easter time. I

will plan to see you then. I cannot wait for graduation.
All my best to you.

Give my regards to "little" Julia.

Sincerely,

Nora

Ray brought back Sammie's reply.

Dear Nora,

Thank you for the basket of goodies. I think Ma is secretly jealous of your cookies. The lemons are just what I need in my tea. Thank you for the scarf and hat. I'm sure you made those yourself. My timing was bad, but I cannot gain my strength back. I did not plan to be sick the entire time you were home, but give me another chance at Easter. It is just around the corner.

All my bestest,

Sammie

Back in Oneonta, the girls sat on Nora's bed as she described her Winter Break and what had happened with Sammie. He had now been down with his cough for 5 weeks. The girls were very sympathetic to her predicament and tried to stay positive when her man was down with a bad cough.

"We have to take it day by day. Today, Sammie was just tired with a bad cough and fever," explained Nora. They certainly had all had experienced that before and came out the other side just fine.

"It's not my job to predict the future; it's my job to say my prayers and not get stuck thinking about the worst possible outcome. We will trust the doctors and wait to hear what they have to say," said Nora trying to convince herself that this was even possible. She prepared herself for the worst but decided to be positive about Sammie's prognosis. The girls all agreed that was a good plan and vowed to be right alongside Nora anytime she needed them. Throughout the coming days, they noticed that Nora simply focused on her school work and didn't participate much socially. Her mind was elsewhere.

Snowy, blustery January gave way to snowy, blustery and colder February and Mrs. Hovey announced a phone call for Nora late one night. It was Ida.

"Hi Dear. I have some news. Papa came in late for dinner. He'd been over to Telfords. Sammie has just been wasting away so Dr. Shaw sent him to Troy today to see a Dr. Irish." Ida then lowered her voice. "He's been coughing up blood and his chest x-ray showed that he has a touch of consumption. *Tuberculosis* is what they call it now. He'll be going up to the Ray Brook State Hospital in the Adirondack Mountains."

Nora was frozen. She had never seen anyone live who was diagnosed with consumption. She stood her positive ground.

"Well, if he's sick, then the special hospital is the best place for him, right?" asked Nora. "When does he leave?"

"As soon as a bed opens up. Apparently, there's quite a waiting list. It could be weeks. I'll keep you posted if I hear anything more... but

Nora..." Ida paused, "Dr. Shaw didn't hold back on painting a clear picture of what Sammie should expect. Sammie cannot afford one of the fancy cure cottages, but he'll receive the same care at Ray Brook. People who go there are usually the ones who have waited too long. He said that, at this point, Sammie's chances are 60/40 in his favor. But he can't wait long for that bed to open up."

Nora was heartbroken at this news, and all the Hovey House girls rallied around her just as Sammie's family rallied around him. His sister, Florence, and her husband, Herb came down from the Hollow to see Sammie and the family the next day. Sammie's 10-year-old niece, Julia, was his biggest fan. She made him a get-well card. Arrangements were made to get Sammie as ready as possible for his trip to Ray Brook, the moment that bed opened up for him. Ma Telford had her list of things that needed to be done to prepare Sammie; Herb would ask the barber to come and cut his hair, Florence would make him a proper bathrobe. Will was exactly his size so he would go to the Falls to buy a new suit, overcoat, and underclothes for Sammie. Sammie would be gone for quite a while, so Pa hired Fremont Meerwarth, including room and board, to take over Sammie's work duties on the farm. Ma and Will welcomed the idea of having Fremont on board. Without saying a word to each other, the women of White Creek dropped off meals and baked goods for the Telfords. White Creek always rallied around its hurting residents.

Ma only allowed visitors in the early evenings. The doctor couldn't emphasize enough how Sammie had to remain still, not cough, and not lift his hands over his head. Luckily, for a farmer, milk was helpful to coat his throat, but Ma had all kinds of concoctions up her sleeve if that didn't work. It was a challenge to arrange, but the grapevine in White Creek passed messages as quickly as the newfangled crank phones. The new phones were still few and far between. Most of the farmhouses didn't even have electricity. Mrs. Cottrell, Elizabeth's mother, was the White Creek operator, and their farm had the nearest phone to send and receive messages. Everyone in White Creek learned that they were to visit only in the evenings. Mrs. Cottrell would be sure to pass along any information she had. In those days, the operator also acted as an answering service and information update service for all of the residents of White Creek.

A few weeks later, Henry and Ray Andrew were over to play cards on a Friday night to help keep Sammie entertained. Ida sent over a pan of hot corn bread and a jar of homemade strawberry jam that Nora had made which they consumed with great pleasure. It was clear to Henry and Ray that he had lost a lot of weight and that he was too weak to play cards, so he just sat in the chair and listened to the boys talk about what was going on in White Creek and on the farm as they played.

Elizabeth Cottrell and her mother showed up that same night with the news from Dr. Irish that there was a bed available at Ray Brook and Sammie was to arrive there on Monday. Mrs. Cottrell knew which calls to eavesdrop on. Dr. Irish had called Dr. Shaw with this news, and rather than wait for Dr. Shaw to bring the news to Sammie, she decided to take it upon herself to deliver the message. It'd save time that way. The news made the seriousness of Sammie's illness very real.

3

Valentines, Raspberries, and Rubies

It felt ominous, but there was a sense of relief all at the same time. There was finally hope for a cure at the hospital. Ma Telford said that Sammie was just becoming "paler and frailer." Mrs. Cottrell offered Sammie her son's suitcase, which Sammie bought for $4. Ma Telford thought Sammie looked too tired, so everyone politely made their exit. Sammie truly appreciated his dear mother. She sometimes stayed up with him all night and made ginger tea for him. They had become very close during his illness. He was her youngest, her "little baby." The Telfords never showed affection outwardly, but they had a deep love for each other. Brother Will, who had been working side by side with Sammie on the farm his whole life, was deeply impacted by this move to the hospital.

That Monday, one month after diagnosis, Valentine's Day, Sammie left for Ray Brook with a Valentine's Day card from Julia and a tin of cookies from Ida. Ma Telford was beside herself but tried to remain stoic. "Ta bron orm," she finally cried, using her old Irish dialect which didn't come out very often. It meant, "there is sadness on me." They had planned to take the train but that would be too taxing on Sammie, so instead, Herb showed up bright and early to drive Sammie and Pa. Sammie was quite pale, which is why tuberculosis was often called the white plague, and the disease often caused its victim to waste away, which is why it was often called consumption; it slowly consumed its prey. Ma and Will stood outside in the cold to see them off. Ma tearfully gave her Sammie a kiss on the forehead not knowing if this were the last she would see him. Sammie and Will locked eyes and nodded to each other. As they pulled out of the yard, Ma broke down in Will's arms. Pa rolled his window down a bit to keep the cold air in his lungs. The trip took nearly all day. They drove the snowy roads to Saratoga Springs and then headed directly north, deep into the freezing Adirondack Mountains which were often a good 10-20 degrees colder than White Creek.

They stopped for gas at a roadside shop somewhere outside of Lake George where there was a thin lonesome bear cub chained to the front porch. Pa, a man who barely every spoke said, "He looks worse than you do, Sammie. Poor thing. There ought to be a law against that."

As the gas attendant came out to pump the gas, Herb lamented at how expensive gas was, but Pa stepped in and paid for it. The mechanic also checked the oil and cleaned the windshield and headlights. The men were all impressed at how well maintained the roads were, even with so much snow.

It was evening before they passed through beautiful Lake Placid where they stopped and ate their dinner in the car. From there, it was a quick trip to Ray Brook. They took a quick tour around the place and saw the Ray Brook rail stop. They all noticed the 6 rough boxes, the size of caskets, piled on the platform of the train station. Clearly, there was a body in each, but none of them said a word. Sammie pretended not to notice. Dr. Shaw had prepared them well for what to expect, but seeing caskets on the loading dock made the gravity of tuberculosis very real to the men. By 6:15 pm, they finally arrived at the front porch of the State Hospital at Ray Brook and two assistants with masks came right out and greeted them in their car with a wheelchair in hand. They made sure that Sammie was on their list and unloaded his things for him.

There was no time for long goodbyes or tours of the facility. Pa was a tall thin man of few words. He put his hands on Sammie's shoulders. For 22 years, they had been milking cows and fixing fences. It was one of those moments that stoic men have all too infrequently. They knew that they loved each other, and were connected for all of eternity, and there was the possibility that they might never see each other again. They could see into each other's teary eyes. They didn't need words. It was "love by osmosis." They hugged. A nurse approached Sammie with a smile and asked him to have a seat in the wheelchair and assured the men that he was in good hands. She led the way back into the hospital with one assistant pushing Sammie in the wheelchair and the other carrying Sammie's things. Herb and Pa watched him until he was well inside and out of sight. Their tall Sammie looked rather small against the backdrop of the huge hospital. They drove in silence for the all-night trek back home.

Sammie felt chilled and alone as Nurse Neurich placed the thermometer under his tongue. She started her intake speech, "We will be taking your temperature 8 times per day for 8 days. Fever charts will show us how you're really doing and, right now, you're at 101. That's not good. 104 is what the dead heads come in with. Here is your sputum cup… that's for anything you need to spit out. Those will be collected each night and incinerated. Alert a nurse right away if you see any blood in your sputum. That includes little specks of blood or lots of blood. Just follow along with your roommate and you'll more than likely do well. Don't worry, if you do something wrong, a nurse will correct you. It's important that you do just as we say. You can recover here, but it's not easy. You need to conserve your ergs and rest your lungs. You have tuberculosis, or what we call TB, and you'll always have it, but you don't always have to be sick from it. Following our plan, Lord-willing, your body will form a cocoon of calcium around the TB bacteria that's causing this whole mess in your lungs. That's why you'll drink 6 glasses of calcium-rich milk per day. Once the bacteria are walled off, it will remain that way unless you get worn down and weaken that cocoon. If that cocoon breaks, the bacteria spills into the rest of your lungs and you die. I'm just telling it like it is, babe."

She marked Sammie's chart and continued to speak. "TB gets into your lungs and eats them from the inside out like a rat gnawing away inside your chest until you can't breathe, causing your chest to fill up with blood and the liquified remains of your lungs. It's not pretty, but I've seen too much to mince words. Every day, the New York Central line drops off dozens of tuberculars right out on our doorstep, far too late in their diagnosis for us to do a thing about it. We keep them as comfortable as possible in Pryor Wing, but they're soon loaded back onto the train in a box headed back where they came from."

She had him stand on the scale. "But you're probably not one of those cases. They might even take someone like you up on the hill, but it'd cost you at least three times as much. Probably more. And don't worry, the same doctors who practice up on "Hemorrhage Hill" at Trudeau's place practice right here at Ray Brook..." She paused to write some notes. "We need to get your weight up. We like to say, 'eat once for yourself, eat once for the germs, eat once to gain weight.'" Sammie just looked at her, listening.

"One winter is worth two summers up here. Once allowed, you'll be taking the cure out of doors for 6-8 hours per day, no matter how low the mercury goes. Be thankful that it's not like the old days; everyone lived outdoors in tents day and night. For this first week, do not lift your hands over your head. Do not cough. Do not get up to use the bathroom... and most of all, stay optimistic." *Optimistic!?* wondered Sammie incredulously.

A nurse casually stepped into the doorway,

"We've got a raspberry in 4."

"I'll be right there," said Nurse Neurich.

Sammie waited a bit and asked what that meant.

"I'm gonna give it to ya straight," she said.

"I would expect nothing less," said Sammie.

"In someone's final moments of TB, the code we use is 'tossed a raspberry' referring to the bloody cough or heavy hemorrhage just before the end. Sometimes you'll hear, "threw a ruby." That's code for a grave final hemorrhage. You're up against a terrible disease, but if you follow your instructions, we just might get you out of here and back home." She left the examination room. Sammie sat in the exam room and didn't have any notions of disobeying any orders after that.

While Nurse Neurich was gone, he wondered if life on the farm in White Creek had prepared him for this cold, sterile world he found himself in. He truly wished that he and Nora had been able speak just one more time before he left. He wished he could just hold her. Eventually, a nurse came and wheeled him to his room in East Wing. After the nurse got Sammie settled for bed, she informed him that the first 8 days were the toughest with temperatures being taken every three hours.

"Here's your record book. You keep this. You are to note any symptoms such as vertigo, change in sleep habits, nervous heart palpitations, or stomach upset. Be sure to make notations about decrease or increase of expectoration into your sputum cup, if there's blood, or if you have shortness of breath. Also, no exercise is allowed for you for a while. How's your appetite? Keep track of your weight and pulse rate here in these boxes. And most of all... stay optimistic!"

Sammie sighed and shook his head in confused wonder. She handed him a pen and his health record book. Sammie held up the pen,

"Great. I can use this to write my postcard to Nora."

"No writing or reading for the first 8 days." She lifted the pen out of his hand. "You just tell me, and I'll write it for you. Writing takes up too many ergs," said the nurse as she turned on her heels and was out the door.

"Well, at least I know what 'conserve your ergs' means now," said Sammie to his roommate.

His roommate, Charles, spoke up with two pieces of advice. "The more letters you write, the more you'll receive, and don't get caught smoking."

It was unbelievable but some doctors outside of Ray Brook actually promoted the benefits of smoking at the time.

"The first week is the worst. I've been here 5 months and it gets much better. The food is good, some of the nurses are babes, but I do have to sneak out to smoke. They can't keep their eye on every one of the 320 beds so it's not hard to get up to the roof or sneak off behind a tree. If I'm brave, I'll go down to the porch at the end of West Wing if the wind is blowing in the right direction. Shall I write that postcard for ya?" So that night (as well as every night that week), Sammie dictated his postcards…

Dear Nora,

Happy Valentine's Day. Long drive from home.

It's much colder here than at home. Not far from Canadian border.

Very strict schedule.

All my bestest,

Sammie

(Written by Charles Cunio, roommate)

Charles said, "This Nora Andrew sounds like a lucky girl, although she has a boy's name for a surname. And pal, don't you worry about the post. I swipe stamps from the nurses' desk all the time."

Sammie, in his exhaustion, didn't realize that he dictated Nora's White Creek address instead of her Oneonta address. He was somehow grateful and terrified to have such a helpful weasel of a roommate. He drifted off to sleep, exhausted from his trip, and barely woke each time they took his temperature throughout the night. The cotton sheets were nicer than he had ever slept on.

The next morning, he was awakened for his breakfast tray. "Absolute Bed Rest" meant that he wasn't to sit up and eat but, rather, awkwardly lie on his side to take in the ample portion of fresh eggs, toast, a glass of milk, orange slices, and what appeared to be a shot glass of cod liver oil. He was only allowed to use the bedpan. Sammie found that his day passed quickly with the routine of meals, doctor's visits, and the never-ending temperature taking, a routine he learned all too quickly. He was happy to absorb the rest.

Sammie watched as Charles prepared to go sit outside for 2 hours even though it was 20 below 0. As he put on several layers, he announced, "I'm about to partake in the elixir of mountain air. Don't worry, partner. You'll be up and around in no time freezing your ass off taking the cure with the rest of us. And to be clear, they take all the x-rays and track your temperature, but they don't know what the hell they're doing. 'But stay optimistic!'"

And off he went in his fur boots and his floor length beaver coat with wind-blockers sewn onto the sleeves to the porch where he would plop himself in a cure chair, very much like a chaise lounge, and wrap his legs in a rug and his upper body in a horse blanket for warmth.

"I'm going to conserve my ergs," said Sammie and drifted back to sleep.

Ida was none too happy when the post for Nora arrived at the farm and not Oneonta. She went right out and harnessed Maude to the buckboard and rode her right down the road to Cottrell's and placed to call an unsuspecting Nora at the Hovey House.

As she tore out of the barnyard, Seth said to the boys, "I don't know what that's all about, but I'm glad I'm not on the other end of it."

Henry added, "I hope the wagon's in one piece when she gets back."

Nora took the phone from Mrs. Hovey and Ida gave her an earful.

"Nora. Do you know what I'm holding here in my hand? A postcard from one Sammie Telford addressed to you for Valentine's Day. You know tuberculosis and young men are not a good match, dear. You know better!" She suddenly dropped to a whisper. "There's a very good chance that Sammie may not return from Ray Brook, he's wasted away so. I won't have you longing for a man who isn't long for this world. I can't just stand here and watch you get your heart broken. We all know and love Sammie and we wish things were different. But you can't be hitching your wagon to his horse at this stage of the game." Ida realizes that her rant wasn't getting through. Ida takes some breaths. There was only silence from Nora.

Nora was so thrilled at receiving the postcard from Sammie that she couldn't take in what Ida was saying. "Mother, can you read me the postcard, please."

Ida was quieter and begging now. "Please, dear, don't let yourself fall in love with a sick man. Who knows what his future will be? Think down the road. You're not head over heels yet. Why on earth would you take up with a dying man? Every woman's fear is that her man will be taken ill. And consumption no less! Let things cool down. Let Sammie just be our wonderful neighbor boy, which he is. Because if he doesn't come back, dear, you'll be devastated."

"Mother, what does the postcard say!?" Nora asked again. Ida reluctantly read it to her, and Nora was thrilled but played it cool. "Mother, don't worry so much. Sammie is a strong young man and has been fit as a fiddle. He'll do well at the hospital. They wouldn't have sent him otherwise. We know I have to graduate first. And trust me, if he had proposed marriage, I would be in the same uproar that you are, but this simply is *not* the biggest thing since electricity."

"*We* know? Who's *we*? You're already a *we*? You girls these days think you know everything. Did you see how frail he was before he left?"

"No, because you wouldn't let me see him!" came Nora's reply.

They sat in silence for a bit until Ida let her anger go and said softly, "I'll let you get back to your studies. I'll put the postcard in the envelope with some other things I'm sending along to you."

"Please tell Ray to call me. Thank you for calling, Mother." And that was the end of the conversation. Nora hung up the phone and yelled, "New gossip!" And all the Hovey House girls came running to hear about Nora's mother not approving of Nora and Sammie's connection, which made their romance even meatier.

As the days and weeks passed, Sammie came to like the Ray Brook Hospital and his doctor, Dr. Bray, who was always in a great mood. You could always tell when he was coming by the clunk of his favorite putter that he used as a walking stick. Sammie had great respect for Dr. Bray. Sammie hung on his every word. It was the same for all the other patients, your doctor was your friend, priest, confidant, and miracle worker all rolled into one magnificent wise old sage. Your doctor's word was like Moses handing down the 10 Commandments from God himself to you. There were no patterns, no guidelines, everything depended on what your medical man said. To the consumptive, he was jailer-omniscient and had the power to put you in "solitary confinement" which was absolute bed rest or sign your exercise prescription card and let you walk around town for the day. Sammie clung to Dr. Bray's instructions and slowly started gaining weight. Eventually, he was allowed to sit up for 1 hour per day and put on "basins," which meant he could stand and wash himself with a washcloth. He could look out his window and see the patients outdoors amusing themselves on their cure porches laughing. He longed to be with people. Eventually, he got up to use the toilet and take a bath. As he gained more strength, he could sit up all day, and then go for short walks. But he was always warned that if he got tired, he must stop what he's doing immediately, write it down in his health record, and go back to bed.

Once off bed rest, he was able to take the cure and was assigned to a porch where he made friends and felt like he really got the lowdown on life at Ray Brook and nearby Saranac Lake. His porch mates were Mr. Titus, a newspaper printer from the Bronx, Mr. Nathan, a baker from Manhattan, and Senor Lorenzo, an Italian-speaking man who smiled a lot, had constant visitors, and understood almost no English, or, at least, it appeared that way to Sammie.

Sammie's first day on the porch was quite an experience. The nurses showed him how to wrap up to stay warm. They told him to save newspapers so he could tuck them under the mattress of his cure chair because *wind can blow right up your bum through a mattress.* Once wrapped up with his head smushed between two fluffy pillows, a nurse packed hot bricks around his feet to help keep them warm. They would come through every hour to replace the bricks when they checked on everyone.

Once the nurses left, the men introduced themselves as they corrected some of the "flaws" in the nurses' wrapping technics. Sammie was grateful for the help. Mr. Nathan explained that their wide-open view included Scarface Mountain and down below was the snow-covered 9-hole pitch and putt golf course.

"I don't know nothin' about golf," said Mr. Titus.

"Neither do I," said Sammie, "just that Dr. Bray must like to play it." The men all agreed. They grilled him with questions about farm life and listened intently to "Mr. Sammie's" description of White Creek and the daily farm chores. Sammie explained that his older brother

Will would take over the family farm, and he would like to buy his own farm someday. That sounded like a beautiful plan to each of the men.

Mr. Titus added, “Did you know that there’s a dairy set up here that milks 465 cows?” Sammie couldn’t believe the size of such an operation.

Sammie asked, “So why do we all call each other Mr. along with our first names?”

“It’s just the way this porch has always operated. We go by ‘Mr.’ to show respect and use our first names to show friendliness. Not really sure how it started,” replied Mr. Nathan. “But one of the nurses told me that this porch has been doing it ever since she’s worked here.”

“Mr. Nathan, I can’t help but notice that you look healthy as a horse,” remarked Sammie.

“Well,” said Mr. Nathan, “the good Dr. Brown always says, ‘get yourself a good chronic disease and take care of it and you’ll outlive everyone else.’ We’re building up our health every hour that we’re just lying here.”

“I’ve never been to New York City. What’s it like there?” asked Sammie. Mr. Titus held up his copy of the day’s newspaper and talked about the grueling night shift he worked at the Tribune running one of their presses. It was hot in the summer and freezing in the winter and it took a lot of men to produce a daily paper. His hands were permanently stained with ink.

Mr. Nathan added, “I also work all night baking in a crowded hot kitchen. I clean the floors and ovens constantly and do my best to keep the rats away.”

"We have rats on our farm too," added Sammie, "If you're storing food that rats like, there's no keeping them away. If you see one, there's a hundred more ya don't see."

"That's comforting," said Mr. Nathan sarcastically. "Senor Lorenzo!"

"Buongiorno!" replied Lorenzo with a smile.

"That's literally all we are going to get out of him," said Mr. Nathan. "He just pretends to read the newspaper most of the time." It was quiet for a bit, they all had newspapers except for Sammie who turned to Mr. Titus and asked, "What are the headlines today?"

"Oh… uh… why don't you see for yourself?" He handed Sammie his newspaper. "What you read today will help keep you warm tomorrow," he added.

Two well-dressed men brought chairs out to the porch and chatted with Senor Lorenzo in Italian. Sammie tried to nap. He wasn't interested in anything from the newspaper man that came around. He asked the men what there was to do for excitement while curing. They laughed.

"Well," said Mr. Nathan, "you could do what some do, they flag a car out front for a rendezvous with a tomato from an up cottage in town."

"Up cottage?" asked Sammie. "Just like it sounds. A cottage where the patients are up and walking around town," replied Mr. Nathan.

"Oh, I gotta girl back home," insisted Sammie.

"Oh, even a wedding ring doesn't seem to stop many of us," said Mr. Nathan. "We may not be here tomorrow, so we take advantage of today!"

A talkative nurse checked on everyone complaining about the outlandish TB "cures" that other patients had been discussing. "Lungers have come through here with every kind of home remedy for TB known to man; some swear by sniffing herbs or taking opium, someone even ate wolves' liver boiled in wine. Someone else ingested arsenic and another creosote and copper salts! I heard just now that someone ate the beating heart of a rattle snake! Can you imagine? No, thank you! I'll inhale tar vapor, drink turpentine, and eat chlorine, before I'd do that! Ernest Hemingway thought that sleeping with a prostitute would heal his TB. I don't think that he really thought that. I think he just wanted a woman of the evening! Don't worry; we've got our cod liver oil, but we don't offer any of the rest!"

"What's a 'lunger'?" asked Sammie.

"Why, you're a lunger, my friend. Anyone with TB," replied the nurse.

Mr. Titus started coughing every now and then. The nurses weren't concerned at first but, eventually, brought him some slippery elm to suck on and took his temperature.

"Let's bring him back inside before he gets bad," said Nurse Neurich. "A man who coughs all day works as hard as a man who climbs a mountain. Here Sammie, this is for you," she said, handing Sammie a letter. Mr. Titus looked so defeated to have to return to bed that he got a little teary.

"Mr. Titus, you know the doctors warn against tears; a crying infant doubles his metabolic rate, and that's a bad thing for a galloping consumptive. We're going to bring you back inside so you can get some rest and bring your fever down. You'll be back out here in no time." She adjusted his blankets and off they went. It was completely quiet except for his coughing they could hear for several moments even after he was gone. It was always quite a poignant matter when someone regressed from the porch back to bed rest. It was an ominous reminder that they could be next. Sammie wondered if that might be the last time he saw Mr. Titus.

Mr. Nathan spoke, “Poor guy. He’s one day on the porch, three days on bed rest. I also don’t think he can read. He lived in a small apartment with many others sharing the rent. Running an offset print machine doesn’t bring in a lot of money. He waited too long to get checked out by a doctor. It’s sad, people would rather remain sick than spend money on a doctor. This bitch of a disease knows no discrimination. It takes us all black, white, Italian, Irish, rich or poor. We’re the ‘poor’ ones here and the rich ones can afford to live up at the Trudeau San. Trudeau doesn’t take the really sick ones like the dead heads we take here and plop them over in Pryor. And if his patients take a turn for the worse, he ships them down here, so his report card looks good.”

Sammie couldn’t pay attention; he opened his sweet-smelling letter from Nora and started reading it silently.

“No fair,” said Mr. Nathan. “All letters read on the porch must be read out loud!”

Dear Sammie,

It's good to hear that you have continued to stay on the mend.

Did you know that we have notorious ancestry? Mother called me the other day with the most fascinating story after the boys had gotten into a fight over something silly. It turns out that my great-great-Uncle Charles was shot by his neighbor, Mr. Case, back in 1866 in a dispute over Uncle Henry's chickens feeding in Mr. Case's cornfield. Apparently, the two had been at odds for years. Mr. Case brought a pistol to scare the chickens out of his corn. It all came to fisticuffs. As they were fighting, Mr. Case's pistol went off and hit Uncle Charlie in the back; all right in front of his two sons. Uncle Charles died two weeks later, and Mr. Case was charged with murder and went to jail for 2 years over this silly nonsense. It was in all the papers. How's that for some family history? I guess that'd teach anyone to not let their anger get the best of them!

Bernadette and the girls all send their regards.

Nora

"Are you getting teary too?" asked Mr. Nathan. "There's no crying in curing! If there's one thing we've heard here a thousand times: crying is a bad thing for consumptives."

Sammie started to make an excuse but was interrupted by the laughs from the Italian men, "Com'è bello non fare niente!" (how wonderful it is to do nothing) one of them declared taking a swig from his flask.

"What do you think their talking about," asked Sammie.

"I have no idea, but those guys visit all the time. I think they have some sort of business together. Judging from the clothes they wear, they're much wealthier than anyone else here." Sammie pondered that for a while. He was getting cold.

"Don't worry," said Mr. Nathan, "it's almost time to go inside. And just think, 20 years ago this building wasn't even here. The place was covered with poor sots living in tents!" And with that, a bell sounded, and they went inside to warm-up and prepare for dinner while Senor Lorenzo stayed outside talking with his visitors looking over some ledgers.

The nurse with the book cart approached, "Can I interest you boys in a book?"

"No way!" said Mr. Nathan, "My doctor back home warned me that books are the biggest carriers of TB germs. Lungers read them, handle them, and cough and sneeze on them and pass their germs right on along to their next victim!"

"Oh, you believe that fairytale?" asked the nurse. The men smiled but not one of them took a book. The nurse continued, "Tuberculosis has been around since ancient times, and we keep learning about it. It almost never is called the same thing twice! It was called 'the King's Evil,' in England and France, because they thought that only a royal touch could heal you. It's been called the 'Robber of Youth,' the scourge, the white plague, consumption, phthisis, scrofula, Captain of all these Men of Death… the list goes on."

"We keep learning about it. Doctors used to tell people that it *wasn't* contagious, that you could share a bed, and you were *never* to open the windows. Doctors told Trudeau himself that he was to exercise and that would increase his appetite and he would gain weight and strength. But the opposite happened. His fever remained high, and he lost strength and weight steadily. Anyhow, there's so much wrong information brought into this place that I can get on my high horse to correct it. You gents enjoy your view here in the Switzerland of America!" She made a grand gesture toward the mountains and made her exit.

Sammie continued feeling better and wrote to Nora in Oneonta frequently. As Sammie regained his strength, he was put on work duty; making 3 beds per day and carrying trays of food to those who were unable to make it to the dining room on their own accord. He proved to be such a good worker that he was put to work polishing the Solarium when he wasn't outside curing. Being on 'trays', he was able to see some of the less fortunate patients and he was quite happy with his early diagnosis. So many others were much worse than him. He was also learning the inspiring details of Saranac Lake and shared his inspirational trivia with those he brought trays to. Patients began requesting Sammie by name.

"Today's Tidbits feature musicians in the Adirondacks. 1-The one and only John Philip Sousa directed his band on the very first steamboat to cruise around the lake. 2-Cole Porter, the great composer and lyricist for the Broadway stages of New York, found inspiration in the Adirondacks and summered here. 3-You know the Pontiac Theater in town? If you can guess one performer who appeared on stage there, I will score you an extra piece of pie." The stars most frequently guessed were Sir Harry Lauder, Al Jolson, and Eddie Cantor, and all were true.

Dear Nora,

I'm finding that it's easier to write than speak sometimes. I suppose thinking before I speak is not a bad direction to go in! I am anxiously anticipating restarting a new life back in White Creek. We talk about deep things here taking the cure. I have so much time to think about who I want to be, my reputation, church, but mostly how I want to live when I return. Mr. Nathan asked me to consider that there are meaningful Life truths, but they've unfortunately been reduced to a list of empty church rules. Are we following empty church rules? I don't want to live that way any longer. There seems to be a way that's more meaningful and it doesn't depend so much on appearances and avoiding the Biddie Bunch, but my motivation and contentedness and state of being. Just call me Mr. Philosopher. I still have a lot to think about. There's a better picture I can see now. It might not look terribly different, but it will feel different.

All my bestest,

Sammie

Back in his room after curing, Sammie hung up his coat and hat and splashed some warm water on his cold red face. He asked Charles about who his previous roommate was. "I've had a few roommates during my time here. My favorite was Jacov (Yah-kov). He was a good man; a mensch, so they say, an Orthodox Jew. First one I ever met. Every morning he would put on his tefillin and his prayer shawl even when he was at his worst."

"Wait. What's tefillin?"

"It's a small black leather box prayer thing that he fastened to his forehead, and it had leather straps that he wrapped around and around and around his left arm and hand while he prayed in a whisper in Hebrew, I think. But it was only on weekday mornings. He took weekends off. The box had tiny scrolls of parchment inscribed with verses from the Torah, the first five books of the Bible."

"I think it was a Jewish group of patients that asked if they could start a 'good cheer' club and the doctors instantly approved it. But anyhow, he was older than me. He waited too long to get here though. He was assigned absolute and utter rest of mind and body—no movement except to use the can once a day, no sitting up except propped by pillows and semi-reclining, no deep breath. He was basically leading the life of a log, but the chaps on the ward and I really enjoyed his stories of life in the Bronx."

"We told him that His wife was much too pretty for him. She visited with a fancy dessert and wine. Wine with dessert; have you ever heard of such a thing? He wasn't supposed to have the wine, but he shared it with a bunch of us on the ward. We didn't have any glasses, so we drank the wine out of extra sputum cups I swiped from the nurses' desk. That's all we could find. It was after lights out so we lit a few of his candles so we could see what we were doing and tried to keep our voices down. Wine and some sort of dessert called halva. It wasn't halfa bad." Sammie ignored his lame joke.

"And when did he go home?" asked Sammie. Silence.

"He never got out of bed. He just got worse and worse from the time he arrived. But what a great attitude he had. His coughing was horrible, but his outlook was fantastic. I miss him."

"In the end, the very last thing they did was wheel in a huge chunk of ice on a creaky cart and placed it on his chest hoping to stop the coughing. It didn't. All of us cough up blood now and then, but I saw how it ended for him. It was terrible. Not how I want to go. He was wheeled away immediately. They say our bodies are very contagious once we die. I think the nurses call them 'Plus-4s' or something like that."

Silence.

"I cringe every time I hear that squeaky ice cart come through. That means someone is close to the end."

The two sat in silence.

"Martin was here before him. He was an older man. He didn't talk much. He kept to himself. He died in much the same way, except a few days after he left, they came to me and asked what I knew of his family and where he was from. I had to think for a moment. I didn't know anything about where he was from. He didn't like talking, so I left him alone. I asked why and they said, 'We have no address to ship his body to and there was no one to pick up his remains. Did he ever have any visitors?' I guess not, I said. I found out later that, on occasion, there are families that drop off their sick and leave them here to die…and they don't reclaim their body. On one of my visits to Saranac Lake I went and saw his grave in Pine Ridge Cemetery. It's on Pine and River. There's a bunch of other unclaimed 'Martins' over there."

So many friends, so much death. Sammie was filled with incredible sadness at these stories. He realized how close he was living to the permanence of death. There was always someone you knew of being wheeled away on a stretcher to the morgue. He wanted to get as far away from death as possible and live the best life he could.

Sammie and his porch pals were well aware of the new faces that emerged from their beds as they healed enough to become upright and mingle about. You could see them all during meal times and during church. Everyone went to church to see people socially, not necessarily for spiritual guidance. Sunday church services and mealtimes in the dining hall were the only times that you saw the opposite sex so everyone tended to dress up a bit, especially for Sunday dinners. Then, after Sunday tea time, there was usually some sort of relaxed entertainment involving a piano solo or two that created a beautiful atmosphere that promoted some good conversation, or a lighthearted poem read aloud called something like "Conserve Your Ergs" that generated lots of laughs, a humorous monologue delivered, perhaps then a sleight of hand, a short skit mimicking one of the doctors putting someone to bed for a whole year, or a skit about boredom and consuming so much milk and eggs and cod liver oil, all performed by talented patients and usually hosted by someone who told lots of funny stories and off-color jokes. Patients got up and gave reviews of the latest Chaplin movie, rumors of what movies were being shot over at the old Ampersand property, or they passed along rumors heard from taxi drivers about local bootleggers getting caught or killed. Some got up and announced they while they were at the Berkely, they were sure they saw Laila Lee, the movie star from the *Perils of Pauline*. It was true that early adventure films found the Saranac Lake location ideal and one of the movie companies built a studio complex along Edgewood Road. Some of the locals appeared in films made there.

Sammie worked things out so that he could deliver trays to his favorite patients, who were the folks that he would never meet had it not been for getting TB and coming to Ray Brook. He encouraged them to remain hopeful. After all, despair used up more ergs than a good, positive attitude. He continued his friendship with Mr. Titus who had to go back on bed rest.

"I can hear Mr. Sammie coming down the hall with my lunch!" Mr. Titus shouted.

"How can you tell I'm coming before you see me?" asked Sammie.

"You're always whistlin'. Don't you realize that you whistle when you're bringing us our food?"

"I guess I didn't realize that. I know I whistle when I milk the cows back home. Must be you remind me of my cows," he kidded.

Mr. Titus asked what the trivia questions for the day were.

"Well, my friend, I'm glad you asked. Today's questions are focused on Saranac Lake 's Olympic Speed Skater, Ed Lamy. Question #1-Ed Lamy set a world record in 1912 in what event, earning him a spot in Ripley's Believe It or Not?"

"No idea," stated Mr. Titus flatly.

"Ed Lamy apparently has wings because set a world record in barrel jumping; 27 feet 8 inches."

"I didn't even know barrel jumping was a sport," said Mr. Titus.

"Neither did I," added Sammie. "Question #2-Mr. Lamy broke how many records in 1919? These records were broken in Saranac Lake and Lake Placid.... If that helps."

"Oh sure, that helps a lot... I'm going to say 12," guessed Mr. Titus.

"Close! 3," said Sammie with a smile. "I had to write this part down. He set records for the quarter mile (34.8 seconds), three quarter mile (1 minute 55 seconds) and three mile (14 minutes 15 seconds).

Sammie added, "Mr. Titus, you get an A+ for consistency in getting wrong answers every day, and for that, you get your extra piece of pie! And I'll finish with a couple of Ed Lamy facts. Ed and his brother put on shows. His brother, Ernest would say, 'Ed Lamy will now break another record.' And Ernest would fasten a literal victrola record onto the last in a row of barrels. Ed would jump all the barrels and kick the record as he landed, thus 'breaking another record.'"

Mr. Titus looked at Sammie nonplussed.

"Well, if that didn't inspire you to get out of bed, then this, my last story, will really change your life. Everyone knows that Caribou Bill has a camp on Edgewood Road where he films all kind of outdoorsy adventure movies. In the film *Yukon* they hired Ed Lamy to dress as the female lead in a fur hat and coat, and the character was to escape on ice skates from a pack of wolves, which were really just Caribou Bill's pet huskies. 'She' skated away and leaped over a huge break in the ice on Moody's Pond and got away from the 'wolves.'"

"People pay to see these things?" remarked Mr. Titus.

"Well, I'm impressed," said Sammie. Mr. Titus just shook his head. "He even set a record skating backwards a half mile in 1 minute and 26 seconds. And with that, I will leave you to your lunch and your extra piece of pie," concluded Sammie as he made his exit with a smile.

4

KISSING COUSINS

Romances were not allowed, but many went under the radar of the head nurses, or so the patients thought. Your lover was called your "cousin." Cozen means one who deceives, cheats, or defrauds. Many, whether married to someone back home or not, would meet up in dark corners or gazebos to consummate their "cousining" afterhours. Others would take a car to a cottage up at Trudeau's San and romance the evening away. No one was ever known to become pregnant, although it was thought that TB was an aphrodisiac. Everyone seemed to know who was with whom. Even the nurses were involved with patients at times. Poor Charles fell in love with a nursing student who often visited their room for late night chats while Sammie pretended to be asleep so he could eavesdrop on their conversations. They had sneaked out one night and got caught on the roof. The head nurse found out about it and had Charles sent home to Manhattan for "smoking." The head nurses knew a lot more than they let on… just like the police chief, James Coughlin, with that whole bootlegging thing.

Sammie was learning that holidays were celebrated to the fullest, and St. Patrick's Day was no different. There was a competition between the wings of the hospital. Patients, who were able, were tasked with cutting out and taping together green paper chains for the dining hall. Some made cards for the patients on bed rest. The leprechaun team was to cut out tiny green footprints and tape them to the walls. Another team was to cut out HAPPY ST. PATRICK'S DAY in large letters that would hang over the nurses' desk. A tall-membered ladder team was charged with hanging up any decorations too high for anyone else to reach. Sammie had never paid much attention to this holiday but remembered his Irish friends in Hoosick Falls looked forward to it each year. He'd been curing for a month and was ready for any kind of distraction. He was on the team that put the green table cloths on every table in the dining hall, which would be serving green food… and not just naturally green vegetables, but green mashed potatoes, green cake, and the like.

In the dining Hall, Sammie was at a table with some of his new friends. The topic came up, "who was the worst doctor to have?" It was quite clear, though none of them had ever been under his care, that Dr. Kinghorn was regarded as some sort of evil masochist. The story goes that he once put a patient to bed for two years. As the story went, that patient wasn't allowed so much as to crook one finger after one year, and the other finger after the second year. Another patient was buying a new suit at Finnegan's but once he was recognized as a patient of Dr. Kinghorn's, he was sold a pair of pajamas instead. It is rumored today that some of Dr. Kinghorn's patients are still tucked away in rooms about Saranac Lake. One of his patients was to be out curing when it was -30 degrees. Instead, he wrapped up his pillows and taped a book to empty coat sleeves and basically left a scarecrow with a fur hat pulled down over its ears. The scarecrow was curing, while the patient sat inside by the fire with his love interest. Dr. Kinghorn found no humor in it and dismissed him immediately.

"The man clearly had no sense of humor," remarked Sammie.

"He forbade his patients to knit because it burned 9 calories per hour and that was 9 calories they needed to heal," said one of the women.

"I wish I could have known some of the famous authors that have cured here," remarked another one of the ladies. "Mark Twain, Somerset Maugham, Ernest Hemingway, Oliver Holmes, or Ralph Waldo Emerson. Why aren't you fellas as clever and famous as any of those intellectuals? Huh?"

"Reading their books is probably what got you sick with TB in the first place," replied Mr. Nathan, knowing he was spreading an old wives' tale.

"Those authors done wrote their books, coughed on them, and passed them onto you! That's how clever they are!" replied another one of Sammie's mates.

A dining hall worker chimed in, "Everyone in town is frightened to death of catching TB. I don't see why then they would patronize Sullivan's Loan Library in town if you could actually catch TB from books."

The gang got quiet. "Well now, there goes that theory!" remarked Sammie.

Another one of the ladies piped up, "I hate it that my *Gibson Girl* magazine is showing all the latest fashion trends on beautiful, *tiny* little women and my goal in this place is to gain weight like a fat dog. I'm not even sure I could fit into a broad-rimmed hat at this point." They all laughed. And then the bell rang.

A kitchen worker was cleaning the tables and said, "you all best get yer talking out now and grab a book because it's quiet hours now. Be sure to enjoy your shot of cod liver oil on the way out." They all agreed, rolled their eyes, and took their shot of cod liver oil; some took it straight and some floated it with orange or tomato juice. A nurse marked each patient's cod liver oil intake on their chart. They meandered off to the library or back to their rooms. The dining hall was where many matched up with their "cousins." Often, pairs disappeared into the library to plan their clandestine rendezvous. These intense love affairs were more often than not just emotional because it wasn't always easy to find a time and place to consummate, plus there was great worry that exertion would overtax the healing. But your cousin always had a listening ear.

Eventually, Sammie was able to get an exercise prescription card for a half day off here and there, which he noted in his diary. He either walked or hitched a ride to Saranac Lake to the Episcopal church. One of his drivers proudly offered him a bit of a tour giving Sammie the inside story and hopefully a decent tip in return.

"They say that up here in the Adirondacks we have two seasons; July and winter," joked the taxi driver. "Since Saranac Lake is so popular for those with tuberculosis, I saw travelers speed through town with their kerchief over their nose the other day. They were hoping they didn't catch nothin'. Saranac Lake is home to some of the nicest people on earth; if you have a bite to eat at one of the hotels and leave your umbrella behind, someone's bound to find ya and give it back to ya. But on the front stoop of that same hotel, you might get shot by a notorious New York gangster. What a town, eh?

"Even during Prohibition, thanks to that 18th Amendment, Saranac Lake proudly features seven fully operational stills and enough death to support three undertakers. One undertaker is right up on the second floor there. And see those young boys right there?"

Sammie looked where the driver was pointing.

"Those boys are paid to collect those nursing bottles and bring them to the drugstore where they are filled with whiskey and sold over the counter for a nice price. It's one of those things where the cops 'unofficially' know all about it but choose not to do anything about it. You can pay a special price at the dry cleaners and get your coat back with a pint tucked inside the breast pocket. If yer willing to make the drive, you can make about a $100 a day just driving the 130 miles north to Montreal, loading your car up with 20 cases or so of liquor and bringing it back here...if ya get caught, ya can just pay off the damn patrol officer from Malone. A buck a case will get you out of that jam or else it comes to fisticuffs and ya make a run for it. That sometimes ends with a bullet in yer head though. Would you like to see where the speakeasies and loose women hang out?"

Sammie replied with a smile, "Oh, thank you but I'm just headed to church this morning." The driver remained silent the rest of the way.

After church, he met up with some of his Ray Brook buddies out with their exercise passes. They peered in the windows of the shops: long john underclothing, wool socks for bed, hats with ear flaps, and Klondike blankets for wrapping up while taking the cure. You could buy cure chairs or home window tents that allowed you to sleep with your head sticking out of the window while not freezing out your entire house. Eventually, they met up with another crew of men and walked down to the Berkely Hotel for lunch. It was one of the only hotels that didn't bear the "NO TUBERCULARS-NO HEBREWS" sign on their door. Sammie looked across the tables that his buddies filled. He was the only farmer amongst a bank executive, a writer, a couple of newspaper printers from New York City, an Orthodox Rabbi, a not so orthodox Rabbi, a garbage collector, a few young fathers, and a few college students. All were young healthy men of various races, ages, and nationalities and religions getting a second chance at life.

Nearby, female "lungers" were enjoying their meal as well. Clearly, tuberculosis didn't discriminate. There was great camaraderie amongst these "lungers" as they enjoyed their nonhospital meal together. Sammie thought they might be too loud as he noticed people whispering and pointing at his table. Sammie faded in and out of the conversation as he wished that he and Nora could be enjoying this moment together. He was feeling like he had more energy than ever.

His thoughts were interrupted by a screaming eavesdropper, "Why don't you Ray Brookers stay put? We don't need your kind here!" Sammie was stunned as was everyone else at his table. Silence. The Orthodox Rabbi, all too familiar with discrimination, replied kindly, "I could definitely understand your concern, sir, if we were contagious, but we can only receive our exercise prescription cards if we are noncontagious. Look at us. You won't find a healthier-looking mensch than any you see here."

Sammie was angry and held out his exercise prescription card. The group all followed suit and held up their prescription cards.

"It doesn't matter. You're all going to die from it one day. Everyone does. You'll be contagious then," the local and his buddy started packing up to leave. "You should think twice before serving tubercular from Ray Brook. We're never coming back here again," he screamed at the manager and stormed out.

There was terrible awkward silence, until the manager said, "Well, good riddance!" And the dining room erupted with laughter.

Sammie had never experienced any hint of discrimination like that before. Clearly, locals regarded Ray Brook TB differently than Trudeau TB.

"That's why they treat us like lepers," said the Rabbi. Sammie and his pals couldn't see how Ray Brook was a place to be feared. Their lunch conversations turned to explaining why they were grateful for curing at Ray Brook and other times when they were discriminated against.

***

In Oneonta, the girls in Mrs. Hovey's House were preparing for their debate on the values taught in Common Schools; three of the girls were to be for the values of teaching biblical lessons from their daily readers, the required use of the King James Version of the Bible (objected to by Roman Catholics and Native Americans), and teaching "the 3 Rs."

"Wait!" exclaimed Bernadette from the "against" team, "What is this 3 Rs?"

Nora leaned in and explained, "Reading, wRiting, and 'Rithmetic."

"This does not translate well inside my head," replied Bernadette. "Only 'Reading' begins with an R. Perhaps those who say '3 Rs' must go back to common schools. No?" All the girls laughed. She continued, "Plus it's only 3 Rs, but it also includes geography and history? Why do we not call it '5 Rs': Reading, Riting, Rithmatic, Reography, and Ristory?"

Nora could hardly keep from laughing and tried to explain it to her to no avail.

"The more you explain, the more I don't understand! This makes no sense!" They all laughed. They all discussed the pros and cons of the McGuffey Reader, different grading systems, and the value of end-of-the-year recitations as a way to inform parents about what they were learning. Nora kept watch over Leah and Bernadette and absolutely loved Oneonta Normal. She was coming into her own, was appointed to be the speaker for their debate team and was comfortable with that. But she missed Sammie and longed for the days when they could be together back in White Creek.

By April, Sammie had gained 17 pounds, and in May, Mr. Sammie and Mr. Nathan sat in the dining room with their new bunch of friends, who happened to be joined by William Morris. Mr. Morris was scouting out places for a concert to be given by Sir Harry Lauder of "Keep right on to the end of the road" fame. Sammie knew that song from the various radios that played in the air shaft for all to hear before lights out. Mr. Morris told a wonderful story.

"Sir Harry wrote 'Keep Right On to the End of the Road' after the death of his only son, a Captain in the Argyll and Sutherland Highlanders, killed in action in December 1916. His son, John, was then 25. What courage Sir Harry must have had at that time, to have been able to move through his own grief through writing these words which have become such a strength and inspiration to countless others in their own struggles."

Sir Harry Lauder was the Scottish entertainer who, at that time, was the highest paid entertainer in the world. He was a singer songwriter, comedian, author, and film actor.

"I brought him to Saranac Lake for a fundraiser for the building of the first United, Methodist Church. Apparently, there's a local livery man walking around town, his name is Giles Bombard and is said to look just like Harry Lauder," remarked Mr. Morris.

During the meal, Mr. Morris, a real swell guy, let Sammie know that 20 years prior, he had had consumption, cured up in this same Adirondack air, and recovered just fine.

"Just don't ever over do. Tuberculosis is like a circus tiger performing just as you'd expect, but the second you turn your back, it jumps and devours its trainer. Optimists don't lose hope; pessimists only see failure ahead. Optimism sees a rough road ahead; pessimism sees no road at all. Hope fuels the journey on that road. And on that note, I'll hit the road," he said as he stood and left a handful of Dutch coffee candies on the table. Sammie was encouraged by his story of recovery and stood up shook his hand and said farewell. He went back to his room and immediately sent Nora a letter, assuring her there was hope for his long-term recovery.

Nora, on the other hand, was having a wonderful year at school and enjoyed it very much once she learned that Sammie was recovering just fine. Her debate team won, and it was time for her Oneonta classes to come to an end. And then final tests were to be taken. The girls had one final night of dancing at Bernadette's favorite speakeasy. Again, there was much dancing and celebrating. But Nora was going to desperately miss Bernadette who was going to finish her schooling in Paris and would be on her return voyage the next day. Nora knew that she was better for having known Bernadette and Bernadette for knowing Nora. There were many tears, and Nora felt a sorrow that she'd never felt before.

5

Will You Love Me In December As You Do In May?

On the third week of May, Sammie proudly weighed in at 177 pounds and both Dr. Trembley and Dr. Bray signed off on his "Apparently Recovered" release papers and allowed him to go back home with the caveat that he would "go real easy" and not overdo. His returning to arduous farm work was of great concern to them, and they made sure he knew that he could *never* go back to the hard-working lifestyle he once enjoyed. Every 6 months, he was to have an exam by Dr. Irish in Troy, and after two years without a relapse, he would receive his "Apparently *Cured*" papers from Dr. Irish.

"Now don't go thinking that 'Apparently Cured' means that you're absolutely cured," Dr. Irish warned. "Again, we can recover from TB and show no symptoms, but that's just because the TB is latent inside you. TB will live inside you forever. Your doctors didn't cure you; you cured yourself up here in the mountains."

Sammie was too excited to be going home to feel the enormity and true impact of the words the doctor was saying. All he could think about was telling Nora and his family that he was recovered. He missed his family sorely.

There was no telling Sammie twice. The very next morning, Sammie caught a ride into Lake Placid to hop on the early train. Having an entire day on the train gave him time to realize how close he had come to death, and he now found a new lust for life, a great desire for a slower pace, and enormous gratitude for his everyday chores.

He couldn't wait to tell all of his stories to Nora and his family. He knew they had all been praying for him in whatever way they spoke with God and would love to hear his tales from Ray Brook. He noticed the hustle and bustle of passengers loading and unloading and watched the hours on the train pass by. He remembered the doctor saying, *the energy you lose in one hour of travel takes 2 hours of curing to regain*. He made it to Hoosick Falls by 6:00 that evening with a resilience of spirit matured by the sobering realization that he had walked side by side with death since Christmas. He was never so happy to see Will and Pa who were beaming ear to ear, and both hugged him without hesitation. That night, there was a joyful Telford family homecoming dinner with Herb, Florence, Julia, and Fremont who was now a part of the family. Sammie felt right at home, yet he was soon exhausted from all the travel and social energy. He hadn't been to any kind of party since the Church Christmas decorating back around Thanksgiving.

The Telford farm had been running smoothly in Sammie's absence thanks to Fremont's help. He would continue to work at the Telford farm but rent a room from the Andrew family. Seth and Ida were happy to work out a good price for him. Sammie was eager to help out as much as he could, so the next morning he started by carrying the cream on the back of the farm truck. Each day, Fremont would lift the 10-gallon milk can on the back of the truck and Sammie would take it from there down to the White Creek Creamery where they could currently get the best price for their milk. It didn't seem like much, but it was important for Sammie to feel useful.

Ma didn't want to overwhelm Sammie, so she kept the guest list short for Sunday afternoon's Welcome Home/Birthday gathering for Sammie. It was Memorial Day weekend as well and folks were out in numbers visiting. He was turning 23. Ma's guest list for the "small" gathering included Fremont, Peter, and Reimer Meerwarth, Aunt Maggie, Aunt Jennie, Herb, Florence and Julia, Uncle Jim McCracken, Clarence and Elsie Harwood, Uncle Jim, Willie and Dewey McCart, Ralph and Rena McCart, Lillean and Edith and Jean, Joe and Harold, Warren, Raymond and Elizabeth Cottrell, Reids, Ralph Andrews and wife, Lottie Peters, Kenneth Potter, Aunt Sarah Fischer, Shermans, Matilda and Elsie Brown, Laura Andrews, Fryers, Dundases, Bertha Gafkha, cousin Anna Collins, Aunt Lizzie Fryer, Ruth Masten, Prebbles, Mrs. Mann and Mrs. Hill, Tuttles, Ralph Andrews, Seth and Ida Andrew, and, of course, Nora, Henry, and Ray. But the "short" list isn't of any concern because when there's a party in White Creek, *everybody* comes!

On the afternoon of the party. Sammie was chatting with Fremont about war veterans and their alcoholism. Sammie noted that the war vets at Ray Brook were known to have had alcohol secretly brought in for them. It was also known that alcohol and TB were not a good mix. Fremont noted that he was glad he picked up cigarettes rather than hooch after the war. It was much healthier. Sammie told some of the stories he learned from curing at Ray Brook. "

You could buy a case of Canadian ale for $240 in a Canadian border town and bring it just across the New York state line and it instantly became worth $700. You could then distribute it along the Rum Trail which ran from the North Country right through Glens Falls, Saratoga, and Albany.

Fremont's eyes got big, "Sammie, we're in the wrong business! Who cares if we get shot? We'd be rich!" The two laughed.

The Andrew family arrived, and Sammie and Nora's eyes met the instant she showed up on the lawn. They played it cool as they didn't exactly know how to act. Nora had finished her exams and was back home, but she still had another couple of weeks left before her high school graduation. Nora thought Sammie looked better than ever and he couldn't take his eyes off her.

Nora and Ray approached Sammie and Fremont.

Ray said to Sammie, "Well, for once there's good news about you all around town and everyone's glad to have you back!" Fremont had a good laugh at that. They all shook hands. "Nora's got some news of her own," added Ray.

"Oh Ray, this isn't the time or the place," she said.

Sammie couldn't let that go. "Well, why don't you tell me your news and then I'll decide if it's the right place or not."

Nora heaved an embarrassed sigh.

Ray answered for her, "They announced this week that she's the valedictorian of the senior class of 1921."

"Valedictorian!" Sammie exclaimed. "Well, this is the perfect time and place for that news. No one ever thought anything much would come of an Andrew, but look at you!"

Seth called from across the yard, "Hey, I heard that!"

Nora ignored her embarrassment at having the attention drawn to her and continued, "The worst of it is that I have to deliver a speech in front of everyone as part of the graduating exercises. That will be more of a challenge than my Oneonta exams were."

"I'm sure you'll find a way to do just fine," added Sammie.

Just then, Ma Telford swooped in and asked Sammie if he needed anything and suggested that perhaps he remember to tend to his other guests as well, and Ida came over and asked Nora to help with the refreshment table. She then asked Ray to find Henry and Elizabeth. They were last spotted headed toward the orchard.

Sammie just smiled at Nora, took her hand, and said formally, "I look forward to hearing your speech, Miss Nora Jane Andrew," and kissed the back of her hand. She did a cute little curtsey. They held eyes for just a moment longer and then walked about enjoying the party.

As Nora finished her last weeks of high school in Hoosick Falls, she decided to drive herself to school with Maude on the buckboard. Henry would get Maude harnessed and then Nora would trot off to Hathaway's where she would catch the trolley over to the school. For a nickel a week, Mr. Dunfey, the hotel stable manager, would take the harness off Maude, put her in a stall with hay and water, and then have her harnessed and ready to go for Nora when she got off the trolley each day.

She received a letter from Sammie in the post which she was able to hide from her mother.

Dear Nora,

I'm still thinking a lot. You can blame Mr. Nathan for all my rattling on. He called it 'quotidian' living; finding joy in the ordinary routine of life. I don't have to wait for some great future thing to happen. I love my life today and I want to keep it that way. Shaving. Eating. Field work. Feeding Cows. Milking cows. Carrying the cream...I want to enjoy it all. I think this is what Mr. Nathan called 'living right now' He also spoke a lot about being grateful and looking for beauty everywhere. It's like part of me died off up here and I'm walking in different shoes now. Actually, I do have new shoes now!

All my bestest,

Sammie

Unfortunately, there wasn't a lot of extra time for seeing Sammie aside from church, Ida made sure of that. She knew that a relapse was common with consumption. She wanted Nora to keep her distance from Sammie until there was no sign of relapse in sight. She was trying to protect Nora from future heartbreak. She didn't know that they were writing to each other. Although Sammie and Nora did find time for fishing up in the White Creek flowing through the rough countryside of Pumpkin Hook with Julia trailing along showing Nora how to worm a hook. The White Creek actually started in VT and flowed through Black Hole Hollow along Ash Grove Road and McKie Hollow and was joined by the Pumpkin Hook Creek which flowed along Chestnut Hill Road. The White Creek then flowed south of Cambridge where it emptied into the Owl Kill River and flowed down to Eagle Bridge.

Sammie brought them to the place he loved the most on earth that everyone called, "the notch" up on Chestnut Hill Road. Bald eagles landed there and sometimes nested close by. Sammie was always gob smacked that the national bird that represented freedom and beauty for the whole country would find its way to tiny Pumpkin Hook and make its home. They saw two eagles that day. Ma Telford cleaned their fish which Florence poached that night for dinner. Florence knew just how to cook fish so that it melted in your mouth. Florence was certain that Sammie and Nora had fallen for each other but decided to keep it to herself and watch to see if things developed.

Sammie and Mason went along to the Hoosick Falls senior picnic with Nora and Leah up at Hedges Lake. The group was large enough that it didn't cause too much of a stir. For Nora, graduation meant that she'd soon be able to be official with Sammie. According to the unwritten White Creek "law," June 20 would be too soon to be courting and cause the Biddie Bunch great outrage. But after the graduation ceremony on June 21, 1921, she would have earned her rite of passage into womanhood. Nora had been working her whole life on the farm and in the house. She was anxious to get to work in her own schoolhouse. She was assigned the red schoolhouse with white trim, School #13, over on Brigg's Corners with the row of chestnut trees across the road and where the students stored their metal lunch boxes above the wash bench. She would be taking over for Susie Lake who got married and moved to Cambridge. Julia was excited that Nora would be her teacher.

Nora's duties included being at school by 7:00 am and leaving at 5:00 pm for the 143 required school days. Of course, in addition to teaching, her daily duties also included sweeping the classroom floors, filling oil lamps and cleaning the lamp chimneys, cleaning the blackboard, and, in winter, starting the fire before 7 a.m. so the room would be warm by 8 a.m. when the children arrived. Once each week, teachers had to scrub the classroom floor. She was to complete all of these tasks wearing the required dress uniform. She was required to take out a large portion of her pay for her later years so that she wouldn't become a burden on society.

On top of her duties inside the classroom, in 1921, Nora and the other White Creek teachers were also to set a moral example outside of the school building as well. A female teacher wasn't allowed to frequent the ice cream parlor, and neither male nor female teachers could smoke, drink, play pool, or participate in any of those activities considered by the board of education to be immoral. She wasn't to be seen in a car with a man other than her father or brother. A female teacher wasn't allowed to be seen dating, become engaged to be married, get married, or become pregnant. A male teacher, however, was allowed to have one evening per week for courting purposes, or two evenings per week if he went to church regularly. Males were allowed to become engaged and get married. And Nora signed her contract to do all this for $75 per month (which was about $1,000/month in modern money). Back at Oneonta Normal, Bernadette had pointed out the unfair allowance that male teachers had over female teachers.

The world was changing fast, even in White Creek. The graduating girls faced a whole new set of rules with the passing of the 19th Amendment in 1920. Women now had the right to vote and had entered the workforce. Margaret Sanger and "birth control" were considered dirty words by many in White Creek although Bernadette had shown them where not every woman was in the same circumstance as the women in White Creek. Prohibition had changed things with the rise of speakeasies, jazz, and the proliferation of illegal alcohol sales. There was a huge divide for women between "having a good name" and being viewed as a promiscuous flapper. Nora wasn't quite sure what "having a good name" meant anymore but was determined to be certain that she thought through what she did before she did it.

Nora was half scared to death about her graduation speech. She didn't show it, but her anxiety often got the best of her. She needed help. In the past, she always managed by figuring things out on her own if she just had enough time. But Nora couldn't handle her stage fright. Her nerves were getting the best of her. She pulled Rev. Manning aside after church one Sunday and asked if he had any advice for her regarding nerves and speaking in public.

He said, "Fear is mentioned 365 times in the Good Book; one for every day of the year. The Bible warns us against it because it prevents us from doing great things. It freezes us up. You have great things to say, and fear doesn't want you to succeed. Fear is a nasty little booger, ain't it? When I feel fear, and I do plenty of times, I thank God for it because if the devil is afraid of what I have to say, then I know that I have something really special and positive to contribute with my words. And if what I have to say has a positive impact AND takes the devil to the woodshed, well then, that's a good day in my book!" They both laughed and Nora was able to rethink her speech as an opportunity, and not an assignment that would be graded publicly.

So, though quite nervous, she stood up bravely and gave her speech on "Americanism." She had it all typed up and delivered it flawlessly. She made the most of her opportunity. Of course, her entire family attended, and Sammie was there, as Henry pointed out to Nora with his finger after the ceremony. Both Sammie and Fremont Meerwarth were alumni of the high school so there was an animated crowd around Sammie asking about his time at Ray Brook as there was a crowd around Fremont asking about the war and his time overseas. After a while, Sammie politely excused himself from his admirers to congratulate Nora on her AMERICANISM speech. He especially liked the part about being neighborly and taking pride in your work. The Andrews and the Telfords were proud of their farms and helped other farmers whenever they could by sharing equipment and labor when possible. There was never another farmer the Telfords or the Andrews wouldn't help.

All the girls talked about the short list of eligible bachelors in White Creek. Nora was completely enthralled with Sammie but, just like all the girls in White Creek, kept a mental account of all of their limited options. Mason Robertson was interested in Leah. He was musical and handsome with deep ties in the community and interested in farming. Fremont was certainly a consideration at 5'9" (much closer to Nora's height) and was handsome as ever with his blonde hair, gorgeous smile, and ruddy complexion. He was a good worker and helped out at the church on occasion. He served in the armed forces (that was a big deal). But as far as financial security went, he didn't have a farm to work, through no fault of his own, although neither did Sammie, and her father had pointed out to her the importance of owning rather than renting a farm. Nora shook her head clear. *What am I thinking? Fremont rents a room from us. We're living under the same roof. I can't even entertain the thought of courting him! No wonder Mother put me in the rear bedroom by the back stairs and Fremont in the very first bedroom next to theirs!*

Sammie spent the entire next day helping Nora prepare for her graduation party. Mother didn't like the fact that they had become an item so fast, but she accepted it.

"Think about what it was like when we were young," said Seth.

"I am!" said Ida. "That's why I want to protect her!"

As people started gathering in the yard, Nora realized how odd it felt to be seen in public with Sammie. But she was soon distracted by gifts and entertaining her guests. Sammie kept folks entertained with his stories as well. Folks were sitting and talking, playing cards or up and running around playing games. All was going well better than expected when Frank Blake appeared to show off his motorcycle and did tricks back and forth on the dirt road in front of the Andrew's house, an unexpected entertainment. Everyone was thrilled for the private show and was impressed with his skill. But tragically, he hit a rut and was thrown over the handlebars against an old roadside tree. All went running to his side. Seth yelled to Ray to get the truck. Florence was at Frank's side, Elena on the spot and started giving directions authoritatively.

"Please back up and give him some air. Someone turn the motorcycle off. Nora, grab blankets and pillows and bring them to me straight away!"

Nora's eyes got big. Farm girl that she was, she couldn't stand the sight of blood and was feeling queasy. She ran into the house to gather the necessary items. Once she got outside with an arm load of blankets and pillows, she starting handing off the items to some of the young men who were watching from a distance.

Florence said, "Nora, come now. You come."

Nora was obedient but felt like she was going to throw up.

"Put one pillow under his head. Lift his head and put the pillow under it."

Nora had to get his blood on her hands to do that. But she didn't want to let her fear get in the way of helping Frank. The truck started backing up to them. Florence cleared away all well-intended helpers but for those needed.

"Nora, wrap this clean towel around his arm. That should help stop the bleeding. Once Nora had a good bit of blood on her, she could feel that her queasiness was all in her head, and she got right into helping.

"We need to get a blanket under him so we can lift him onto the back of the truck."

Nora and Florence were the only females helping turn Frank carefully on his side, slide the folded blanket underneath, and then roll him the other way and pull the blanket through, just as if he were in a hospital bed. They called in a few more helpers and carefully lifted Frank into the back of the truck where a bed of pillows had been made by Sammie and some others. Frank was unconscious but they did the best they could with what they had as he was in for a long trip to the Troy hospital. He died that night.

At dinner, Ida went on a rant, "First the flu, and then TB takes out our young people, and then something as foolish as a motorcycle kills a fine young man."

"Mother, I see your point. These are modern times we're living in, and our kids need to find their way," Seth replied.

As it turned out, no Andrew would ever get on a motorcycle for many a decade after that. Not for fear of the motorcycle but for fear that Ma would kill them. Nora really didn't care that her graduation party was ended by the accident, she was just in disbelief and sad for Frank and his family.

Sammie planned their first real date alone…to the north cow pasture. Sammie was to go out and clear the leaves and debris out from around the spring up by the woods. It was a messy job digging out mud and leaves from around the spring, but he loved watching the water flow more freely which was important as it watered all of their animals. He told Nora what he would be doing,

"You come too," he said. She agreed.

There was a nice warm breeze and off they set up the hill, shovel in Sammie's hand and a picnic basket with a snack in Nora's. They walked slowly and talked about Sammie's new motivation for life. It was really a one-person job, so she sat on the stone wall as he worked digging the leaves and sticks and mud and rocks away from the spring which came up through the ground.

Nora enjoyed the sun on her face and her heart was pounding with her newfound "graduated" freedom. Once he got the spring flowing, he joined Nora on the big rock for the snack that Nora had prepared. She brought hard-boiled eggs and salt, corn bread and jam and iced tea to drink from mason jars. As they chatted, Sammie noticed that Brown Cow was down in the tall grass by herself. He couldn't see her that well, and he knew she was getting ready to freshen, so he and Nora walked down to see if she had had her calf.

"Pa says every farmer ought to have a brown cow, but Lord knows they can be a pain in the neck," he said.

Off they walked, and indeed, Brown Cow had her calf that was already standing and taking milk. With much concern from Brown Cow, Sammie threw the calf up over his shoulder and around the back of his neck to carry the calf back to the barn. Nora noticed that he didn't seem fazed having the calf's wet umbilical cord right on the back of his neck.

"Shall I help bring Brown Cow in also?" she asked.

"No need to worry about her. She's not going to let her heifer calf out of her sight. We couldn't stop her from coming with us if we tried."

So, Sammie led the way and carried the calf to the barn with Nora carrying the shovel and picnic basket and Brown Cow following closely behind. All in all, they both thought it was a nice afternoon.

Later that week, Fred Masten's body arrived via train in Hoosick Falls. He had been killed in the war and it had been some time getting him back home from France. Mrs. Masten kept her chin up at the funeral as best she could. She was proud that her son served his country but could not comprehend the loss. Fremont Meerwarth was at the funeral in uniform and read a few words of scripture as he was asked by the Mastens. Nora and Sammie spent time with Fremont during the social hour following.

"Everyone asks me what the war was like. I tell them, it's like coming face to face with death several times per day. It changes you. Many of my men couldn't handle it and had real mental problems, and many took up alcohol."

Fremont was feeling a bit of survivor's guilt. He felt shame that he was alive and Fred wasn't. That was hard for him to explain.

As the summer moved along, Nora and Sammie were expecting to spend time together, yet life kept unfolding in unexpected ways. Sammie was selected by Rev. Manning to go to the esteemed Epworth League Institute to learn about church leadership. So, he was gone for 10 days of leadership training for that. When he got back from that, Nora was already camping for the week with Leah and their girlfriends up at Hedges Lake, much to Ida's delight. Then Sammie, Florence, Julia, and Aunt Maggie took a week-long trip to Niagara Falls to visit the McCracken relatives there. Florence had been looking forward to the trip for a long time. They prepared all of their food ahead of time and stopped alongside the side of the road to eat. When it was too late and too dark for Sammie to drive, they pulled well off the road and camped. Early the next morning, they awoke bright and early, as all farmers do, and see that they pitched their tents underneath the tree with the NO TRESPASSING sign. Whoever the owner was seemed none the wiser as no one bothered them. Julia gathered sticks and branches for their fire where Florence and Aunt Maggie made coffee and fried up some eggs.

Once they arrived at McCracken's house, they piled out and gave them a gift basket from their farm: fresh eggs, homemade jams, homemade butter, and canned meat. After warm greetings, they were shown to their rooms in the large rambling manor. Julia was escorted to the converted attic where the McCracken daughters slept. Uncle Eliphalet was sick from breathing the dust from CARBORUNDUM WORKS, where he was employed. He planned all kinds of tours for his guests. Of course, they enjoyed a day at Niagara Falls, but Julia's favorite tour was of the Shredded Wheat Factory. At the end of the tour, they were served a warmed shredded wheat biscuit with butter and cream and sugar. A delicious memory for Julia and her giggly cousins.

Sammie was happy to have some male companionship from his cousin, Clausen. They were able to get away and see some sights on their own. Everyone convened at dinner time for stories and great food. Julia loved to tell tales about learning in a one-room school-house with a teacher who taught 8 grades. She told how the boys once got in trouble for putting chestnut burrs in her hair after school.

Florence added, "She once got a spanking at school and, no doubt, needed it!"

Julia continued, "Once a new family came to school and after the very first day, the entire school went home with lice. Mother had to wash my hair twice with kerosene. She scrubbed so hard that I'm surprised I had any hair left!"

Uncle Eliphalet so enjoyed the stories from White Creek, his boyhood home, and encouraged Julia to share her experiences. The neighbor boys, the same ones who put burrs in her hair, had just recently gotten old enough and were allowed to harness their surrey to their horse named Nancy, and drive to and from school on the condition that they bring Julia with them. Eliphalet loved that and laughed until he had a coughing spell.

Florence added, "Julia now has built up a little flock of sheep for herself. It started when Ray Taber walked across the field with a lamb. His ewe had had triplets and not enough milk for all three, so he gave one of the lambs to Julia. She named her Cora. Once word got out to the other farmers that she was a good caregiver, her single little lamb quickly turned into a six-lamb flock."

"Even with twins," said Julia, "the ewes don't always have enough milk to feed both lambs, so rather than letting the weaker one fade away, they give it to me to bottle feed. I love my sheep. I'm trying to train them to pull me in a cart, but they don't like that very much." They all laughed.

The McCrackens loaded up their car with gifts from Niagara Falls, including three bushel baskets full of peaches, hand me downs from the older cousins to Julia, a car catalogue from Clausen to Sammie, and quilt pieces for Aunt Maggie. Cousin David McCracken was the Niagara Falls postman and supplied Julia with stamps from Niagara Falls and many postals or postcards from the places she saw there.

Julia was excited to make a presentation to her class once school started again. Once everything was packed in, there was barely any room for everyone. By the end of the trip, Sammie was ready to spend some time alone in the barn away from women!

Upon their return, Sammie was busy helping with chores and hayin' it. He was careful not to overdo and couldn't help in the hay loft lest he have a coughing fit. He was just driving the tractor with loads of loose hay from the field to the barn where brother, Will, unloaded it with a pitchfork.

Though Sammie seemed to have recovered just fine, Ida had seen all too many times that consumption often came back with a vengeance, and she was now trying to protect Nora from that. In her memory, she had never seen anyone recover from TB as Sammie had. But she was still concerned. She was pleased that Nora had many restrictions placed on her as a teacher. She had to wear skirts that were hemmed no more than two inches above her ankles and had to wear at least two petticoats underneath her skirt. Her contract read that she was encouraged to read the Bible during her free time. After all, she would be setting an example for the little ones. Ida was pleased that the school rules for teachers seemed to be on her side when it came to keeping Sammie and Nora apart. But Ida had to be honest with herself; she was more concerned about keeping a proper eye on Fremont and Nora now that he was renting a room from them. She didn't want the Biddie Bunch to have any gossip on her.

In July, Nora and Sammie and Julia went strawberrying and Ida cut some rhubarb for strawberry rhubarb pie, Seth's favorite. And the following week, though it was hot, they also had a nice time picking blackberries along the edge of the woods as each picked about 2 quarts which would become pie in no time. Nora was annoyed that they didn't have enough time together, and Sammie just encouraged her to accept it.

"Good things come to those who wait."

In July, word came that Jack Holton's barn was struck by lightning and burned to the ground. And despite Seth's ineluctable attitude toward the science behind lightning rods, he couldn't take the risk of having his barns burn down. Sammie was able to encourage him just enough to buy the lightning rods. Without a word to his boys, the next day, Sammie helped him put the lightning rods up on the house and barns. It was Fremont's day off from Telfords, so he helped as well. After all the convincing, arguing, and debating, Henry and Ray just looked at each other in disbelief and shook their heads.

"What magic powers do you possess that could convince our father to buy lightning rods? We've tried to convince him countless times," asked Ray.

"I must have caught him at just the right moment," said Sammie.

Nora was more than happy to provide refreshments of iced tea and sandwiches for the men as they worked, since she didn't mind seeing their sweaty, shiny, shirtless torsos. They came in out of the sun for lunch. After they devoured the lunch, she prepared as well as two whole gallons of iced tea, the men took a break. Nora and Sammie went out front and sat on the porch swing. Nora felt extremely awkward, but Sammie had found a new boldness at Ray Brook, and he would have gladly had a conversation with anyone who had a problem with the two of them sitting together.

"Are they holding hands?" said Ida incredulously spying on them through the pass through.

"Take it easy, Mother," said Seth assuring her that the kids were just fine. "Nora has a good head on her shoulders. Sammie-no. Nora-yes."

Ida didn't find any humor in what was happening.

As the summer progressed, the new couple's plans continued to be thwarted. Nora and Sammie planned a day together at the county fair, but then Julia got sick and needed a trip to the doctor's so Sammie and Nora drove her to Bennington.

"Blessed are the flexible," Sammie said.

They postponed the fair to the next day, but Nora was needed to go along to help take care of Leena Willoughby who just had a baby and needed some looking after. It seemed they were destined to only be together on the porch swing as every "away" trip seemed to be fraught with obstacles. Sammie missed talking to Nora so much that he ended up sending her a letter.

Dear Nora,

We keep missing each other. I enjoy our talks. I received another letter from Mr. Nathan about quotidian living. He pointed out that the Lord's Prayer is just about having enough for today because that's where we are. I want to live my life in a meaningful direction not by a burdensome punch list. While in Ray Brook I went to an Episcopal church service with a priest wearing a robe and nice stained-glass windows and the whole gold chalice thing. In a quiet ritual, everyone got up and was served communion. It took a long while. But even after everyone was back in their seats, we waited and watched the priest clean up and wash the cup as a part of the ceremony. This formal ritual required a public display of doing the dishes! That's when I really grasped the meaning of "quotidian" and how important every little daily task is. My thoughts are a bit jumbled but I'm hoping we can talk more. I've never written to someone who lived just around the corner. This will really make the postman wonder about us!

All my bestest,

Sammie

After a long hot day in August, Sammie got cleaned up, had supper with the Andrews, and he and Nora retired to the porch swing. Back and forth they glided while watching the occasional car or horse ride by. Ida never said a word. She was convinced that she would have to wait this whole thing out and prayed for the best.

By the middle of August, however, they found their groove and found time and energy for a day or two at the Saratoga racetrack, and, of course, they attended the Grange picnics and the Strawberry Social at the White Creek Creamery. Sammie and Nora, Henry and Ray spent a day together at the Great Cambridge Fair and truly had a wonderful time. Nora was so happy to see her brothers and Sammie enjoy each other so. They all cheered as Henry swung the sledgehammer and rang the bell on the High Striker game. Sammie could hardly even lift the sledgehammer let alone swing it. He was amazed at Henry's strength. Henry, actually, didn't know his own strength and was admired by many for his handsome looks and brute force. Elizabeth Cottrell certainly fell into that category.

No matter what the week brought, Nora and Sammie always relied on their Sunday ritual. Of course, they did their morning farm chores and Sammie always picked Nora up for church where it was now *acceptable* for them to be together. They then had dinner at either the Andrews or the Telfords and then, after evening chores, they headed out to a picture show at night. Sunday was their favorite day.

The Telfords, Dundases, and Andrews worked together and threshed 500 bushels of oats from the Telford ground and then they rotated and worked each of the three farms together; Sammie was getting stronger and always finding chores he could do. As summer started to wind down, Nora eagerly began preparing to teach at Schoolhouse #13 in Brigg's Corners and Leah was to be at Groveside. They were excited.

Uncle Jim and Aunt Edith McCart invited Sammie and Nora to their 500 Card Party. 500 was a popular game at that time. It was the social event of the summer, and all of their friends would be there to play. They were one of the 24 couples there. What fun everyone had. Sammie and Nora were feeling comfortable being seen together as a couple outside of church. Shy, yet clever, Nora learned to talk trash right along with the rest of them.

"C'mon. Play one. Look at the rest," she would always say, prodding someone to make a hasty decision and misplay their hand.

As she was maturing, she was finding her voice. The party lasted until 3:00 in the morning and Sammie was quite happy to have such a good card player as a partner. They didn't win the final game, but they sure gave the others a run for their money. This was the final night of the summer for Nora, as she and Leah had a district-wide teachers' meeting the next day. She was quite excited and nervous. But time passed quickly, and as the days of teaching school turned into weeks, she realized that Oneonta Normal had taught her how to be tough when it came to student discipline and earning respect.

6

School Days

Thus, with the daily grind of school routine, the hours passed slowly, but the weeks passed quickly; Sammie loved working on the farm planting potatoes, filling silo, husking corn, and milking cows, while Nora taught school, prepared lessons, graded papers, and cleaned the school building. Together, they led their church youth group leadership gatherings called Epworth League meetings named for the British birthplace of John and Charles Wesley, the forefathers of Methodism. They also attended White Creek grange meetings (a grange is simply a house with outbuildings) and worked the degree team. Following Robert's Rules of Order, the first four degrees, or levels of study, focused on teaching young people about farming in each of the four seasons. Mason and Leah worked right alongside them, and the two couples quickly became the talk of the town. Nora and Sammie grew closer together, and, as more and more time passed, even Ida *almost* forgot all about Sammie's previous TB diagnosis and Sammie joined the Andrew family and their boarder, Fremont, for dinner just about every night.

On a cloudy October morning, Henry was coming back from town where he had the Bay Team shod, when he found a riderless horse grazing at the side of the road. Now, it wouldn't have been odd at all to find a horse that had gotten out, but a riderless horse with a saddle was a different thing. He poked around the burdocks and tall grass and found King, the fishmonger, lying in the ditch nearby. He had got his drunk on and was passed out in a pool of his own vomit. Henry picked up King's frail body that reeked of fish, vomit, and alcohol and laid him in the back of the buckboard. Henry took the grazing mare by the reins and tied her to the wagon and headed for home. Everyone knew that King hit the bottle too much and too often. Many thought he was gruff and didn't talk that much.

Seth frequently said, "every man has his secret sorrows which the world knows not; and, oftentimes, we call a man cold when he is only sad," as he helped Henry bring King up the stairs.

Neither of the men could believe how frail King was as they laid him down in Henry's bed to sleep it off. Henry told Mother to set an extra place at the supper table that night. King very much needed the bed to sleep in and greatly enjoyed a good supper that night. He stayed all night and Henry took the couch. Seth asked him to stay on a few days to help on the farm, which he did. Ida made a point of buying more fish from King after that.

November meant that Sammie had his six-month appointment in Troy with Dr. Irish. Nora paced the platform anxiously awaited his return on the train. He had been taking it easy physically and helping where he could but left the hard labor to the strong and able-bodied. He stepped off the train and said to Nora, "I got the 'all clear' to keep doing what I'm doing. X-ray looks good. Next visit in 6 more months." And off they went to share the good news with their families.

Just before Thanksgiving, Florence was busy getting her geese prepared for sale. She loved raising them and turned a good profit having them dressed and oven-ready for everyone's holiday table. She always kept her favorite goose, Gary, as a pet, however. Julia was out doing her chores when Gary decided that he was in a pissy mood and started hissing at her. Julia decided that she was in a rather pissy mood herself, "You scoot!" she shouted, "Get away!"

She threw sticks and rocks at him to no avail. Gary started chasing her. There's a reason why a goose is called a goose. Julia was running all over the barnyard with Gary's beak nipping at her backside. Florence watched out the kitchen window laughing as little Julia battled it out with Gary. Julia ran as fast as she could and hopped over the wood-rail fence into the hog yard where six giant sows were sleeping the day away. Surely, the fence would keep Gary the Goose away from her. But, surprisingly, Gary flew up and over the fence and chased her across the hog yard. Julia screamed and jumped up and over the fence on the other side to get a way. The sassy gander followed her and hopped up onto the top rail of the fence in hot pursuit. Florence was still enjoying the show from the window. Julia turned and looked back and to the horror of all, one of the sows grabbed onto Gary by the tail feathers and pulled him down to the ground. Feathers were flying and pigs were squealing, and it was over in one final screaming HONK. Both Julia and Florence froze in disbelief as Gary was no more.

At dinner, Herb said, "That's why we don't keep farm animals as pets."

After Thanksgiving that year, Cousin Ed finally arrived with his equipment to wire both the Telford and Andrew houses for electricity. Everyone was over the moon at the new modernizations that seemed to be happening everywhere. Sammie learned everything he could about electricity and Cousin Ed taught him how to install light fixtures. Both Ida and Ma Telford had their eyes on the new electric washing machines.

"Turning two loads of laundry a day really sucks," Ma Telford said to Ida who agreed wholeheartedly. Back in the day, the washing machine worked with a hand-operated crank and a lot of manual labor.

When Christmas rolled around, Henry, Ray, Sammie, and Nora went out to the woods to cut down a Christmas Tree for Nora's school entertainment. They came across brother Will, rabbit hunting while out in the woods.

"You're scaring all my rabbits away!" he kidded.

Ray suggested that rabbit hunting over on Tuttle's Hill, but Will had already gotten four rabbits so was none too disappointed and was happy to help with the tree. Like his father, Will was a man of few words and was more comfortable with dragging the tree through the snow than he was talking about it. It wasn't so easy dragging it out in the snow, so they took turns dragging it two by two.

On New Year's evening, Nora and Sammie wanted to be alone, so they went up to Nora's school and lit the cast-iron potbelly stove. The tree was still up, and the schoolhouse smelled of Christmas. Soon, the school was toasty warm. Sammie sat on the floor up against Nora's desk by the tree and she snuggled up close to him. There were no nerves. There was no forcing it. They snuggled under his coat and the kissing they experienced was effortless and right and perfect and slow. Had there been records kept of White Crikk's most romantic evenings, surely this would have registered as at 10 out 10. But it had to come to an end, as all good things do. The fire got too hot, and they had to open some windows for a bit. They didn't stay too late as Sammie had to draw a load of sawdust early the next day for the ice house.

In February, once there had been a good long spell of below-freezing weather, Pa Telford announced that the ice was "ripe" and the Andrews and Telfords joined forces cutting ice from Wolfrum's pond. They had to wait for a good long cold spell until the ice was almost a foot thick, usually about the middle of February, each year. First, they all gathered to scrape the snow off the ice which neighbor kids usually enjoyed helping with. Then the two-man cutting crew used the one-horse ice plow to score the ice with a pattern of giant rectangles. One man led the horse while the other steered the ice plow. A long saw, about 4 feet in length, and a very strong arm was used to complete the final cutting. The first block was always the most difficult, but after that, as each block was cut, it would drift on the surface of the water.

At this point, a second cutting team used long poles with spear-tipped ends to secure the floating ice blocks and then hoisted them up and out of the water and onto the surface of the ice with ice pics. It was cold, wet, messy, hard work, and all of the men were happy for the extra pairs of dry gloves, snacks, and hot coffee and cocoa that the women had prepared for them. This second cutting team then used a long 2-handled saw to cut the ice blocks into smaller 'ice cakes' that were about 18"x24". The cakes were then pushed up a wooden ramp and onto the sleigh. When loaded, the two-horse logging sleigh bore a considerable amount of weight.

"If one horse can pull 8,000 pounds, 2 horses can pull 24,000 pounds," Seth said. "That's the miracle of teamwork for ya."

The Andrews used their Bay Team and the Telfords provided their team of draft horses for drawing alternating loads of ice. That they sold and delivered to everyone between Wolfrums and their farms.

Nora and Ida cooked all morning together and brought over more food and hot drinks in thermoses. Ida admired Sammie's kind way with the horses and was sure to remind everyone to make sure they didn't fall into the water. Nora made up a special tin of food for Sammie's lunch and brought it over to him,

"I hear you're selling lots of ice today!" Nora said.

Sammie replied, "In Post Corners, it's what we call making cold, hard cash." They smiled at each other's cheesy jokes. While he ate his lunch, Nora sent the young neighbor boys home to eat after she had them bring up buckets of water for the horses. Nora fed the horses from the canvas feed bag while the men rested.

The first goal of the day was, of course, to fill each Telford and Andrew ice house (and not fall in the water). The second goal was to sell the ice for a fair profit to the houses between Wolfrum's pond and the Andrew and Telford farms. Sammie had gone door to door earlier in the week to make his sales. The Telfords had been selling ice for some years now and this side business was growing quite nicely. Most families ordered enough ice to fill their ice houses and Sammie paid the older neighbor boys to stack the cakes inside each ice house. Sammie supervised while they did all the heavy lifting. Sammie oversaw the dispersing the sawdust between layers of ice. This year, using the two sleigh teams, they totaled 245 cakes at 2 cents per cake with $4.90 going to Wolfrums. Both families filled their ice houses, and they sold enough ice to pay for the entire endeavor all by evening chore time. The home fires felt wonderful that night!

Ice houses, if insulated with enough saw dust around the perimeter and between each cake, could keep ice all through the spring and summer and up to the next winter. When needed, a cake would be brought inside and placed in the "ice box" which was a large wooden tin-lined box for keeping kitchen groceries cold. Ray always found it a pain in the neck when it was time for another ice cake to be brought in from the ice house. He and Ray often arm wrestled over who would have to bring it in. Henry always won, so Ray was stuck with that chore most often.

That Friday night, Nora treated her older students to the movies. There was plenty of snow, so Sammie drove his sleigh and picked up the children who all lived near the school. They had the sleigh bells on the horses to warn pedestrians that they were coming, as sleighs don't always stop quickly enough. It turned out that only the girls were able to go, as none of the boys could attend. The girls thought that was odd. So, Sammie and Nora, with a sleigh full of girls, headed to the Falls for the picture show.

"Who needs the boys, anyway?" the girls exclaimed. They laughed and huddled together under a heavy blanket. When they came around the corner by the frozen White Crikk swimmin' hole, they were ambushed by the boys with snowballs from behind the stoned wall behind the hedge row that ran alongside the road. Nora had set the whole thing up. Ray had picked the boys up early to make snowballs and lie in wait for the battle. The girls were screaming. Nora and Sammie didn't show up for their fight empty handed, however. They were prepared with two bins of snowballs under the seat, and the girls were able to fight back.

All too soon, the girls were out of ammunition and Sammie asked, "Should we make a run for it?"

"YES!" the girls called out.

The surprise attack turned into a race to see who could make it to the movie theater first: the boys' sleigh or the girls'. It was all good fun and Nora was just happy that no one got hurt with the horses running full tilt down the road and through town. She made Sammie slow down when their bob sled went around the corner on just one runner. The students were red-cheeked and cold when they arrived at the theater and had a wonderful time.

The following day was Saturday and Sammie was down at Byron's in Hoosick Falls getting his haircut when Nora arrived delivering the unfortunate news from Niagara Falls that his Uncle Eliphalet McCracken died. Ma Telford had received word while over at Cottrell's and knew Sammie would want to know. She stopped at the Andrews, thinking Sammie would be there and Nora volunteered to bring the news to Sammie down at the Falls.

"He was 61 years old. His funeral will be on Monday. Your mother surmises that you'll probably want to go," said Nora.

"I'll definitely go, he was a great man… but I'll miss you. I'll send you a postcard every day," he said.

"You'll be back before they arrive!" Nora said from her practical side, but her heart certainly appreciated the gesture. Nora was happy to see him off the next day and they both joked that maybe she would get caught up on her work if Sammie wasn't taking up all of her time.

Nora did get a lot of work done and missed having Sammie around that week. She knew that he would actually mail her postcards every day, so she jotted down a short note for him each day. After a week, Sammie returned, and a few days later, as his postcards arrived each day, they sat on the porch swing and read each other's notes for that day. The postcards and notes read as follows:

Nora, Bitter cold here today.
Staying with Sarah and Clauson. He's got a Model T Ford.
I read scripture at the funeral.

Day 1 with no Sammie.
Florence and Julia both sick with the grippe
and I went up and stayed all night with them.

Nora, Bitter cold.
Went around Goat Island and the foot of the falls.
Heard jazz music at a restaurant with Clauson and Sarah.

Day 2 with no Sammie
Ma Telford went up to take care of Florence and Julia.
Both sick with a grippe in the head.
Aunt Maggie came over to cook for the Telford men.
Ray fell and hurt himself,
so Fremont is working here a couple days.

Nora, Bitter cold here again.
Sarah gave me a tour of Niagara Wall Paper Co.
Niagara Falls High School burnt down.

Day 3 with no Sammie
Edward absent from School with bad cough.
I got all of my schoolwork done, finally.
Helped mother wash and churned in evening.

Nora, Bitter Cold and sunny.
Sarah and Clauson took me to Hippodrome Theatre in Buffalo.
Had a fine time.

Day 4 with no Sammie
Mrs. William McCart had a baby.
Mason and Leah took me to picture show at night.
Father delivered a load of sawdust from Eddey's to your father.

Nora, Bitter cold.
Spent the day with family in Tonawanda.
Rode in Clauson's new Model T.

Day 5 with no Sammie
Edward absent from school again.
Took my students ice skating.
Farmer's Inn on Hoosick-Bennington Road
burned to the ground.

They both realized that there was no future for them in publishing romantic poems, but, deep down, they appreciated having someone to write for and share their everyday with. They so enjoyed just being together and making plans for their next adventure. Nora and Sammie were able to feel deep connections with each other and all the people they encountered.

Sammie was bitten by the automobile bug after riding around in Clauson's new automobile and he called up Ralph Weir and had one of his salesmen come over and write up the paperwork for buying a brand-new auto. The farm was doing well, and Sammie was always good at knowing where to spend his money. He bought a tobacco brown Chevrolet model 490 for $598.10. A few days later, when the car finally arrived, they were swept up in the excitement and drove it over to Herb and Florence's to show off his new purchase. They were on their way to show Harringtons and Boots when Nora remembered that according to her school contract, she wasn't to be seen in a car with a man other than her father or brother, so they scooted back home right away.

Now, for sure, there was debate over whether or not Sammie should purchase an automobile, but the general consensus in town was that it was about time he bought himself something; a fine young man ought to have his own auto to go about doing business. After his initial drive, showing off the car he was so proud of, Sammie parked it in the barn to keep it as pristine as possible. He wanted it to last forever and he was determined to work harder than ever to pay it off early.

And the year went on just so, with Nora teaching in her one room school house and Sammie working on the family farm each day, and the usual prayer meetings, picture shows, card parties, and White Creek Grange meetings. But it was after the Rock Fry at Jermain's Watering Trough one night that Sammie and Nora got into an "imaginary" discussion about what they each saw in their ultimate "future."

Sammie started. "Well, I like the idea of trying to have lots of children."

Nora slapped his leg. "Get your mind out of the gutter!"

"Okay, okay, okay, I guess we're going to be serious about this then?"

"Of course, we are," replied Nora.

"I do want to have a family. Have a farm that makes so much money people come up to me on the street and ask me about how I get so many apples from just 6 apple trees and why my potatoes fetch such a good price. You can be married 30 years without really being married 1 day. I don't want a marriage where we just live together in the same house, I want to really be 'married every day' to my wife. I want us to have plans. I want to know what she's thinking… so I can go off and do my own thing!" He laughed.

Nora didn't laugh. "Well now, you were on the right track until you gummed it up with your foolish talk. You're never going to get your family that way!"

Sammie was interested to know why Nora wanted this conversation. "Okay, okay, okay," he said. "I'll be proper. What is it you want your future to look like."

Nora took just a moment and then gave her best case scenario. "I think life is meant to be lived with a partner. I see myself with a farm and a family. I want my students to be so smart and score so high on the Regents Exams that other teachers come to me and ask me how that was possible." Sammie was listening. "Many people try to farm it and leave as soon a bit of hardship comes their way. I want to have a family farm that has a good name for… a long, long time."

Sammie interjected. "Wait. Clarify. What's a long, long time?"

"Oh… I don't know… a long time," replied Nora.

"I need more to go on than that," pushed Sammie, "like 30 years? 40 years?"

Nora joked, "I don't know… 100 years."

"One hundred years!?" Sammie exclaimed. "That's a nice round number but, we'll both be dead in a century! How could I promise that?"

Nora replied, "And what kind of good name would we have built for ourselves if our family farm still was in operation with our good name long after we were gone?"

"That's a tough one, out of my reach, but okay. I like a challenge. That goes back to having children, which is the first thing I brought up, and you hit me! And you keep saying "good name" what makes a good name?"

Nora paused here… "Well, not a bad name! 100 years of a bad name would be a terrible thing but a family that keeps their name out of the police blotter and out of the paper! A family that works hard and goes to church; that doesn't disappear when they hit hard times; that has grit; that has deep roots in White Creek and leaves things better than when they found them."

"Okay, I'm good with that."

Nora concluded with, "And I like what you said about being married every day."

At that point, Julia and her friends invaded their space with news of homemade pie and ice cream being served inside.

7

The Bridges of Washington County

When Sammie wasn't on for chores, Sunday afternoon drives became a big deal. On Sundays, after church, when the weather was good, not raining and not too muddy, Sammie's car came out of the barn and they would take an excursion created by Nora with selected family and friends, often, Henry and Ray or Will and his sweetheart, Rena. Other times, Mason and Leah, and Ma and Pa Telford would laugh the afternoon away with them cruising around the countryside exploring roads none of them had ever taken before. Nora would scour the paper and keep her ears open to find unique destinations like the Gladiolas Farm in Berlin, NY and they would drive direct and then she would create a scenic route home through every hook, hollow, hamlet, hill, and dale. They always brought their supper and cooked it on the side of the road and had a grand time.

Once they drove up to have a tour of the Salem Jail where they learned that back in the day, the sheriff operated the jail, basically, as a boarding house for the homeless. He billed the county on a per diem basis for those he incarcerated, so he filled up the jail with tramps from Pumpkin Hook or what's now known as Cobbtown, which had a reputation for being filled with whores, thieves, bootleggers, and swindlers. The Smart Brothers from the Presbyterian Church, who had a column in the Washington County Post, referred to Cobbtown as a "sinkhole of iniquity." The hobos didn't care if they were imprisoned as long as they had four walls and heat to survive the subzero temperatures of winter in upstate New York, and they certainly weren't particular about what they ate.

During the month of May, what many call the "season of mud," the nearby babbling, yet still cold, White Creek was particularly popular with tramps who would have recently finished wintering in the county jail. There were no bathing facilities at the Washington county jail back in the 1880s, so the tramps would head to the river to bathe. And then back to Cobbtown they'd travel for the summer.

On this one particularly hot Sunday afternoon, Nora and Sammie and Mason and Leah packed their dinner and took a trip Nora had laid out to see all of the local covered bridges in Washington County starting locally and then heading North, and then 5 more covered bridges coming back south on the Vermont side. They welcomed the ride because they found relief from the heat with the windows rolled down at their top speed of 40 miles per hour. The breeze on their faces felt good. Mason and Leah were not getting along too well, and Nora thought that if they had to sit next to each other, that would get them feeling closer.

First up was Van Buskirk's Covered Bridge. They had all seen it a hundred times, but Nora was nothing if not thoroughly prepared to start off conversation that she knew all would agree on. None of them could figure out why the Methodist Episcopal society built a church at Buskirk's Bridge on the Washington County side of the road, while the Dutch Reformed Church was already right there but on the Rensselaer side of the road. Why such a tiny hamlet needed two churches was beyond them. Nora planned to sit close to Sammie in the front seat setting the tone for Mason and Leah, but it was just too darn hot for that. Maybe today was the wrong day to attempt promote closeness!

The girls spoke about the frustrations they faced at school while the boys spoke about the frustrations they faced with farming when it was so dry. They all talked about their frustrations with church. They crossed over the bridge and headed up over Oak Hill Road, where there used to be a toll over to Stevenson's Corners, recently renamed Coila.

They continued north where they crossed the Main Street Bridge in lovely Greenwich. Big disappointment.

"Not really a covered bridge, is it?" remarked Mason and Sammie.

Nora had spent a lot of time putting the trip together, so she was disappointed that her choice was a letdown. Leah became defensive on Nora's behalf. Nora had spent a lot of time planning the trip so she remarked that they wouldn't be able to see the beautiful waterfall if the bridge were covered. Now, neither couple was feeling any too close.

After they drove through Greenwich and got out into the country, Sammie said, "Look there. That's Albert Harrington doodlebugging around that barn up there. They must want to be able to water their livestock inside the barn." He pulled over to watch for a bit to see if he'd find water.

Leah asked, "Doodlebugging? That doesn't sound like something I want to watch!"

Mason said, "Ya know, water witching or water dowsing? He holds out a Y-shaped stick called a divining rod and walks around waiting to feel a downward pull. That's where the water is."

Beautiful white face mares came across the field to see their four visitors. The women fed the horses apple slices, and Nora took some pictures while the men chatted about the validity of water dowsing.

"There's groundwater everywhere around here. It's not a matter of where you drill, it's a matter of how deep you have to drill," said Sammie. Mason didn't agree and they didn't stay very long.

They continued north to East Greenwich and crossed over the Rexleigh covered bridge near Salem.

"Did you know that the Granville Quarry, just north of here, is the only quarry in the US that produces red slate?" asked Nora.

"Really?" said Leah, "My dad used to have red slate on the roof of the barn. It spelled out '1865.'

"It's too bad that barn burnt down," said Mason.

"Sammie said, I wonder what makes Granville so special that God gave it red slate of all things?"

"We'll have to take a tour of the slate quarry one day," noted Nora. "On that trip, it'd be nice to cut over to Rupert, VT and Dorset, VT as well. I hear that it's a special part of the world. The men had to stop to pee in the woods.

When they got back into the car, the women were sitting in the back and the men took the front chatting about other farmers' field work. Nora navigated all back roads on her map to the beautiful Shushan covered Bridge and more backroads along the Battenkill River to the Eagleville covered bridge where they planned to take a swim. Sammie and Nora had quite the tiff about the best way to go; Sammie arguing the shortest route, Nora arguing the scenic route. So, when they arrived in Eagleville the men were happy to go off on their own and let the ladies fend for themselves, which was fine with the women. There were many people at the Eagleville Bridge, and they were all delighted to find many friends there taking a break from the oppressive heat. Mason and Sammie helped provide entertainment by jumping off the bridge with the other males into the deep flowing Batten Kill River and the women, secretly drawn to their heroics, urged them to be careful.

Meeting up with other folks at the popular swimming spot seemed to put both couples in a good mood. They dried off and held up towels creating an impromptu dressing room so they could change into dry clothes. They decided to have a bit of a snack there. Then Mason wanted to drive so Leah sat in front with him and Sammie and Nora took the back seat. Nora guided Mason over to the Vermont side on Route 123 where they crossed the Arlington Covered Bridge and then the one in nearby Chiselville that none of them had seen before. As the conversation shifted to all-things Vermont, Sammie mentioned that he had attended a new church in Saranac Lake where they were making a fuss about their bell tower made from Vermont marble.

Nora asked, “Why is it that our rocks are the most interesting thing about us?”

Sammie was giving Mason instructions on driving from the back seat and Nora kept telling Sammie to leave him be. Leah didn’t like Mason’s driving so Leah and Sammie and Nora and Mason were teamed up against each other. Then down the Ethan Allen Highway heading south toward home, they crossed three more bridges over the Walloomsac River in the Bennington area: the Silk Road Covered Bridge, Paper Mill Village Bridge, and, lastly, the Henry Covered Bridge. They would have to come back to the Battle of Bennington Monument another day as it was getting late. Sammie took over the driving again for the back roads he knew well through Walloomsac to North Hoosick and then home to White Creek. Everyone was cooled off from swimming, windblown women rested their heads on their man's shoulder for the final leg of their trip. All in all, it was a good day, and both couples were holding hands by the time they dropped off Mason and Leah.

8

Ma Telford

With their houses being newly wired for electricity, the big news in White Creek was that Ma Telford and Mother Andrew got on the farm truck, drove to Troy and both bought electric Maytag washing machines on the same day. They were rather fed up with asking their husbands over and over for the new washers. The current system of turning laundry was taking its toll on their arms and backs having to turn daily loads of laundry. So, when the Andrew men came in from fixing fence, they found a new washing machine in the house and Ida made them connect it right away! The women had paid the Bowker boys to unload the washers off the back of the farm truck. Nora didn't know which was more worthy of gossip; that these meek and mild mothers would go buy washing machines, or that they would do such a thing without any real discussion with their husbands!

Seth said, "Well, I thought you were just making a lot of racket about wanting one of those new machines, but 'Noise proves nothing. Often a hen who has merely laid an egg cackles as if she laid an asteroid.'"

"You and yer sayings," said Ma.

Right around Sammie's birthday was time for his 12-month check-up, so off he went to see Dr. Irish. This time, he took Nora with his automobile, and they spent the day in Troy. The doctor explained to Nora that the TB is still in Sammie's lungs, that's why he couldn't ever overdo. If he were to even start up coughing again, he could dislodge the healing that his body had formed around the TB bacteria.

"I didn't know that the TB was 'latent' inside you," commented Nora afterwards. "That's a bit disconcerting."

"It's just the nature of the disease," said Sammie. "My release papers say that I'm 'Apparently Recovered' or healed. My body has healed itself. They tell me that no relapse for the first 2 years is as close as I'll get to being 'cured.' I'm sorry if I don't remember to tell you everything. It seems like if it's in my head, it must be in your head too." Sammie was happy to share his good report from the doctor back home with his family.

While Sammie, Nora, Henry, and Ray were working the first and second degrees at the White Creek Grange, word was received that Ruth Masten's husband died of heart problems. They all agreed to pitch in to send flowers to Ruth. Most of the town planned to attend the funeral as well as Sammie and Nora.

"First, her son is killed and now her husband dies," said Nora. "How can the woman face another day? I can't imagine."

Nora didn't expect an answer, but Sammie thought for a moment and replied, "I asked that same thing a Ray Brook. So many died. The nurses said to think of sorrow as a tunnel, not a pit. You just have to keep putting one foot in front of the other to move through it."

That summer, Julia was 11 years old and started riding horses. She couldn't find a saddle and was warned never to ride side saddle, since one of Byron and Fannie's girls in Brigg's Corners was thrown from her horse when the saddle slipped. Herb rented a work horse named Sally from Seth Andrew at $10 for the season. Sally was a cribber, which meant she obsessively bit down on whatever board or railing she could find, which destroyed her stall and fencing, so she had to wear a leather cribbing collar to help with that. Cribbing could be bad for a horse's upper teeth if they did it enough. Herb used Sally on the dump rake as she was meant for work and not riding.

"Then let me run the dump rake," said Julia.

And that was Julia's foray into the world of "men's" work. She enjoyed her long hours on the seat of the dump rake being pulled by Sally. They got along famously, and Sally's cribbing became much improved.

"Clearly, Sally and Julia each needed a friend this summer," said Florence. "They're kind to one another and they keep each other entertained all day long."

Herb actually received some comments that Julia's windrows looked better than his!

Just a few days later, they called Dr. Shaw in to see Ma Telford, who was taken ill. She hadn't been feeling well at all for some time now. She'd had a terrible grippe in the head for weeks, wasn't eating anything, and just wasn't right.

"She must have a complete rest," said Dr. Shaw.

So, Sammie and Nora brought Ma up to stay at Herb and Florence's. A relative, Matilda McCracken, who had served overseas during the war came to nurse Ma as well. Aunt Maggie moved over to keep house for the Telfords for the duration. It was accepted that Ma was very sick. Very sick.

However, one thing that farming teaches us is that life never stops. Never. The cows always have to be milked and fed morning and evening. The crops always need to be planted, harrowed, and harvested. You have to keep putting one foot in front of the other. So, while Ma Telford was on her bed rest, the men stayed busy and hayed it. On a hot Sunday afternoon, Nora and Sammie, Henry, and Ray wanted to go help Pa Telford take his mind of things, so they went out to pick cherries. Ma loved cherries. Nora, Aunt Maggie, and Sammie canned 31 cans. Being productive like that was always admired. Sammie and Nora brought a few quarts of fresh cherries up to Ma and two pies for Florence when they visited that night.

Sammie and Nora were in church on a very hot July morning, Herb came in and tapped Sammie on shoulder. They stepped out into the foyer. Ma Telford had taken a turn for the worse. She had been seen by three doctor's and none of them could identify the problem. They immediately went up to see Ma. All the Telfords were there. Nora keeping little Julia occupied with a game of dominos while the adults talked. It was very serious. Matilda thought it might be a growth on the brain. Nora overheard the conversation with Pa Telford and Dr. Shaw deciding if they should bring her to the hospital or not.

Nora's heart paused for a moment. Life and death are something you learn very early on a farm. You raise pigs and chickens to butcher them. You order 200 chicks and some of them don't arrive alive. If calves aren't fed too much milk, they get scours and die. You have a puppy that runs in front of the tractor and Little Jack is gone forever. But saying goodbye to Ma would be tough on everyone. They all hated seeing her suffer so. Nora knew Sammie and Will were very attached to her. When Will was bothered by something, he went racoon hunting. He got over $100 worth of furs in one weekend.

Eventually, when the men had to leave to do evening chores, Florence kicked everyone out to give Ma some peace and quiet. Each night, they expected the news to come that Ma didn't make it, but day after day, she kept pulling through.

Sammie and Nora went up each day to see Ma for just a short visit. In August, they brought her some fresh picked blueberries. Visitors were coming in from all over to see her. Sammie and Nora escorted the Niagara Falls folks from the train to Herb and Florence's place to see Ma. It was nice to see Meredith and Clauson again but Nora wished it had been under better circumstances. As visitors came and went, the men all continued to cut oats together during the day and Pa stayed with Ma all night. The men moved the Dundases' binder from one field to another, one farm to another, working together. The women kept the men watered and fed in the summer's heat.

In between visitors, Sammie went for a walk alone to pray. *God, I'm confused. Why can't you take the good ones quickly? Better yet, why don't you heal the good ones? Ma is a hard worker and always goes to church. She might gossip a bit too much, but she's suffering something terrible. Please take her now. I can't believe I'm saying that. I don't want her to go. She's a good mother. I hate seeing her suffer so. It's tearing me up inside. Please take her quickly. Ta bron orm.*

The start of school was just a couple of weeks away and Nora went up to stay with Leah Harrington at Hedges Lake. The plan was to prepare for school, but mostly they talked about what it was like to be engaged and weddings! They went blackberrying and talked for hours. Leah was to marry Mason and start a farm, but she was concerned that his "want" to farm outweighed his "knowledge" of farming. Nora's concern with Sammie was that he seemed to be out of the woods with his TB, but it was always possible for him to have a relapse if he overdid, and he was forgetful.

"I swear he'd forget to eat if he weren't called in at every meal time!"

For Nora, year two of school started without a hitch and Sammie was preoccupied with the work he could do and visiting his mother. Since Sammie was over a year out from his TB, he was allowing himself to work a bit harder. And then, on September 13, 1922, a little over two months after she had been at Florence's, Herb came down in the morning to tell everyone that Ma died at 2:00 am with Pa and Florence at her side. Florence and Pa made the funeral arrangements with the Baker's. He bought six burial plots up in Cambridge. He liked the idea of family sticking together even after death. Nora and Florence took Pa to buy a new suit. He looked so handsome. He was quieter than usual. It took so much energy for him to receive all of the relatives and condolences. Jeannette Horton Hunt, a neighbor, dressed the body and prepared it for burial.

They had a service a couple of days later right there in the parlor. People from all over White Creek and beyond came to pay their respects. People dropped off food and flowers and gifts. Before the funeral service, the close family members gathered upstairs while they waited for the funeral to begin. As the family came down the stairs and took their seats, they saw that even more family from Niagara Falls and Philadelphia were there. It felt like the whole town showed up for the funeral and there were people outside in the yard.

Sammie and Will were quite pensive. They had never lost anyone this close. Sammie just wanted to be alone with Nora. But, as usual, after the funeral, the families gathered and had a splendid time, sharing memories and catching up on life in their part of the world. Nora helped in the kitchen, took a lot of pictures, and kept an eye on Sammie. A few of the neighborhood farmers got together and did the Telford barn chores and milking that evening. Sammie and Will sat with Pa as they told their stories and listened to how much everyone appreciated Ma. They all enjoyed it and looked handsome in their suits.

Everyone got up the next day and firmly put one foot in front of the other. It was daily chores that got them out of bed and got them moving. The women had to cook, clean, wash, and take care of the chickens, while the men took care of the cows and had corn to cut. After a full day of cutting corn and then evening chores, Sammie took Nora up to the cemetery to water the wreathes on Mother's grave that Nora helped make. Nora knew that Sammie, especially, would miss his mother. He was devoted to her. Sometimes, they brought Pa and Julia and Florence. They brought sweet cider to enjoy. Florence was tough but she cried sometimes. It was a good opportunity to answer Julia's questions about death and heaven and God. Sammie remarked on what a perfect and peaceful view it was from her spot on the hill.

"Yep. She was a good wife," said Pa.

On a beautiful cool breezy October day, Florence let everyone know that she was going to be refinishing the old chairs Ma gave her that she had been storing in one of the sheds. The air was dry, perfect for sanding without having it stick to you.

She said, "These are the chairs with the engraving on the back that Ma loved and passed down to me, but they need so much work."

She was going to honor Ma by refinishing and caning those chairs. She had already put Herb on chair repair and that much was done. Now it was time to sand and stain and varnish them, so Sammie and Nora, Herb and Julia joined her in the forenoon for that job. It was messy hard work, but the chairs were in good shape and looked amazing for the next Saturday when the same crew gathered to cane the chairs. Caning is a beautiful weaving technique used to make the seat of a chair. Florence had purchased the caning from the Crikk Store and taught her little class how to cane just like Ma taught her. And in a few hours, she had five chairs that were as good as new and five people that were quite proud of their accomplishment.

"Good job, Florence. Ma would be pleased," Sammie said.

As time marched forward, Nora was proud of Sammie for continuing his generosity with helping the local farmers. He got the Dundases going with their field corn and kept particularly busy fixing the tractor, helping Nora's father fill silo and went to the Paper Mill to sharpen the ensilage cutter knives when needed. He was definitely mechanically inclined, which comforted Nora and helped her feel secure.

"Your Ma is proud of all you do," said Nora.

9

Santa Claus and Nurse Nora

Soon, it was Thanksgiving time, which meant that Sammie had his 18-month check-up. Nora had been watching him work harder than he had been and anxiously awaited a good report from Dr. Irish, which Sammie gladly delivered to her. Their plan to build a good name together was on track. But Nora thought it wise to wait for his 2-year anniversary of being released from Ray Brook so that Sammie would have his Apparently *Cured* papers. Once Nora received word that Sammie's TB was still latent, she could feel the tension leave her shoulders. Now she could focus on preparing her students for her school's Christmas Entertainment.

As a second-year teacher, Nora really wanted to make a great impression on her students' parents. The first 3 weeks of December were quite busy for her. She selected readings and recitations for her 13 students plus a short play for the school Entertainment, which was always the last night of school before Christmas vacation. She had to make sure there were materials for students to make decorations, and she got started writing Christmas cards to each of her students and making them presents. She knew to let her students play outside until they were good and tired. They she would let them inside where they could hang their wet socks and boots and coats to dry by the potbelly stove while they sat and learned their recitations for the program. She just wanted to make sure it was a nice evening for everyone. Susie

Lake had been very popular with the parents and students, and Nora knew she had big shoes to fill.

Nora got Sammie to agree to be Santa Claus. She found cheap red fabric and made him a new suit. The school board and parents thoroughly enjoyed having Sammie participate in the school activities but thought it best to refer to Sammie as one of Nora's "brothers" when he helped at the school. Early in December, Henry and Ray brought over the Victrola from the living room. Nora was no musician, so when it came time to rehearse the singing portion of the program, she just wound up the old Victrola and let the records lead the singing. Henry, Ray, and Sammie went out and found a nice tall Christmas tree and dragged it out of the woods as they collected ground pine in burlap sacks, which they delivered to the school. The children got busy winding the ground pine while "Miss Andrew's brothers" put up the Christmas tree and fastened it to the wall for safety.

The few days before the program, Nora was fitting Sammie with his Santa suit and Sammie found himself assuring Nora that her program would be just fine. She packed the students' presents into Santa's draw-string sack, thinking, *If ever there was a contest for the skinniest Santa in White Creek, Sammie would be the winner.* Even with a large pillow tucked into his shirt, he just looked pathetic. Unfortunately, he had been having a terrible sore throat for days, so he'd make a raspy Santa for sure. Sammie went to the school at night and Nora walked him through the program and his role. He would enter through the front door with a loud "HO! HO! HO! MERRY CHRISTMAS!" immediately following Jingle Bells. She would help him hand out the students' presents that were on the tree and then he would hand out presents from his bag. Easy-peasy.

Well, on the day of the entertainment, Nora's students rehearsed all day and seemed to forget everything they had been working on.

They didn't sing well. They didn't remember when to stand or move to the platform. Half of them were sick. She had to make a lot of changes. A frustrated Nora came home to find that Sammie had completely lost his voice. Nora refused to panic. She got on her sewing machine and whipped up elf hats for Henry and Ray and they would help Sammie along with his role. *God bless Henry and Ray!* Nora knew that kids were kids, and it was acceptable to have lots of things go wrong because of it, but she felt like the evening was going to be a big letdown for the students and reflect poorly on her. She just resigned herself to the fact that this year would be a disappointment.

***

Here is an actual excerpt from Nora's 13-year-old Elizabeth Howard's 1923 student composition book entitled: OUR CHRISTMAS ENTERTAINMENT

A few weeks before Christmas, we were wondering whether it would be best to have a Christmas program or not. We asked our teacher, Miss Andrew. She said if we would get busy and learn some pieces we might.

Miss Andrew thought maybe it would be best to have it with another school. She said we would not have to learn so much. But finally, we students decided to have it alone.

Miss Andrew found some songs and pieces and dialogues were selected and assigned and we started memorizing. Now we must think of trimmings for the school room.

We wanted it to be different than the year before. Miss Andrew's three brothers got us some ground pine and put up our Christmas tree. We wound the ground pine into ropes and swooped it along the chair railing around the whole room. We

placed a poinsettia shelf where each swoop came up to the railing. We cut long strips of paper and stapled them together to make a long chain. Miss Andrew's brothers got a ladder and tacked our paper chain to the high ceiling, crisscrossed from corner to corner. She promised to bake them a pie. At the back, in cut out letters, was "WELCOME." At the chimney we had a wreath and inside this wreath hung a bell. We also fixed up a beautiful fireplace which Miss Andrew painted on a wooden black board and set it by the tree. We wrote "MERRY CHRISTMAS" on both of the slate blackboards.

One corner became the stage for our program. Our curtains were hung so there was a wing on each side and a place between was the platform. We practiced our singing with the Victrola. Miss Nora said she wasn't a good singer and she was right.

The morning of our entertainment we brought in our presents. We practiced nearly all day. Then, we trimmed the tree and put our presents on it. We were so excited. Then we went home to do our chores. When we came back at night the whole school was lit with 100 candles and it smelled like magic. The schoolhouse was filled with our relatives and friends whom we had invited. Everyone was there.

Finally, it was time to begin. We sang loudly with Miss Andrew's victrola and then we recited our pieces. Our parents laughed many times. Rachel had stage fright, so Julia went up and sat with her during her recitation and helped her get started. We sang Jingle Bells while Miss Nora lit the candles on the tree, then Santa and his elves burst in and just about broke the door. I've never heard Pa laugh so loud.

The Christmas tree was the best part for the children. They stared at Old St. Nick and his elves handing out the presents on the tree. Some of the gifts were tricks and people had jokes played on them. Some got potatoes. Some got doughnuts or lollipops. The school sang a "Good Night Song" to Santa and his elves.

We were a little tired but very happy for we had had a good time and received many nice presents. Ma and Pa said that they had a fine time.

Everyone went home but Sammie's throat was so uncomfortable, that he went to the Troy hospital the next morning and had his tonsils out! He came back the day after Christmas and stayed at the Andrew place so Nora could take care of him for the week. It was Nora's first real experience nursing someone back to health. She asked her mother what he should eat. Custard was all he could get down morning noon and night. For the most part, all they discussed was the outrageous $22 hospital bill that covered his surgery and 4-day stay. Everyone could see that Nora had a knack for taking care of the sick. Every time Sammie rang the little bell from the guest bedroom, Henry would call out, "Nurse Nora! Nurse Nora!" just in case she didn't hear it.

The winter of 1923 proved to be a snowy one. It was bitter cold and snowy with lots of hail and ice storms. Since autos were new, so were winter drivers. Seth took Ida out for a Sunday drive over on Potter Hill and the auto skidded completely around and went over the bank. They were not hurt and walked to the nearest farm. The folks there were nice enough to harness up their well-trained dapple-grey team and pull that car right up and out of the ditch with no effort at all.

"Maybe I should have stuck with horses," said Seth, and a terrified Ida agreed. He offered to pay them for their help, but they refused like all good Crikkers would. Seth said that he would have to thank them with potatoes or chickens or something from the farm. Ida had plenty of ideas for a basket of canned tomatoes and preserves and eggs they could bring back in the spring when the roads were clear. There was no damage to the car, so Seth wanted to continue their trip.

"Not on your life!" exclaimed Ida. The only place we're going is back home. And don't run with the car." Ida was clearly done with winter driving.

On Valentine's Day, Sammie, Nora, Mason, and Leah planned a trip into Troy by train to avoid driving on slippery roads. Mason and Leah arrived at the Eagle Bridge train station just in time to park their car and catch the train. Sammie was very protective of his car, so he and Nora arrived early at the station in the carriage with Maude leading the way. They boarded Maude at the Eagle Bridge Inn for the evening and walked across the street to catch the train. They went to a clever show at Proctor's Theatre, a car show that even the women said they enjoyed, ate dinner out, and then saw another performance at the Palace Theater. They caught the late train back to Eagle Bridge where the sleepy couples parted ways. The stable boy had Maude harnessed to the carriage waiting and ready to go.

"It's really dark tonight. Would you like a lantern for your ride home?" asked the stable boy. Sammie accepted and assured him he'd have the lantern back in the morning when he carried the cream. The lantern provided an orange glow to the sleepy travelers and then it started to lightly snow. Sammie and Nora snuggled together for warmth. The clomp-clomp of Maude's hooves, the lantern glow, and the large flakes were mesmerizing. They were in no hurry to get home even though they were tired. They were finally alone. The rest of the world was asleep. Maude seemed to know that his passengers were not paying much attention to her or to the road.

When they finally reached the Andrew's Farm, the snow was really coming down and it was very dark.

Nora asked, "Shall I run inside and ask Mother if it's okay that you stay here tonight?"

"No, I best go home. I can put Maude in our barn and bring her back in the morning." They kissed good night, Nora stepped properly out of the carriage, and went up to her room to watch Sammie's lantern light head down the road. Each was head over heels with the other. Nora scooted up to her room, ignoring her father sleeping in in his chair, who asked her what time it was. Sammie, somehow knew that she would be watching him through her window, so he stood up in the carriage and faced backwards waving the lantern to say one last "good night." Her heart was full and warm. But as he was waving the lantern, Maude went too fast over the frozen washed-out gullies at the bottom of the hill, and it rocked the carriage so that Sammie was thrown out of the carriage into the snow bank. Nora looked puzzled. All she could see was the path of the lantern light which proved quite confusing, yet entertaining. Sammie had to run to catch up with the carriage. Maude knew exactly what she was doing. It was a story that he and Nora kept to themselves and laughed about frequently.

A highlight for Nora were Bernadette's letters. Ida was all about inspecting the ritzy stamps from France. Ida could get lost in thinking all about what European life was like and wanted to know what Bernadette had to say. Nora took the letter up to her room and jumped onto her bed thrilled to hear from her Parisian Normal School friend. She opened the envelope and out fell several blank postcards of the Arc de Triomphe, La Madeleine, La Seine et l'Hôtel de Ville, and Notre Dame. Nora would examine those later with her mother. She wanted to hear what Bernie had to say.

Dear Norrie,

How I miss you! How are things in White Creek? Are you enjoying teaching? I hear that Sammie has continued to be your beau. That is so exciting! Tell me everything.

My English is already fading away quickly. I need you to write to help keep me in practice.

I also have news. I met a wonderful man named Henri. He and I have gotten very close. I am carrying his child and we live at my parent's house. We are looking to get our own flat after the baby is born. I know that's not the way things are done in White Creek, but I am so happy. Please be happy for me. Write soon!

Yours,

Bernadette

A couple years back, it was no secret around town that Sarah, Nora's older sister, was being courted by Howard Evers when she sat her parents down to tell them that she needed to get married. She was carrying Howard's child. Seth and Ida were devastated. Ida cried.

Seth yelled "How can a daughter of mine who has been brought up in church get pregnant? Everyone will think I've raised a whore! What is the matter with you? God Damn it! You are no daughter of mine any longer. I hope that every child you ever have gets sick or dies!" Ida continued to cry.

"Hey now! Let's take a step back for a moment and gather ourselves," said Nora as she came down from her bedroom to help defend Sarah. Sarah didn't deserve the abuse she was getting. Sarah was weeping and trying to leave. Nora was weeping for her and directed her up the back stairs to get her away from the verbal stoning she was receiving. Nora was in an awkward position. She didn't at all approve of Sarah's unspeakable actions and was shocked when she learned of it, but she also was her sister. "Respectable" single girls don't get pregnant in White Crikk. But, at the same time, a respectable girl would never abandon her family, especially her own sister.

Nora mitigated Sarah's situation with her mother and father after everyone calmed down. However, to avoid more family conflict regarding the wedding ceremony, Howard and Sarah ran off to the justice of the peace and got married that week. Sarah had Nora stand up with her and Howard had his brother. Seth had said from the start that he would never attend her wedding and other family members as well would not attend such a disgrace. Sarah was happy to get the paperwork over with and move on with her life. The rest of the family was glad they were officially married now and that there was no wedding event to attend. And no wedding shower and no baby shower. She was never a large part of life at the Andrew family farm after that.

Nora could see Bernadette's situation a bit differently now that her eyes were opened to at least considering that anyone who does something "wrong" or just different doesn't deserved to be abused or shamed. The Biddie Bunch was always counting the months between wedding and the first baby. Nora appreciated the European way of life that was quite different. Bernadette had told them so many stories during their days in Mrs. Hovey's House together. Bernadette accepted the White Creek girls as wonderfully old-fashioned and loved them dearly.

Sarah and Howard were certainly not the first couple to jump the gun and become pregnant before marriage and they certainly wouldn't be the last. The latest well-known secret was that John Dundas, one of the hardworking Dundas brothers in his early twenties, had gotten his girlfriend, Odette, in the family way. It wasn't even proper to speak the word "pregnant."

Odette and Nora graduated high school together. Now that Sarah's boy, Andrew, was 3 years old and a precocious red-headed ball of energy, Nora had eased up even more on how women should be viewed and treated when found in difficult circumstances. *We can never stop accepting people who do things differently than us.* She still felt that a woman should know how to keep her man's hands to himself. Odette was six and a half months along, and they planned to have a small Dundas family wedding.

Sammie had dinner with the Andrews, as usual, and took Nora aside.

"I'm going to stand up with John at the wedding. Odette is going to ask you to stand up with her."

"She's 6 months along already… I don't think I can do that. My sister was one thing, but people would think I was actually standing up for *that kind of behavior*. What would the school board say?"

Sammie thought for a moment. He was angry and Nora knew it.

He calmly said, "What *would* people say if you stood up *with* her? They will *see* that you care more about being a true friend than what others will say. You're not standing up for her behavior, you're stand up with her. Half the hypocritical Biddie Bunch probably had to get married themselves. But you're not a hypocrite. Let 'them' say whatever they will. Just because they say it doesn't mean it's true. Be your own woman and proudly stand with your friend rather than shame her."

Nora saw the wisdom in what he said, yet she still didn't understand how women could let themselves get pregnant.

She answered honestly and softly, "If I let myself stand up with her, I'd actually, feel guilty for not wanting to punish her by ignoring her."

"That's the Biddie Bunch talking in your ear," he said.

After much thought, Nora added, "I certainly don't want to end up as an old Biddie." And after more discussion, Sammie and Nora agreed to stand up with John and Odette Dundas as true friends. It was just a family wedding, but John and Odette also agreed to have Henry and Elizabeth attend as an arranged date with plenty of supervision.

Nora was prepared to have the school board come down on her and replace her, but she did what she thought was right. The next time she saw Mrs. Sisson, she asked her about the situation. The response was, "Oh it was brought up at our board meeting by… someone who was very upset by it. But as a board, we decided that, as the old saying goes, 'The art of being wise is the art of knowing what to overlook.'" And Mrs. Sisson gave her a wink and a smile.

Leah sent word that one of her school children from the Moses farm next door in Eagle Bridge was selling off a few calves and wanted to know if the Telfords or Andrews would be interested?

"Interested?" asked Sammie. "Thomas and Anna have one of the best farms in Washington County! They've got some good ground over there by the river. Of course, I want to look at their calves." So off he and Nora went to buy a calf or two for Pa Telford. They harnessed Maude to the buckboard and off they trotted to Eagle Bridge.

When they pulled into the Moseses' barnyard, Anna was hanging out the laundry. "Hello there, Anna!" called Nora.

"Why, hello there neighbor; how's life over in your neck of the woods?"

"Well, just about the same as it is here, I imagine," answered Nora.

After some more small talk, she told Sammie that Tom was around the side of the barn attempting to cut a whiffle tree for the wagon. While Sammie wandered over to the barn, Anna put Nora to work helping her hang a large damp quilt on the line.

"Hello there, Thomas," said Sammie.

Thomas looked up from his work.

"Why, hello there. We didn't know if we'd ever see the likes of you again!"

"Yes, well I made it back to the land of the living; whether or not that's a good thing or bad depends on who you are, I guess."

Thom laughed.

"I suppose you're here to have a look at those calves I have for sale."

"You suppose correctly!" said Sammie.

After a good look at the four Holstein calves, Sammie decided to buy two of them. They settled on the asking price for one and a whiffle tree for the other. As they entered the pen to separate the calves, the animals got spooked and one of them pushed right through the gate, breaking the latch and now there were four calves on the loose.

"Well now, it appears that my gate is about as useless as tits on a boar hog," said a perturbed Thomas.

"Anna!" he yelled. Anna and Nora both came around to the barn. The women knew all too well the tone in a man's voice that needed help like it was the end of the world.

The ladies came through and saw the calves frolicking joyously in the field. The ladies thought their celebration of freedom was beautiful and humorous. Thomas was a bit angry and started yelling instructions on where to stand so they could maneuver the playful calves back inside. As everyone moved into position, Sammie shook a pail of grain that was in the barn and the calves knew what that meant. Food! Sammie sat right down at the entrance of the gate swishing the grain around, and as soon as one calf came, the rest followed. The others just watched Sammie work his magic. They eventually came up to the bucket and sniffed the grain. Sammie stayed low but moved a few more steps toward their pen. They followed. And little by little, he had them inside the pen and Thomas held the gate closed. Anna applauded.

"You just can't be in a hurry. They seemed pretty happy doing their dance in the field. I wasn't sure it would work," explained Sammie. Anna kicked Thomas in the ankle.

"See, you don't have to call me every time there's a problem." They all chuckled. Nora got a couple of lengths of rope from the buckboard and made lassos. They secured their two new calves, Thomas put Nora on gate duty and he and Sammie carried the calves over to the buckboard.

After the calves were secured, they all walked back over to the front porch. Anna asked Nora into the house, and they soon emerged with iced tea and cookies. It was a beautifully warm Saturday in May and the four of them had a good visit. Nora admired the beautiful quilts she had and the way her house was decorated.

"I go to those quilting bees at Jermain Hall. It's easier to start with some help. That's for sure. I'm not sure what my next project will be, but I fear I'm too busy and too old to take on something new; arthritis and all," said Anna.

"Age is just a number. You can do anything you set your mind to," replied Nora. "So says the 20-year-old," said Thomas and they all got a chuckle out of that.

"You've got good ground here. I've seen your crops. Do you get as many stones as we do higher up?" asked Sammie.

"Oh, my word, yes. My fields frost up just like yours and those blasted rocks come heaving up and out of the ground every spring," Thomas answered. Anna handed Nora a piece of crewel work to inspect. Apparently, she liked to embroider as well as quilt.

"We're fortunate to have taken on such good ground. Our predecessor took good care of it, and we should too. This ground lies between the Hoosick and Walloomsac rivers and was first claimed and populated by the Mohicansacs as their most sacred ground. Where the two rivers come together is known as the mystic cross, right here in Eagle Bridge, which the Mohicansacs called 'Tiashok.' I always feel it's important to pass along the stories out of respect for those who came before us."

Thomas chimed in, "Don't get her started talking about Indians. She'll never stop!"

"What other stories?" asked Nora.

"Well, of course, you've heard of Saratoga Springs down the road just a bit?" Anna continued, "It's one of the few naturally carbonated springs in the country. I believe it was the Mohawk Indians who claimed those springs to be medicinal and bathed in them. Even George Washington himself was an advocate of its restorative powers.

'Taking the waters' was reputed to cure just about everything: kidney and liver complaints, rheumatism, diabetes, heartburn, scrofula, cancer, malaria, hangovers, and weakness of women, whatever that is!?

"Maybe you should go take a dip, Nora," chided Sammie to an unresponsive crowd.

Thomas interjected, "Well, right in your front dooryard, practically, there was the Tabor Mineral Springs. Just the same thing. Thousands of people used to come to bathe in their springs. Back in the day, people used to come and fill their jugs of Tabor Mineral Water."

"Right in White Creek?" asked Nora incredulously.

Thomas continued the story. "That's right. In 1860 someone once offered Mr. Tabor $40,000 to purchase the property—"

"$40,000!?!" Nora and Sammie exclaimed in unison.

"Yes, $40,000, but he wouldn't sell because, good Quaker that he was, he thought all people should be able to share and enjoy his mineral springs free of charge."

"$40,000!?" exclaimed Sammie one more time. Thomas shook his head,

"I bet he's kicking himself now for not taking that deal! Forty thousand dollars for water that tastes and smells like rotten eggs," said Thomas shaking his head.

Anna continued, "The Tabors still farm that same White Creek ground today. Why it runs right up to Herb and Florence's farm. There are some magical and wonderful things that have happened around here. I sometimes wish I could share it with the world."

Thomas turned the conversation to Sammie, "Now, tell us about that bit of a scare you had here a couple years back. We thought we might lose ya."

"Yes. Well, I'm coming up on 2 years with no relapse. Knock on wood," replied Sammie, leaning forward and knocking on the porch rail.

"I went up in the Adirondack Mountains to take the cure."

Anna joined in, "If I recall, and pardon me if I'm talking too much. I do like to talk. But I think there was a fella born right in Bennington, I think one of the Patterson granddaughters married him in Hoosick Falls. Lewis…Lunar…Loomis. That's his name, Loomis. I think he had something to do with starting a sanitarium up there."

Sammie perked up. "Yes. I heard about him while I was up there. I had no idea he had ties to this area. He wanted a sanitarium closer to New York City and easier to get to, so he built one near Liberty, NY. Of course, Trudeau is the big name in Saranac Lake. I was at Ray Brook State Hospital right next door. No matter how cold it got, we were outside 6 to 8 hours a day!

"It gets darn cold up there! I can't imagine." Thomas added, "Well, kid, they sure done right by you because you're still on this side of the soil."

The two couples chatted the afternoon away until it was time to go.

"You two drop in anytime you're out vistin'," said Anna as Maude trotted out of the yard with her four passengers.

10

Because

Later that week, Ida got right into her spring cleaning, took a tumble down the wooden step ladder while washing windows and hurt her back something terrible. Fremont found her and helped get her into the house. Nora finished washing the windows for her ailing Mama. She would be laid out for a while, so, her duties were divvied up between Papa, Nora, and the boys. It fell to Nora to take over the spring cleaning and planting the garden. She didn't mind gardening but wasn't in love with the idea of doing it alone, so Sammie volunteered to take on the garden alongside her. Together, between the Telford and Andrew families' gardening tricks and experiments, a new way to plant the garden was born.

The two began to plot out the garden on paper and Henry went out and plowed up the garden ground with a horse drawn plow.

Sammie said, "Basil and tomatoes go well together, in and out of the garden, as the basil keeps the hornworms off the tomatoes.

"We've always planted parsley near the tomatoes for that same hornworm reason," added Nora, "plus no one really eats parsley so let the hornworms have it! And, of course, marigolds are pretty and keep the root bugs away from the tomatoes, so Mama always planted marigolds in row 1 and tomatoes in row 2.

Sammie jumped in, "Asparagus and tomatoes are good for each other too... I have no idea why, it's just something Ma always said."

"We can put the asparagus in a bed at the end of the row," added Nora. Sammie added his final thought on tomatoes,

"We want to be sure to plant our cabbage far away from our prized tomatoes also! Again, I have no idea why, Ma just always said it."

"There is nothing better than a delicious homegrown tomato sandwich."

Seth came in from refinishing some old chairs with varnish and asked, "You two are still talking about the damn tomatas?"

In May, Mama still was recovering from her sore back. Nora and Sammie were cooking dinner. Sammie was peeling potatoes and Nora was checking the roast and the biscuits. Sammie set some papers on the counter.

What's that?" asked Nora as she flipped the papers over and read them.

Nora gave a yelp of excitement. Enough of a yelp to make Mama wonder if Sammie gave her a ring. Sammie had left for Troy that morning after Nora left for school. He saw Dr. Irish and received his "Apparently Cured" papers. Nora fixed up a plate for Mama and told her the news. Ida was truly happy for Sammie and was certainly relieved with actual certified papers that read, "Apparently Cured." At dinner, Sammie told the men his news and they all congratulated him by toasting him with their milk glasses.

It was a Sunday after church, school had just gotten out, farm work was well underway, and Nora thought Sammie was acting weird but didn't say anything. Sammie announced on the way home that he had planned the afternoon. Ida had fixed them a picnic lunch. They parked the car at the side of the road and hiked up to the top of Perry's Hill.

"It's beautiful up here! Beautiful view of the Nichol's Place," she said.

"That's a nice farm right there. It takes up the whole valley," Sammie agreed.

They spread out their picnic blanket and ate their lunch and commented on what a good cook Mama was.

"Poor May," said Nora. "First, she loses her husband in the war, and then she's forced to rent out their farm. Thank goodness they hadn't had kids yet."

"She's just taking the next right step for herself. That's the best any of us can do..." said Sammie.

Then there was a long awkward silence. Sammie took a deep breath and said, "Well, I haven't had a relapse for two years now. What do you think about making some future plans to have a farm and... get married?"

He held out the ring box and handed it to her. She took it, smiled ear to ear, and opened it up. In the box was a simply beautiful gold ring with opal, her birthstone.

She said, "It's beautiful. I knew it was coming, but I didn't think it would be so soon. Why today," she asked.

"Because. I think it's good to have a plan." Sammie pulled out his hanky and wiped the sweat off his brow.

"Are you in a hurry?" she asked.

"I'd be good with a week or two," he joked.

"How about 6 months?" came Nora's practical answer. They finished their lunch and went back to their families and showed everyone the ring. Seth and Ida were genuinely delighted.

The summer was a busy one with gardening, planning a wedding, and farm work. Of course, Nora wouldn't be allowed to teach during the 1923-1924 school year, as she would be getting married, so she had to arrange to take the whole year off. Later in the summer, Nora's sister Sarah stopped by with little Andrew. She was pregnant again and explained that Howard was drinking a lot and was becoming rough with Andrew. So Nora gladly kept track of Andrew for a good part of the summer while Sarah and Howard worked things out. Sarah was going to have a talk with Howard about his drinking.

"I don't see how Prohibition is doing any good," said Sarah. "He just goes up to Cambridge and buys all he wants."

Ida was back on her feet at this point and said, "He can stay with us as long as you like. We might not give him back!" Nora had a wonderful time. Andrew was sweet and helpful at age 4 and helped with all the chores. Nora knew that she would need to tire him out before he tired her out! But the next day, when Sarah came to check on him, Nora noticed that she was moving rather stiffly. Nora was going to invite her in for lunch, but Sarah didn't even get out of the car.

After she left, Ida commented, "I think her cheek looked swollen."

In July, Nora received a call from Florence. "Odette is having strong, frequent birthing pains and she's home alone. Herb has the car so I have no way of getting to the Dundases to deliver the baby and I can't reach any of the Dundases."

"I don't like where you're going with this. Why me?" asked Nora uncomfortably.

"Because. Maude will get you there quicker than me. Can you ride over and call me? If you can keep her calm, I think Herb will be back soon so I can get there for the delivery."

"You *think* you can get there for the delivery? You *best* get there for the delivery!" Nora could feel that her face was white as a ghost, but she knew how to pull herself up by the bootstraps. So, she saddled up Maude and rode over to Dundases's place. Blood still made her queasy at times, but she knew that she would be okay if she just stayed focused on the helping part, and not the blood part.

She arrived at Odette's and went right in. Odette was lying on her side and in a sweaty panic.

"Nora! My water broke."

"Oh, that's a good sign." Nora surprised herself with how calm, cool, and collected she could stay. She put a cold cloth on Odette's head and assured her that all would be A-OK, but Odette would need to take some deep breaths. Nora spoke softly and moved slowly to get her to calm down. She tried to reach Florence on the phone many times but soon Odette was really pushing. Other than keep Odette calm, Nora had no idea what to do other than gather sheets and towels and boil a bunch of them. Florence finally arrived and showed Nora how to deliver a baby. Nora had seen many animal births: puppies, kittens, calves, horses, goats, and pigs, but never a real baby. Nora was grateful to witness the miracle of life. Odette gave birth to a bouncing baby boy, John Dundas, Jr.

Nora asked, "You could have called anyone in White Creek, why did you call me to help with this blessed event?

"Because. I know you have what it takes to be an excellent nurse," Florence said, "I wanted you to see a birth. Birth is beautiful and messy all at the same time, kind of like death. Death can get messy too."

"I'll try to remember that," said Nora.

As the hot humid summer progressed, Sammie worked harder and harder on the farm and enjoyed blueberrying up on Waites Hill with Nora, Julia, and Pa. The first week of August, word came that President Harding died of a heart attack in his hotel and there was no autopsy, which fed all kinds of rumors. The country was shocked by the sudden death of such a popular president in his third year of office. Vice President Calvin Coolidge was sworn in as the 30th President of the United States. Crikkers liked the idea that the new President was from Vermont. Nora and Sammie listened to the radio all evening and reported any new details. White Creek knew the importance of voting and were quite religious about it. Women, now more than ever, were quite interested in politics. Women had always been interested in politics but only through the lens of knowing how to steer "their men" to vote.

Sammie taught Nora how to drive his auto that August to much criticism and joking from the male drivers.

"Why are you teaching a woman to drive?" they asked.

"Because," replied Sammie every time.

"Aren't you afraid that eventually your woman will be running everything," the naysayers asked.

"Not in the least," said Sammie, "and Nora is her own woman, not mine."

Nora knew that the only response was just to be a good driver and ignore all of the negative comments. She was glad that her parents stood by her. Nora was looking forward to her big excursion which was to drive her mother and father and Sammie up to Mason and Leah's wedding at Hedges Lake on the weekend. There was a party in the pavilion afterwards with dancing and boat rides. It was a grand time.

Nora and Sammie were in charge of the Croquet Game they learned from Bernadette. They were setting it up with Henry and Ray's help. They were hammering the stakes in when Nora and Ida realized that some of the wickets must have fallen out of the box in the car.

She called to Seth, "Papa, can you fetch the wickets in the car?"

She got no response from Seth who was listening to someone finish their story. Nora asked a little louder.

"Just a second, Nora," came Seth's best attempt at trying to not look annoyed.

Ida repeated Seth's words, "Just a *second, Nora.*" She got a chuckle out of that.

Nora asked, "What's so funny about 'just a second, Nora'?"

Ida explained, "Because you're the *second* Nora."

"Whatever do you mean?" The boys wanted to hear what this was all about.

"Well, you know that in 1890, my first baby, a girl, died at 2 years old. Back in those days, we didn't name our babies until they got to be 6 months or a year old. We wanted to see if they would live before we named them. We named her Nora when she was 1. She was our first. Everything was going fine until she got a fever just before her second birthday and I was already carrying Henry. Then, eventually, all you kids came along; Sarah, Ray, and then you. You looked just like our first Nora, so Seth wanted to name you Nora as well."

"I guess you're not as unique as you thought," said Ray to Nora.

"There's two of you?" yelled Henry.

As August came to a close, Nora was very much in wedding-planning mode. November 7 would be here before she knew it. As the school administration required, women were only to teach school if they were single or married. Women who were engaged to be married weren't allowed to teach. So, Nora didn't teach in the fall of 1923. Instead, she made arrangements for the large wedding they were planning, helped run the house, since Mama Ida's back still bothered her on occasion, and took care of Andrew as frequently as possible.

Some of Sammie's New Jersey family came up for a visit and brought a large truck load of peaches. Nora was on the job of cutting up and canning over 90 cans of delicious peaches and baked so many peach pies that they couldn't give enough of them away. When it came to wedding invitations, Sammie asked why they were sending so many invitations to those far away who would never be able to come.

"It's always nice to stay home with an invitation," came Nora's reply.

Sammie and she spent a lot of time addressing the invitations until she decided that his penmanship was lacking and finished them herself.

"My plan worked," said Sammie cleverly.

On September 14, Leah and Verna made a surprise wedding shower for Nora over at Jermain Hall. Over 40 were there and Nora received many fine presents. Many friends including Odette and her baby, Anna Moses, and lots of school moms were there. Her sister Sarah didn't come. The Robertson boys were invited to provide music and there was much square dancing that night. Seth and Sammie were there.

There had been much talk about Sammie's future. Sammie's brother Will planned to stay on with Pa and run the Telford farm, so it was up to Sammie to step up and buy a farm of his own. But there were only a couple of farm possibilities between Bennington and Cambridge that they would consider. The closest one and obvious choice, the Nichols property over in Post Corners. It had a 12-stall barn with two box stalls, well-built outbuildings, a nice large house, and plenty of tillable land with good drainage, good fencing, a pond, and a wood lot. Seth, Pa Telford, and Sammie discussed the value of that farm and a good purchase price.

A few days after the shower, Seth, Sammie, and Nora took the auto up to Greenwich to see May Nichols, the owner of the farm to discuss a purchase. She had been renting out the farm for the last couple of years. They needed to convince her to wrap her head around the idea of selling rather than renting, as a Mr. Fuller was currently renting it.

"A farm is a lot of upkeep and that can get expensive," said Seth. "I can already see how the fences need upkeep and the house has some roofing shingles missing. As fine a renter as Mr. Fuller is, renting is just not the same as owning."

Sammie spoke very little and watched Seth convince her to sell. Of course, they would have to have a lawyer write up their agreement. But in a few days' time, they had Lawyer Green write up their purchase contract for $4,500 for 125 acres, including the woodlot. Each party thought that they got the better deal, which is how every fair deal should be.

But not all things were as exciting as buying a new farm, and soon there was a lot of corn to be husked! So, the Andrews and the Telfords, with the help of their families and friends, as they did every year, hosted an evening barbecue and invited all of their friends over for a husking party. It started in the forenoon with a break for lunch and then all afternoon and late into the evening sitting on stump stools. Even the children helped husk the corn out on the barn floor with the rest of them. Kids made the best huskers but tired quickly. Nora had Julia show the kids how to make corn husk dolls. The boys gathered the husks in hemp sacks. By the evening, the faithful huskers were doing so by lantern and candle light. They took roped hay and stuck the handles of pitchforks straight down into them. They slid candles down onto the tines of the pitchforks to provide impromptu light. Once it got dark, the inappropriate stories started, and the women and children retired to their homes while their Irish friends from Buskirk were taking nips from their flasks and speaking Gaelic to each other and singing their Irish songs and telling stories. Nora and Sammie sat on the porch and listened to the men sing their songs interspersed with gossip and laughter. By night time, Seth was exhausted, the corn was all husked, and everyone knew too much about their neighbors.

Wedding plans were really moving along now. Sammie and Nora went over to look at the house they were buying. It was being rented by the Fuller family, so they didn't spend a lot of time there. They measured rooms and talked through all kinds of ideas. And of course, along with the purchase of a whole farm, what followed next was trips to auctions, as the soon-to-be newlyweds would need to fill the house with furniture, the barns with animals, and the outbuildings with farming equipment.

Not only that, but Sammie was also faced with the issue that Mr. Fuller was renting the property until March 1, so he and Nora had to find a place to live for the 4 months between the time they got married and the time they could move onto the farm. Sammie was a bit overconfident thinking that that wasn't going to be a difficult challenge. Nora left the living situation in Sammie's hands. She had pickles to can and a beautiful trellis to adorn with flowers for the wedding ceremony. The day before the wedding, everything was bustling. Sammie and Nora went up to Cambridge to get their marriage license and then over to Walloomsac to vote for Coolidge.

"You can never be too busy to vote," she said.

On November 11, 1923, Nora, 21 and Sammie, 25 were married at 8:00 pm. Leah Harrington and Verna Lowe and Ray Andrew and Will Telford stood up with them. Seventy-five people were there at the house! There was a special prayer of remembrance for Ma Telford. It was a fine time. All of Nora's hard work paid off and she was eternally grateful to all who helped her make the preparations. Ray drove the newlyweds to the Mayo Hotel in Troy late that evening and the next morning they hopped on a train for Philadelphia. Sammie was still unable to secure a house or apartment to rent from December – March, so he made a deal with Ray that, while they were gone, if he were to find a place for them to rent, he'd receive a nice fat finder's fee. Neither Sammie nor Nora wanted to move back in with her parents after their honeymoon.

It was common for folks to leave White Creek to get married and move south to warmer weather and try their hand at business closer to larger towns and cities. Harry McCart got married some years back. He and his wife, Jill, met Sammie and Nora at the Philly train station. They went out for supper and then to the Cross Keys Theatre. Sammie and Nora wanted to take in as much live theatre and city life as they could. While visiting family in the coming weeks, they were taken to the Aldine Theater, Keith's Theatre, Locust Theatre, as well as the Museum of Natural Science, the Aquarium, a lecture on the bird life on the Island of South Georgia, the Philadelphia Zoo, Independence Hall, and City Hall. They had a wonderful time.

During their second week, Uncle David hosted them and continued their intake of theatre experiences at the Palace and the Lyric Theatre where they saw *Up She Goes* as well as movies here and there. They bought flowers and took them up to the cemetery where Aunt Ella was buried and then over to Johnnie Telford's Bakery where they bought more than their share of goodies. Then Uncle David took them to Pencoyd Farms and all around Chester, PA. They then took a train to Vineland, NJ where they saw Fred, Sammie's much older brother, and Rena Telford and had Thanksgiving with them. Fred grew up on the farm and had moved to New Jersey for a business venture several years back. Farming wasn't for him.

On a crisp December 5 evening, Sammie and Nora arrived back in Hoosick Falls at 6:30 pm after their month-long honeymoon. Ray greeted them at the station.

After some updates, Sammie implored, "So, please, Ray, did you find a place for us to rent?"

Ray gave a long pause. "I'm afraid you two will be staying in Nora's room for the next few months," smiled Ray who knew that they would want the privacy of their own place. Anyone would. Sammie and Nora's eyes met. They had previously decided to make the best of whatever living situation they ended up with.

The whole town was abuzz with news that Sammie and Nora were back. In fact, about a week later, they were the recipients of a horning. A horning is a good-natured way to disturb a newlywed's privacy. About 30 of Sammie and Nora's friends collaborated to meet at the church and then drive over to the Andrew's place where Sammie and

Nora were now living. Before they got there, they all switched their lights off. They slowly drove in their circular driveway and parked all around the house and when the signal was given, everyone flashed their lights and beeped their horns. This is what passed as fun for White Crickkers in 1923. Then, after all the cows and pigs have had heart attacks, the "horners" bring cider and cookies and all sorts of goodies inside for the newlyweds. Nora and Sammie enjoyed telling them about all they saw on their honeymoon.

The rest of December was eventful as well. Sammie and Nora received two more hornings from other groups of friends and family. Sammie went out and cut a couple of bee trees and got 79 pounds of honey. He was glad that he waited until winter time to go after honey! And Henry, Ray, and Sammie built a new ice house over at their new farm and Nora made lists of items they would need for the new house. The new normal, at least for the time being, was that Fremont went back to live at Telfords and Sammie filled-in doing chores on whichever farm needed him the most. A place called Hoods was where they could now get the best price for their milk.

One very cold December 24 morning, just about the time Nora realized that Sammie should be home for breakfast, she received a call that he was at Dr. Shaw's. Sammie didn't allow his car to be driven on snowy roads, but this was an emergency, and Nora had to see what the matter was. She drove over to Dr. Shaw's and found Sammie bundled up in a chair.

"Good grief! We can't leave you alone for a moment! What happened?"

Sammie smiled a tired, sheepish smile, but he was still clearly in pain.

"I delivered the milk as usual. Then I parked and then went inside to get the milk receipt like I always do. I came back out and as I crank started the farm truck, it kicked back, knocked me to the ground, and broke my arm! Myron Center was there and brought me here."

Dr. Shaw set Sammie's arm and explained that it would ache quite a bit. He even prescribed whiskey for the pain.

"Well, it's a good thing you don't need your arm to go to auctions to buy me furniture," kidded Nora.

No one stayed up to sing "Auld Lang Syne" to usher in the New Year. Farmers don't keep late hours when they don't have to.

On January 1, 1924, the Andrews and Telfords decided to start an annual tradition of getting together for a New Year's celebration. Herb, Florence, and Julia came. Pa and Will. Fremont, Peter, Reimer Meerwarth and their mother also came. Sarah and Howard Evers and Andrew were invited, but they didn't show. Sammie helped as much as he could with his one good arm. But mostly the women prepared the food while the men sat around, joked, planned their spring work, and discussed politics, farming, neighbors, and the next electric gadget to buy for the house and barn. Henry would just sit and listen, and if everyone laughed, then he would laugh. Seth and Pa Telford talked about having problems sleeping and also decided that they each needed water bowls for the cows inside their barns. It was a typical White Crikk gathering.

News came that Odette Dundas died leaving her 5-month-old baby and her husband behind. Dr. Shaw had been seeing her for the last few weeks, as she had an infection. She took a turn for the worse and died of pneumonia. Florence and Nora had delivered that baby and were heartbroken. The news was met with disbelief. She was a good strong woman. That was the main topic of conversation once the women joined the men. They put together a basket of canned food and baked goods to bring over to John. They urged the men to send over at least one of their numbers to help him with his farm chores until he got back on his feet. Nora stepped up to take care of the baby 4 days per week as well as cooking and cleaning and also organized a schedule of other babysitters for round-the-clock care for the children.

At first, Nora felt that it was improper that she stayed all night at another man's house. She was annoyed at the double standard that if men needed help in this circumstance, it superseded all the so-called respectable male/female "rules and regulations" enforced by the Biddie Bunch. If the tables were turned, if a woman's husband died, the woman would have to care for herself and her children round the clock and probably not receive very much outside help. It would certainly be improper for her to have a man come and stay with her at night so she could get rest for the next day. Nora's eyes were opening to the conflicting double standard that she had grown up with. Nora gathered the church ladies and organized regular meals and babysitters for the days she wasn't available. When there was a crisis, no one stepped up to help like a Crikker. Nora did hear a comment about Odette's dying was God's wrath for her getting pregnant before she got married. Nora shut that talk down right away. Even the Biddie Bunch knew that cooler minds must prevail in a situation like this, and only a generous spirit would be proper. In fact, old Mrs. Clark, a widower and self-appointed Biddie leader, was one of the sitters who volunteered to stay all night with the children.

Meat was running low, so Pa Telford butchered one of his bulls and gave Nora and Sammie a hind quarter. Nora canned some of the beef and shared it with John. When an animal was butchered, there was always the liver that needed to be thrown out or eaten. Mr. Tuttle often did seasonal work for the farmers, so the word around town was that Mrs. Tuttle loved liver. Since just about no one else did, all of the farmers in White Crikk dropped by the Tuttle place to drop off liver every time they butchered cow, sheep, pig or chicken as gratitude for his hard work. This would include all of the giblets as well. With each delivery, the Tuttle children begged each farmer to stop giving their mom liver with a chorus of, "Yech! Please stop bringing us liver. You're torturing us! We hate it! She cooks it all the time! It's putrid!"

Even with the new electric washing machine, Mother Andrew couldn't keep up with all of the laundry, so she put Sammie to work turning the old crank washing machine with his one good arm to make use of himself.

"I don't want you to get bored," she kidded. "Think about how strong that one good arm will be."

Sammie was quite good natured and didn't make any fuss. Sammie was able to run errands and make deliveries using just his one arm.

Ma Andrew said, "I don't know how you keep such a good attitude with all the work I'm giving you."

Good natured Sammie replied with the words he grew up hearing from his mother, "Because. Most folks are as happy as they make up their minds to be."

The Ice Harvest was done and that meant that Sugar Season for the Telfords to head up into their woods and tap their oldest Sugar Maple trees. Will and Pa went up with the hand drill to tap the largest maple trees. Sammie carried the buckets to hang on the taps. Soon, February would turn to March when the nights were below freezing and the days were in the 40s and that would kick off the 20 days that sap runs the best. Once tapped, Will and Pa rode horses up into the woods each day, gathering the sap buckets and bringing them down to the house where Aunt Maggie kept two boiling kettles going, one to burn down the sap and then a smaller one for finishing the syrup. Once emptied, Will and Pa rode back up into the woods to hang the sap pails on the taps again.

Aunt Maggie said, "Why do we go through this fuss every year?"

Pa said, "Because."

11

The Great Moving Day

Nora was inspired to start quilting ever since she helped Anna Moses hang quilts on the line. Aunt Maggie was still keeping house over at Telfords and had been there since Ma died. Aunt Maggie had some extra quilt pieces and sent them along with Sammie to keep Nora encouraged. Nora decided to attend one of the quilting bees down at Jermain Hall, sat next to Anna for the afternoon, and enjoyed it very much.

"You can hear all the local gossip and create something beautiful at the same time," said Anna.

Mrs. Rita Smith, the teacher who filled in for Nora for the year, fell ill with appendicitis and Nora approached the school administrators about filling in for her while she was recuperating. They were happy to have Nora, the permanent teacher, substitute for the substitute teacher.

February came round again, and the men drew 115 cakes from Wolfrum's pond at 6 cents per cake. Sammie just about fell over when they started charging triple their previous price. But they didn't let it stop them from buying the ice, and they were able to sell it for a profit just the same.

Sammie was unable to help due to his broken arm, so he turned the wash all forenoon. Then, he and Nora went to an auction and bought a horse named Jennie, some oats, bushel baskets, a sewing machine for Nora, and a roll-top desk. Other auctions throughout the winter included items such as a stove, and a wagon hay rack, and corn sheller.

Riding back and forth between auctions, Sammie asked Nora what she thought about him switching life insurance companies. She was fine with it. Just as long as he got a good deal and he remembered to cancel the old life insurance policy so that he wasn't paying for two policies. The next time Sammie was in Hoosick Falls, he simply walked over to the Metropolitan office to ask for a comparison of his current policy. By the time he left, he had taken out a new life insurance policy with an additional $10,000 worth of coverage.

March couldn't come soon enough for Sammie and Nora. Sammie's arm was out of the sling, the Fullers' lease was up, and the Fullers finally moved off the Nichol's Property to rent a farm in Bennington. It was now time to begin the month-long farm preparations before things would be ready enough for Sammie and Nora to move into the house. The first order of business for Sammie, Henry, and Ray was a day of felling trees out in the back woodlot. They would season for a year and make good firewood.

"Be sure to go easy," said Nora and off the boys went. The boys were so excited that they left without the lunch Nora prepared them. So, Nora heaved a big sigh and decided to saddle up Jennie. *I suppose now is as good a time as any to get to know this giant*. The truth was that every horse was a giant to Nora, but she had amazing brute strength when it came to grabbing a saddle off the saw horse and managing it up onto her new steed. They didn't have a fancy horse block like they did up at Fenton's on Cambridge corners, so she improvised and lugged the saddle up the step ladder and finally got Jennie saddled up. All she knew about Jennie was that she was from a good home and the owner was moving away. She was sure to speak calmly the whole time she was working with her, and she worked out just fine. Off they trotted to the back woodlot and the boys were happy to have their lunch and drinks delivered.

"Looks like you're making good progress out here!" remarked Nora. "I've got to get back to cleaning. Florence and Julia are coming over this afternoon to help me clean that kitchen, but I've got to clean it once first before they get here!" She started to trot off and turned back to say, "Don't let Sammie work too hard!"

A farm is no small venture. The next day, the boys brought over two loads of hay from Telfords and stacked it in Sammie's hay mow, a load of sawdust for the ice house, and a load of oats in the grain room. Many of their farm friends gave them animals as presents but they couldn't move any animals onto the farm until there was food to feed them, tools to clean up after them, a team of work horses, and a manure spreader. The next order of business on their month-long list was to haul some ice from the Andrew's ice house over to their new one. Together, Sammie and Nora went to several more auctions for the needed furniture for which Nora had planned, as well as more second-hand farm equipment, fence posts, and, finally, the animals. It was hard, hard work but they loved every minute of it.

Finally, April 1 arrived, and it was finally time to move in, even though March was going out like a lion with a blustery, windy snowstorm! Not in recent memory had there been a snow storm so late in the year, but the Andrew and Telford Families invited many helpers. First things first, it was freezing so the men got right onto setting up the new stove and stove pipe while the women got busy laying down burlap on the kitchen shelves that Nora had painted that month, before they filled them with pots and pans and the set of dishes Ida bought for Nora as a wedding gift. They brought in ice for the ice box and stocked it with food and prepared meals. Leah and Mason, Howard and Sarah Evers, and even little Andrew were all there. Howard was a great help when he was sober. Hanging Nora's curtains on the windows was a high priority. Once the men finished with the stove, it was time for carrying in the furniture. As the men carried in boxes and furniture, Nora stood in the middle of the house and directed movers to the proper room. Friends stopped by to deliver their animals and Sammie handled those situations. They were quickly accumulating a barnyard full of animals. *Nothing is more beautiful than a barnyard full of animals and no manure,* thought Sammie. He knew all too well how soon the manure situation would change.

With the stove warming the house, and plenty of food out for everyone, the atmosphere was jovial and energetic.

"The first of April is the day we remember what we are the other 364 days of the year," quoted Seth.

The Fryers brought over 20 baby chicks as a housewarming present.

"I made a pen for them out on the barn floor," said Sammie, "until I can build a proper chicken house for Nora." The house was buzzing with energy and a generosity of spirit from so many helpers. Much was accomplished in very little time due to Nora's organization and the White Crikk work ethic. In that one day, they got everything situated that needed extra help. Sammie and Nora could handle the rest. They felt blest and loved by their friends and families. Everyone was certainly tired that night. But Sammie and Nora's farm on the Nichol's Property in Post Corners in White Creek was officially born.

12

Married Everyday

Nora could hardly sleep, as her mind was creating lists of things that needed to be done. The next day brought on the first of the daily chores for Sammie and Nora, which they did together. They got up at 5:00 am, and Sammie got to milking their six cows right away. Nora was on feeding detail. First up, she bottle-fed the three lambs that the McCarts had given them. Adeline and Amos, the bay team, and Jennie received oats and the cows received grain while Sammie milked them.

"We still need a brown cow," they both said at the same time.

Nora watered the chickens and made sure their grain was fresh. She loved chickens and knew these chicks would grow fast and need a proper chicken house. The current set up would do for just so long.

The following days brought on more chores and more animals as Sammie and Nora built up their herd. They bought a brown cow from Robertsons, and two more Holsteins from the auction house. Sammie was running down to the Falls and asked Nora what she wanted. She went along for the ride and bought more wallpaper and paint, Sammie stopped off to pay his life insurance, and also went to the doctor's for the dang cold he couldn't get rid of. That night, after evening chores and dinner, they papered the parlor and Nora kept giving Sammie her home remedies for his cough, but the coughing just wouldn't stop. She gave him tea with turmeric and honey, but the hacking just went on and on. Sammie was exhausted from coughing all night, so Nora did the farm chores with Henry and Ray.

The next day, Henry and Ray brought another bed over from home. Nora wasn't about to put up with a sleepless night again, so the new bed was set up in another bedroom for Sammie on the other side of the house so Nora could get some sleep and take care of him during the day. The family had a good time nudging Sammie about that! They weren't even one week on the farm and Nora kicked him out of bed. Sammie stayed in bed most of the day. Nora didn't want to disturb him once he fell asleep and stopped coughing. She had plenty to do between cleaning, painting, cooking, and the farm chores, which she loved doing. Perry's brought over two piglets as a gift. Nora put them in the hog shed and enjoyed watching them explore their new surroundings. Sammie came out in his pajamas to use the outhouse and had a look at the piglets as well. As they walked back into the house, Nora asked if they should name them.

"We better not," said Sammie. "In the fall, they'll become our ham and bacon. It's easier to eat an animal if it doesn't have a name."

Sammie continued to cough, and Nora called Dr. Shaw to see if he had anything stronger for a bad cough. None of her home remedies were working. Dr. Shaw came over and examined Sammie. He brought stronger medicine and said he would stop back in a week. Sammie was to have a complete rest. The medicine helped Sammie a great deal and Nora was happy to do the chores herself and was busy preparing for Leah and Mason's wedding as the Matron of Honor. Henry and Ray were life savers and helped Nora often. Daily life moved on with Sammie's bad cough keeping him in bed most of the time. He wasn't getting better and then he started having flecks of blood in his sputum. Nora immediately called Dr. Shaw.

Dr. Shaw paid a visit and examined Sammie once more.

"Sammie is to continue to have a complete rest. It's possible that I hear the TB back in his lungs." Nora froze. *TB? How could this be?*

"How frequent is a relapse for a young man that has been relapse-free for two years?" asked Nora. The doctor explained that it was quite frequent. Maybe 80%.

Nora tried to stay calm. "I thought it was 80% before the two years," she said. She tried not to show it, but she was devastated.

"Shall we get him back to Ray Brook?" she asked. Dr. Shaw thought that that was the best course of action. Sammie felt like he had let Nora down. She was thankful that when they bought the house, it already had been wired for electricity and had a phone. She called Florence. Florence came over immediately and stayed the night with Sammie while Nora rested. Word spread fast of Sammie's relapse.

At age 22, Nora pulled herself up by her literal boot straps and poured herself into the daily chores. The farm needed spring work done, so she had "farm meetings" with Sammie to make sure they prioritized the work correctly. What they couldn't manage to get done with help, they would hire done. Herb came down and plowed their oat ground on the flat. William Perry came over and plowed and marked the garden as a favor to his neighbors who had fallen on these hard times. Henry and Ray had a time of it doing the chores on their farm as well as helping Nora with the chores on the Nichol's property. They disked and dragged and sowed the oat ground. Nora went into town to buy timothy and clover. Nora was concerned that all the family friends visiting was tiring Sammie out. So, for his 26th birthday, May 25, she got up a postcard shower for him. When one was too sick for visitors, their caretakers asked folks from all over the Crikk to simply mail a birthday postcard and, thus, *shower* them with postcards. He was deeply touched to receive so many kind wishes. They were waiting for a bed to become available in Ray Brook with the belief that Sammie would respond to treatment there just as he did the first time, as long as they could keep Sammie in bed!

Nora got some good old-fashioned dried-up fertilizer from the barn yard and planted her favorite flowers; hollyhocks, gladiolas, sun flowers, and put tulip and daffodil bulbs in all around the perimeter. She and Sammie had their system for the garden, and she wasn't about to give up the work of a garden just because Sammie was under the weather. Nora was tired. Now that it was spring, they turned the cows out over across the road daytimes.

Even though Nora couldn't stand Howard Evers for drinking and beating her sister, she could still hear her father saying, "Every man has his secret sorrows which the world knows not; and, oftentimes, we call a man cold when he is only sad." She left room in her heart for a man with hidden pain of his own; however, that didn't mean that Sarah had to put up with one more minute of abuse. Howard came over and drew out the cow manure. Nora commented to Sammie on how fortunate they were to have such supportive friends, even if they were mad at them.

The very first Methodist Church north of New York City started in Cambridge led by Philip Embury. Sammie asked Nora to run out and ask Howard to come in and Sammie was forever grateful to Howard for helping he and Nora with the farm chores. Sammie then explained that, though the Little White Creek Methodist Church was too small to hold a gathering, the The Embury Methodist Church held what they called, "bands," small groups of four or five men that watched over each other when it came to their overindulgence in the drink. The church wasn't far from his house and the band met on Wednesday evenings. Sammie asked him if he would attend one meeting and then come back and tell him what it was like. They talked for a bit more and Howard went on his way with some cookies from Nora.

The plan all along was that Nora would return to teaching in the fall. The day came for the August 3 Glens Falls Summer Teaching Convention and Nora and Leah went together. Sammie said he would be fine by himself for the day. He was feeling useless, and he hated seeing Nora and other men do the work that he should be doing. He knew he had TB again and he felt like a failure. He promised Nora 100 years of building a good name together, and he didn't even make it 6 months. He felt he had let down his family, his friends, and, most of all, Nora. Here he was, 26 years old and bedridden and everyone knew it. That God-damned tuberculosis had come back, and he was going to fight it with all of his might. But he had no might. He was mad at God for allowing this to happen to him. He wondered what he did wrong to deserve it. Just when he finally got all that he wanted, a wife and his own farm, he gets TB… and just barely one week after they moved onto the farm. How unfair!

Well, today, he wasn't going to wait around for death to come knocking on his door. He wanted to provide for Nora. He got himself up in the forenoon and took the buck board into town and bought Nora a new washtub and rub board plus whatever supplies he needed to build a proper chicken coop. People knew he was sick and stayed well away from him. The trip was exhausting, but he didn't let that stop him. After a rest, he got himself some lunch from the ice box and went out to build Nora's chicken coop off the side of the barn. He was a good builder. He put up the frame first and built a decent roof with the tin from the old hog sheds that Pa Telford let him have and the door and sides were framed out with the left-over lumber from the ice house. He then put the roosts up higher than usual to discourage the rats from stealing the eggs. Finally, he hammered on a double layer of chicken wire to keep the racoons, fox and coy dogs out. He was driven to do something for Nora but as he dragged in the feeders and waterers, he got the sinking feeling that he had made a big mistake by getting out of bed and overdoing. Just then, Leah dropped Nora in the yard, and he could tell that she was beyond furious.

"Samuel Dewey Telford!" She had never said his middle name before. "What on God's green earth do you think you're doing? You're supposed to be in bed. You are going to cough up a lung. Can you imagine if I came home and found you dead in a sea of blood inside the chicken coop you just built?"

Sammie exploded. "I am so God-damned tired of hearing about how much everybody's doing for poor little Sammie. I wasn't feelin' any worse or better stayin' in bed all day. I might as well get up and do something. I know you need a proper chicken coop, and a husband gives his wife what she needs. I'm tryin' to be useful."

He knew his thinking was off, but it felt good to express his feelings.

"I don't need a chicken coop!"

"Well, you got one now!" he said, kicking a feeder over.

They had never had a fight like this before.

"We agreed that you'd follow doctor's orders again just like last time. You can't decide that you're going to overdo and maybe take the chance of swinging a hammer and dying! You don't get to make that decision alone. We're together in this. Remember? 'Married every day.' No fair leaving me out of your plans; especially the ones that could kill you!"

They both fell silent with their hearts pounding in their heads. Sammie summoned all the ergs he had and limped over to lie on the lawn.

"What are we gonna do? I feel it gnawing at my chest. It's worse than last time. I can't leave you and go to Ray Brook again. What about the farm? What if I die? All I can do is stay in bed and use the chamber pot while you feed the animals and clean the barn and cook and clean, and soon, you'll be teaching school. I can't do a damn thing to help."

"It's hard, but it's what I'm supposed to do. And getting you healthy is what I'm supposed to do. We just do what the doctor tells us."

Sammie sharply replied, "Well, it's easier said than done."

Nora replied 100 times as sharply, "That's no excuse! 'Easy' doesn't have any role in what we've got going on here. We're between a rock and a hard place and even that doesn't begin to describe where we are. This isn't only about you. It's about me and you. Will you please take care of yourself and go to bed and get your rest? I will gladly take care of everything else, but I can't do it if I know you're not getting better!"

"Fine name I'm building for us. We have separate rooms. Dr. Shaw will send me back to Ray Brook and leave my wife to take care of my farm. There's that good name for us alright."

They were both silent for a long time.

"You're a very good man, Sammie. Do you think I'd have married you otherwise? Our fight is with TB, not each other. Let's not let that come between us. We've got to play the cards we're dealt. We can't get stuck in feeling sorry for ourselves or wishing things were different. Your body may be failing you, but your heart and mind are still that of the fine man I married. I knew going into this that you had latent TB. Seeing you sick in your body is one thing, but seeing your mind and attitude get sick is unbearable. You think you aren't any good to anyone, well find a new way to measure how much good you are. Our vows aren't that old, we can see this thing through. Let's be married every day no matter what."

She lay down on the grass next to him and took his sweaty hand.

"Doc Shaw was frank with us. Chances are that round 2 of TB is much worse than round 1. Where do we find courage for that?" asked Sammie.

"Right here," said Nora without skipping a beat. "You're out of courage? Use mine. I still have courage." Her eyes filled with tears and her voice cracked.

"And when that's gone, we'll ask your family for courage, and then the whole town if we need to. We're not the first to live through hard times, we're just living through hard times for the first. I need you. Don't let your heart leave me while your body's still here. You need my courage, I need you. Swear to me that you will not leave me while you're still breathing." She held out her pinky. He paused. He clasped her pinky with his. "I swear I will not leave you." Their pinky swear was complete. "How can I ever repay your father, and Henry and Ray and Herb and…"

"Well, certainly, if you can't take the next right step, taking a deliberate wrong step is not the best option. Right now, all of us want you to get better. No one but you is griping about anything. No one is looking for repayment. Just tell them how grateful you are. You can still read and write and talk on the phone. We have big decisions to make. I don't know how to run the farm, but you do. I don't know how much to feed the dry cows, but you do. Our two heads together are better than just you alone, lost inside your own head. Maybe ask Mason and Leah if they want to rent the farm."

The idea just flew out of Nora's mouth. She hadn't really thought it through.

"We could talk about that. It's not what we planned but… we're making things up as we go along… just like jazz, improvising is all the rage right now."

They stayed a few more moments on the lawn together. They enjoyed the warm breeze. Sammie was cooling off. They could hear their animals stirring.

"Must be chore time," Nora said. "My sheep are getting hungry. Thank you for the chicken coop. It's beautiful. Let's get you cleaned up and back into bed, and I'll do chores. Henry and Ray are coming over to help me do the milking later tonight."

"Hey," said Sammie as he held up his pinky, "thank you."

Nora clasped his pinky with hers. "Chicken coop pinky swear."

"Chicken coop, married every day, pinky swear," he said.

"For a hundred years," she said.

From then on, Sammie and Nora renewed their commitment to each other and kept putting their heads together with their daily farm meetings. It would be best, rather than lose the farm, to rent it out. It was too much work for Nora to maintain alone, so they asked Mason and Leah if they would rent it. It was the peak of the hot August summer and Sammie wasn't improving. Even with Nora's homemade strawberry shortcake with fresh strawberries steeped in sugar, homemade buttered biscuits, and real whipped cream from their own cows, his weight was dropping, and he was still on the Ray Brook waiting list. It seemed like every single decision they had to make broke their hearts more and more, but they remained together in every decision focused on the next right step.

They sat at home together while their friends went to the Saratoga race track. Then, Sammie's grandfather died. It was a small funeral. He sat off to the side during the service and was imagining it as if it were his funeral. He imagined what people would say and what people would feel like when they sang the same hymns. Would Nora cry or would she be stoic and hold it all in until she was alone? *She would cry*, he decided. Most people knew well enough to give him wide berth due to his TB. He didn't sing and if he had to cough, he was prepared with a towel to cover his mouth.

Sarah and Howard were at the funeral as well. Howard pulled Sammie aside and told him all about the bands he attended. "They ask everybody five questions. They made me memorize 'em:

What known sins have you committed since last we met?

What temptations have you met with?

How was you delivered?

What have you thought, said or done of which you doubt, whether it be sin or not?

Have you nothing you desire to keep secret?"

Sammie thanked him for his report and asked him to keep going and telling him about what he heard there.

After the funeral, Nora invited Mason and Leah over for lunch. Afterwards, they wrote up their agreement to rent the farm as of

September 1. Sammie felt relieved knowing that Nora wouldn't have to run the farm alone. Things would have to move fast, though. It was the beginning of August, a bed was now available for him up at Ray Brook, and now Sammie and Nora had to sell their animals that they had grown so fond of. Mr. Perry bought their 6 Holsteins at $50 each. Uncle Willy McCart bought their little brown cow and Sammie watched through the window as Brown Cow was led down the road. Mason and Leah bought some of his equipment. Sammie negotiated all of the sales and watched the animals get loaded up and taken away. They sold Nora's chickens from her proper chicken coop. It felt like they were saying goodbye to their children. It was so sad for both Nora and Sammie. But through it all, they remained "married every day."

After Sammie built the chicken coop and they had their fight, they realized that letting emotions out wasn't such a bad idea. So, he and Nora started allowing daily 5-minute Pity Parties when they each were allowed to express any emotion they wanted in any way they wanted. And when the 5 minutes were up, so was their emotional outburst and it was back to business.

Nora had made up beautiful lists of everything that needed to be sold and Sammie kept track of it all and called the folks he thought might be interested in buying them. There was a list for things to be stored in their barn and it was so well-organized that it was a pleasure for those who were helping them out.

It was the third week of August. Sammie and Nora decided to have their auction the day before they were to leave for Ray Brook. They recreated the living room right out on the front yard with the rug and couches and lamps and coffee tables just so. Folks on their way to Bennington stopped and bought things and visited for a while and folks headed west on the way to Cambridge stopped in as well. Ida was busy offering cookies to everyone. Sammie lay in a hammock all day and when the sun moved, Henry and Ray picked up the hammock at either end and moved him into the shade. Everyone who came along wished him well.

He said, "We're hoping for the best and planning for the worst." He and Nora both stayed as positive as they could. He remembered that optimism was a big piece of Dr. Trudeau's cure success, and he planned on following the rules again. He was losing weight, but he remembered his doctor telling him that tears and fretting used up twice as many ergs as optimism.

Both Sammie and Nora noticed that some people seemed to steer clear of Sammie and were quite rude about it, like they were turning up their nose at a leper. Nora handed things off to her mother and father and Pa Telford for a bit and took a lunch break with Sammie. Sammie was feeling a bit like a leper as people would learn of his TB and look at him like he was a monster. If they didn't leave, then they certainly got as far away from him as possible. Sammie had seen all these reactions before and understood them, but it didn't always make it easy.

He told Nora that with so many consumptives coming into Saranac Lake that the town of Liberty barred them from ever coming into the town. They were afraid that their tourism would suffer as tourists would fear that they might catch it. Liberty's ban on consumptives was even in the *New York Times*. They enacted a law that said no buildings within the village of Liberty could be used as a rest house, hospital, or sanitarium or be fined. TB patients were not allowed to stop at any of the Liberty hotels. Just like in Saranac Lake, spitting in public was a fined offense.

He said, "I feel like a tubercular in the middle of Liberty and I'm at my own house."

Despite Sammie's experience, the auction was a great success, and anything left over, they offered to Mason and Leah to hold onto. Nora got into the hammock with Sammie. Nora knew that she wasn't to get too close to Sammie, but part of her didn't want to live if Sammie were to die. They just quietly rocked with no words. They could hear the quiet countryside singing to them in the breeze, the frogs in the pond and crickets chirping away. They were just... together, until Nora said,

"Hey. Wait a minute. We sold our beds! We don't have any place to sleep tonight!"

"Yes, we do," replied Sammie, and they snuggled right up together and spent the night in the hammock."

Herb and Pa drove both Sammie and Nora over to Saratoga Springs the next morning, where they stopped for gas and then the long haul on up into the Adirondacks through Lake George. Nora had never been to this part of the country before. She was amazed at the steep mountain cliffs and narrow winding roads. The vast pine-covered mountains interspersed with lakes and rivers were beautiful. The massive and mysterious Adirondacks matched the silent fear of the unknown they both held inside. Sammie had been praying for 2 years that he would never have to make this trip again because of TB. Ida had made them dinner which they ate alongside the road where they overlooked a lake. An ominous cliff stretched high above them on the other side of the road which Nora guessed was a corduroy logging road at one time. Sammie was frail and week and barely ate anything. Nora got him to drink some water.

There weren't many words spoken, but much emotion, nevertheless. Sammie now weighed less than he did the first time he went to Ray Brook. He asked to go into Saranac Lake first to buy an authentic Adirondack Reclining Chair for $15, which he really wanted. Herb did his best to keep things as normal as possible. And getting out of the car for some shopping helped snap Nora out of her worry and reminded her to stay positive. Sammie exhausted himself just from pointing out a few local buildings and telling a few wonderful memories from his first trip.

Nora encouraged him, "There will be many more memories this time as well."

In another few miles, they would be at Ray Brook where Nora would be staying with Sammie for a couple of weeks until she had to return to teach school.

Once arriving at the Ray Brook State Hospital, it was the same routine; a nurse came out to greet them with a wheel chair and two assistants came to help bring in their things. They said their goodbyes, and, all too soon, Sammie and Nora were inside the hospital. Sammie had expected to see at least some familiar faces but recognized no one.

"This is my wife, Nora. She's about 5' but her attitude is 6'3". His intake nurse smiled. He asked her if Nurse Neurich were still a nurse there.

"Oh dear," she said, "she's here alright, but she's a patient now and recovering just fine." That made their hearts sink.

"There are over 800 doctors, medical students, nurses, and nursing students at the wrong end of the thermometer these days," she stated rather quietly.

She turned to Nora, "You dear will need to be tested as well. It's best if you keep to the room here and not wander around the facility."

Nora felt sick upon hearing that. Sammie's heart sank. It was getting hard to stay optimistic. But they had gotten in the habit of gently joining pinky fingers, reminding the other that they weren't alone.

Sammie was admitted to Pryor Wing where there was an extra bed for Nora as well. As the nurse left, Nora felt numb as she got her exhausted Sammie into bed.

"This is just a stop on our otherwise exciting journey, babe," Sammie reminded her. She kissed him on his forehead and off he drifted. Nora was tired but not ready to sleep. She unpacked their bags and was grateful that they allowed her to stay with Sammie. She didn't sleep well that night with all of the hospital sounds, squeaky ice carts, and emergency sounds from the nurses' desk. Nora had never felt death so close by and in such a tangible way than in the hallways of Ray Brook.

The next forenoon, Nora stayed and observed the nurses taking good care of Sammie. The doctor will be in to examine Sammie to see if he is a good candidate for surgery. *Surgery?*

"My how things have taken an unexpected turn!" said Nora. "Is surgery really necessary? What kind of surgery?"

"Well, dear, extreme remedies are very appropriate for extreme disease." The nurse went on, "This would all depend on what the doctor says, but they sometimes collapse the infected lung and reinflate it after a certain amount of time. The doctor will go over all of that with you if he's a candidate. There was talk at different times of transplanting the lungs of a calf into humans, but that's just talk! You may hear about removing the infected parts of the lungs and filling in the cavity with ping pong balls. That's true! They used to do that, but not anymore. There's a man walking around Saranac Lake with

112 ping pong balls inside him. He's kind of a crumpled over fella. Any hoo, the doctor will go over all of that with you. Sammie would have to be strong enough to undergo the surgery. The doctor will be in soon," she said as she left.

"Well, I never heard of such a thing!"

"Oh yes," said Sammie, "I heard all about it the first time I was here."

"Well did you think to let me in on any of these 'little' details?"

"I'm sorry, I thought you knew."

In a few moments, the doctor came through and examined Sammie's chart and listened to his lungs.

"If we can get your fever down and your weight back up, we might be able to consider an operation, but until then, you're not a candidate. You're to stay on absolute bed rest. We need to give your body every chance to heal itself again like it did the first time."

In the afternoon Sammie assured Nora that he was in good hands and encouraged her to go for a walk. He winked.

"A pretty girl like you will have no problems flagging a car. Just go outside and look for a taxi and wave at them."

His nurse piped up. "Just ask to go to Finnegan Block. Finnegan owns everything along there. He'll drop you right on Main Street and then you can go about your shopping. You're a teacher, correct? You might want to go over to Petrova Avenue to see the new school. We're growing so fast around here; we're now the largest school district in the state with over 600 square miles of bus routes!"

"Six hundred square miles. My lands!" exclaimed Nora.

The nurse was full of information. "Every child in the village public schools is x-rayed yearly and are taught that coughing spreads the germs. Some of those very same school children deliver milk and newspapers locally to the cure cottages. They're taught to hold their breath during each of their financial transactions lest they breathe in the TB germs. The kids all know that germs can linger in the room for three hours and are projected 3 feet from the coughers mouth. The germs can also be transmitted from spit in the streets, which is why there's a $50 fine for spitting, because TB can be brought indoors on shoes or long skirts, according to Dr. Brown's handbook, and when the maids sweep, they spread the germs all around the house. The doctor figured out that if you nap on the couch that a tubercular had just vacated you run a risk of infection also."

Nora did as she was told, and flagged a car, even though it felt incredibly uncomfortable. She had never done that before. Nora's driver rambled on and gave her an unwanted tour. "Saranac Lake is home to many underworld rumrunners and gangsters such as Eddie Diamond, Legs Diamond's brother. Many around here think if Prohibition was going to outlaw anything, they just should have taken away hard liquor and at least allowed beer and wine." He could tell that Nora didn't care for his stories, so he tried to redeem himself for a better tip.

"You can easily make a day of it shopping here in Saranac Lake. You can see there our beautiful A. Fortune furniture store. Some beautiful tapestries. He's got embalming rooms upstairs. He's an undertaker who sells furniture! The people of Saranac Lake are lovely. Nothing much to worry about. As the saying goes, 'We're all chipped and broken pottery here, but we rattle around and make a cheerful noise.' There was once a band of thieves stealing furs from Edelberg's but their truck was blocking traffic right out front. It was fine until it became showtime at the Pontiac Theater next door. That's when the corner cop came to inspect the reason for the traffic problem. Not realizing what was going on, he ended up helping the thieves load up the stolen boxes onto their truck, so they'd move it along quicker. Even the cops help out the robbers here!" Silence. The car slowed down to a crawl.

"Ah damn. The horse-drawn street washer up ahead. That's why we're going so slow. They wash and sweep the streets daily here. They don't want the TB coming inside on the bottom of some broad's skirt. You won't see old friends running into each other, arms wide open. No public displays of affection for fear that someone catch TB." Finally, he pulled up to Finnegan's Pharmacy. "That'll be 15 cents, please." Nora wasn't impressed, paid the man plus a penny tip, and got out of the car quickly.

She was soon lost in a world of window shopping and browsing at souvenir shops: nature books, deer skin gloves, pine-stuffed pillows with "High Pine for you and Balsam" embroidered on them, bobcat skin rugs, ski socks and thick sweaters. It started to rain, so she stepped inside to look around. Saranac Lake saw an annual rainfall of 34 inches, so if it wasn't snowing, it was probably raining, which helped purge the atmosphere of dust and harmful bacteria. She walked about the store slowly and saw framed crewel work that read, "To cure sometimes, to relieve often, to comfort always".

As she gazed at it, the owner came over and said, "Those are the words of Dr. Trudeau, the doctor who started the sanatorium here in Saranac Lake. Those words are the inscription on his statue that was just unveiled a few years ago. This town and thousands of his patients will be eternally grateful to him. He had TB as a young man. He came up to Paul Smith's Camp and got better after some months. He realized that it was the air and rest that cured him, so he started curing others."

Nora politely smiled.

"He was one step above the village priest. He was a healer for decades and then, finally, TB took him about 8 years ago. He'll be missed."

Nora noticed a sign hanging behind the clerk, "Men, it is up to us. Spitting spreads disease and women don't spit." Nora didn't care to have any souvenirs from the Adirondacks. Her time here was filled with such pain. She bought some mints and magazines and had lunch at the Berkely Hotel while reading her editions of *True Story* and the *Journal of Outdoor Life* showing consumptives out birdwatching and picnicking and even sledding. How she wished she could have enjoyed beautiful Saranac Lake with Sammie under different circumstances. Her heart ached.

Nora brought some oranges and goodies back for Sammie who was sleeping almost all of the time now. She watched him sleep and was comforted that she wasn't alone. Sammie was still Sammie. She went over and ever so gently wrapped her pinky around his and she silently prayed, *God. We need another Ray Brook recovery miracle. Amen.* At supper, Nora told Sammie of her day how she walked along Park Avenue called "Millionaire's Row" where the "swells" lived and that she refused to eat at the St. Regis Hotel once she heard that they refused service to tuberculars.

She couldn't fall asleep being in a new bed in a strange place. She thought about some of the things she overheard on her afternoon out. She learned that there was a great rivalry between Saranac Lake and Lake Placid. One opinion was that it was because there was once a football game with a score of 102-0, and Lake Placid took the shellacking. It didn't help that it was recorded in Ripley's Believe It or Not. But the more probable reason being that Saranac Lake was becoming world renown as being a TB cure center, while just 9 miles away, Lake Placid was becoming known for its vacation facilities and its famous Lake Placid Club with its "No Tuberculars" sign at their entrance. Al Jolson said that he would only perform in the Adirondacks if it were 100 miles from the city of the sick. It seemed that the more people knew about TB, the more they feared it. They knew how contagious coughing, spitting, and the sputum cups that were incinerated each night were.

Each day, Nora walked the grounds through the golf course and around the duck pond. On one hand, she noted the sickness looming in the air inside the hallways of Pryor Wing. Yet, on the other hand, outdoors, there were recovering patients looking alive and well. They were walking about, flirting, playing golf, and laughing, and she even saw some kissing in one of the gazebos. She missed kissing Sammie. *Please God, get Sammie up and around again. I'm pleading for a miracle.* She gravitated to the gazebo by the duck pond; shaded and cool. She met a beautiful young woman crying in the gazebo.

"Oh, my," said Nora, "what have we here?" she said holding out her hand to shake it. "May I have a sit with you? You seem like you're having a rough day."

And just like that, the young lady opened up with her story.

"I'm Joan. I just spent the morning with my husband and our child."

"Are you a patient?" asked Nora.

"Yes," said Joan. "I got an exercise prescription, as I'm feeling better, and I wanted a visit. I've been here 5 months and my 18-month-old son doesn't even recognize me anymore. The doctor warned that I should not even try to hold him lest I jeopardize his future. It wouldn't have mattered; he wouldn't have come to me even if I wanted. I'm a complete stranger to him."

Nora just listened.

"Bill and I planned on having more children, but now we're not so sure. Even if I'm healed, it could break out again if I'm overstrained. Who knows? Is it worth the risk? Would delivering another baby be too much strain on me and bring back my illness? What kind of life would that be? Should I just divorce Bill and let him marry someone who could be a proper wife to him?"

Nora allowed some silence and let Joan's words linger in the air.

"I can see how you would feel that way," she empathized. "But I'm sure Bill doesn't want a different wife. He wants you. Once you get home, your little one will eventually warm up to you so much so that you won't be able to fix dinner without him clinging to your feet! It sounds like today was hard. But you're on the mend. You'll be home in no time. 'Hard days' are better than 'no days.'"

The two continued to talk and Nora did her best to encourage Joan. Deep down, Nora was envious of her recovery and future with her family. She wished she knew if Sammie had that bright of a future ahead.

As she headed back to Sammie's room, she bumped into Sammie's doctor and asked, "Why?"

He waited for her to continue.

"Why does Sammie have TB? He didn't live or work with anyone who had it. It's not like he lived in a New York City apartment with 12 others who had it. He always called his doctor whenever he got as much as a sniffle. He's not homeless. He's been outdoors on the farm his whole life. He doesn't drink."

She was getting louder and angrier.

"WHY? Why has this happened to my Sammie?" She stood there demanding an answer. "Is God punishing us for something?"

The doctor let her get all of her questions out and he calmly replied, "TB doesn't play favorites. It strikes who it strikes. We still have a lot to learn about it, but we're getting there. I'm so sorry that Sammie has to be here. I've dedicated my life to studying TB because I want it gone forever. My mother and father both died of it. I'm trying to make sure as few people as possible have to suffer from it."

Nora's eyes were filled with tears. He placed his hand on her shoulder. "Remember, we do have hope on our side. Herman Melville noted that the Catskill eagle flies so high that even in its lowest swoop, the mountain eagle is still higher than the other birds upon the plain. The sanitarium concept is so superior to any other treatment for tuberculosis, that even, at its worst, it is the best course of action for most patients. Sammie is in the best place."

He excused himself. She composed herself as he walked away. She picked up the day's paper at the nurses' desk and headed back to the room.

Back in the room, she sat next to Sammie and started reading him the interesting articles from the *Adirondack Daily Enterprise*.

A nurse came in to record Sammie's temperature and said, "Your temperature is down for the second time in a row. That's encouraging."

The she turned to Nora and asked, "Did you have a good talk with the doctor?" Nora stared at her. Sammie looked at Nora. "Yes, I did. Thank you."

And when the nurse left, it was obvious that Sammie was furious. "You spoke to the doctor without me? What did you have to ask that couldn't be asked in front of me? I thought we were 'chicken-coop-pinky-swear-together.' What questions do you have for the doctor that you think I can't hear?"

"It's not like that. I was on my way back from my walk and I ran into the doctor. I thought you were sleeping," explained Nora.

"I may be sleeping but I'm not dead. My body is broken but I'm not. I want to know everything that's going on with you and my TB! Don't go behind my back ever again!" He was indignant. He demanded to know what she asked him.

Nora stopped breathing. He understood his point. A nurse stepped in and quietly closed their door without making eye contact.

"I didn't mean to go behind your back. I bumped into the doctor and thought I might save you some grief by talking to him alone."

Silence.

"I asked him why you were sick. You've done everything right. You don't fit the picture of most who are sick. You basically live outdoors. You eat well. You don't drink... Why does it have to be you?" She cried. "I'm feeling sorry for myself and didn't want to burden you with that. I'm mad that you're sick."

Sammie replied, "I want you to burden me with your pity party. It makes me feel useful. I may be sick, but I can always whoop some sense into you when you're feeling sorry for yourself. I'm still here. Let me be here for you."

Nora was silent for a moment. "Agreed."

"Now get over here and hold my hands. It's impossible to hold hands and fight, and I'm a lover, not a fighter," he joked.

13

Sadie, Sadie, Married Everyday Lady

Sammie continued sleeping more and more. Nora went on walks regularly in the afternoons. She would bring her book and sit in the shaded gazebo by the duck pond reading. She would always bring some leftover bread from lunch to feed the ducks. Today, Nora's new friend, Sadie, a kindhearted woman with a cane asked if she could sit and chat with her. Nora and Sadie were both at the Ray Brook State Hospital for the same reason. Nora welcomed her to share the bench.

Sadie started, "My, my, it sure is hot! I understand that the summer season here is shorter than any other in the United States. Someone told me that it's only 110 days between spring and fall frost. And, of course, our men had to get sick in the middle of those 110 hot days of summer!"

Both women agreed, fanning themselves.

"You know, my Harold is not long for this world. He's sleeping all the time, so I get out of his room and let him sleep. I've done some tours around town where apparently the biggest complaints are horses getting unhitched, and pigs and cows being a nuisance out in the street. I wondered why this Doctor Trudeau, who started all of this outdoor cure, chose Saranac Lake of all places. He must have meant a lot to these people. So, I asked myself what kind of man is revered so? He must not have been a complete jerk. He died of TB just about 8 years ago and they already made a statue of the man."

Nora listened as she felt sorry for herself. She split her duck bread and shared it with Sadie. They fed the ducks as Sadie continued.

"They say he was a noble man who saved thousands by bringing the sanitarium experience here and, at the same time, businesses thrived from all of the people coming in and out. Someone pointed out that in the late 1800s, in order to get into medical school, all a college graduate needed to do was pay a $5 fee and he was in. No entrance exam or letters of recommendation needed! What drives a man to go to medical school to learn about a cure for TB?"

Silence.

"I was having lunch the other day at the Berkley, a beautiful place, and I overheard a conversation. They said that Trudeau's brother died of TB, and it broke his heart. At the time, it was believed that TB wasn't contagious and generally incurable. But he didn't settle for that common knowledge of his time. He set out to get to the bottom of it. He was fueled by the love for his brother. He went to medical school and studied TB. He then got married, and on his honeymoon, he found swollen glands on his neck. A year later, he was diagnosed with TB."

Nora resonated with the pain of TB in the first year of marriage.

"He thought he was going to die, so he went over yonder to Paul Smith's hotel. He had to be carried in on a cart through the woods by guides. He weighed almost nothing. He had to be carried up the stairs. He had been to Paul Smith's as a young man and loved it so much that he wanted to spend his last days there. He said goodbye to his wife and went there to die. But, instead, he learned how to rest. He spent his days casually fishing out on the lake being rowed about by one of his guides. He thought he was just enjoying himself, but he was resting. Before long, he gained 15 pounds and felt better than ever. He was getting stronger. In the springtime, he gathered beautiful mountain violets and picked wild strawberries and blueberries. He was in awe of plants and trees and animals. They say he connected with some sort of divinity or great mystery in nature. His son said that this connection to God through nature was the most penetrating influence in his father's life."

Sadie fed the ducks. Nora was listening.

"Anyhow, let's see, where was I… He started taking his meals with the others in the dining room and attended the Episcopal services held at the hotel. He met many rich whom he would later ask to support his efforts. He was incredibly optimistic. He believed that the pines emitted an atmosphere of healing. After several months, he recovered. He was a spiritual man and felt something that he described as "auto-suggestion" or "inner prompting." He got the notion that his experience could benefit others, that he should secure several cottages for wealthy patrons who were interested in his "cure." These cottages were for the well-to-do, not for you and me with our short purses! Anyhow, students started coming to study with him. He called it the 'University of Hope.' Trudeau was a man of overwhelming kindness and gentleness. I'm so sorry, Nora; I'm rambling on and on. I'll be quiet now!"

"No please, please continue. I'm feeling like I need a shot of some Trudeau optimism."

"I agree. Optimism heals not only a broken body, but a broken spirit as well," continued Sadie.

"The guides. Trudeau was inspired by the ruddy Adirondack guides. They lived life for life's sake, and they added to his optimistic outlook on life. He found more investors to start his sanatorium up on the hill there. Initially, he didn't charge for his services, but raised the money. Basically, all he prescribed was mountain air, food, and rest on a bed of hope. He suggested singing and whistling. Nora, even his own son said that he was 'the kindest man' he had ever known. I think he genuinely loved each and every one of his patients. I guess that's what I conclude. He had the right optimistic outlook, and he was motivated most by love, not money."

Nora sighed. "I wish that my story had a happy ending. It doesn't look like it will."

"There are a few things that come to mind, dear. Is it okay of I call you 'dear'?"

"Of course," Nora smiled.

"Please remember that your story is not over just as my story is not over and my Harold appears to be in the same situation. Granted, we've been married now 40-some-odd years, but our story is the same. We got married, bought the business, I couldn't have children, so our church was our family, we did the best we could with what we had and now it's his time. On one hand, I'm devastated that he's sick, but on the other hand, I'm so grateful for the time we've had and the life we built. We kissed each other every morning and before bed every night of our married life. It feels too soon, but even if we were 100 years old, it would feel too soon. We take what we get."

Sadie took Nora's hand. "Dear, from what I understand, you have lived and loved a lifetime in the year that you've been married to your Sammie. You have a farm in a beautiful valley with a man who goes to church with you and is kind and wonderful. God gave you wonderful years of courting and a beautiful marriage, even if it seems to be cut short. None of us knows how long we're going to be here. It's awful what has happened to Sammie, but if I could, I'd like to encourage you to cry your tears, and see if you can accept that Sammie's life hasn't been cut short, but that TB is simply part of the story of his life. A life has a beginning and end. That's life. If we can accept that this is Sammie's story, this is Sammie's time, then we honor his life rather than feeling like something is wrong with it. It's sad and it's beautiful at the same time. What did I hear the other day? 'Pleasure and pain have followed each other like sunshine and rain.' Dear, I know that your story isn't over, and the sunshine will come out again."

Nora held all of Sadie's words close to her heart as she bounced between hope and fear. Nora stayed with Sammie for two weeks and ran into her dear Sadie a few more times. She rested. She and Sammie listened to the phonograph that played music in the air shaft, or sometimes it was a radio announcer with the news or a baseball game. Sometimes, she read to him. Their two weeks together went by all too quickly. Nora tried to bring him local trivia questions about Will Rogers or the first Ice Palace, for his lunchtime meals which he was no longer able to eat.

The day Nora dreaded arrived. It was time for her to return to White Creek to teach.

Nora was by Sammie's side when Doctor King delivered his prognosis, "Ray Brook is the best place for him at this point—"

Nora interrupted, "Don't tell me. Tell him."

Sammie piped up, "I only look like I'm sleeping."

Dr. King continued, "We can keep you comfortable here. Unfortunately, your temperature is back up and you continue to lose weight. You have no other choice than to stay on complete bed rest at this point. I know the news is difficult to take, but Sammie's affairs should be in order."

Nora was choked up.

"He recovered once from this a few years ago. Is there any chance at all that he'll rally and do the same thing again?"

"His TB wasn't as far advanced last time. I've not seen anyone in his current condition survive more than 1-2 months," came the doctor's morbid response. "I would never rule out hope, but it doesn't look good at this point. If you're praying people, now's the time to ask for a miracle."

Nora and Sammie looked at each other.

"I'll call you with an update in 2 weeks," said Dr. King as he left quietly and closed the door.

Nora couldn't catch her breath. She felt as though she'd been hit by a wall. Eventually, she heaved a heavy sigh. She laid down on the bed next to Sammie. She knew it was against the rules, but she needed a good cry. It felt so final coming right from the doctor's mouth. Sammie's eyes were filled with tears. The doctor's words felt like a gut punch. There they were, young newlyweds. Sammie at 26 and Nora at 21, still kids themselves in many ways. A nurse came in and Nora started to get up.

"Don't mind me, dear," she said very softly, "I just have a few things to check. We nurses live by a saying, 'regret can't change the past, anxiety can't change the future, but gratitude can change the present.'" She put some notes on a chart and said, "At 4:00 o'clock this afternoon, the opera La Boheme will play in the air shaft. It's in Italian.

I'm a big opera buff and it was my turn to pick today. Here's my copy of the libretto just in case you want to follow along," and she left silently.

Opera? No wonder so many of us die here at Ray Brook; they kill us with opera! thought Sammie. Nora had now heard this gratitude tool twice at Ray Brook. She decided that she didn't want Sammie to have to speak, so she forced herself to speak out some things she was thankful for, "I'm thankful that we had a wonderful honeymoon. Our families are wonderful. Little Julia, who's taller than me now. She's a real sweetheart."

Sammie agreed but couldn't find anything to be grateful for.

Nora continued, "We have wonderful White Crikk friends, the Grange does a lot for farmers, we're together today, we have a beautiful farm and good people taking care of it for us, I love teaching, church is supportive, we're finally done with the Biddie Bunch!"

Silence.

"I have you," Sammie added.

"I have you," Nora echoed.

The phonograph started playing La Boheme in the airshaft that vented into their room. They didn't understand any Italian. They didn't like opera, but they listened, and it wasn't as bad as they imagined, not even for Sammie. For two hours, they drifted in and out of a sleepy wonderland in each other's arms. At times, Nora flipped through the libretto spot reading.

I love her! But I'm afraid...
Mimì is terribly ill,
weaker every day...
The poor little thing

is doomed...
A horrible coughing
racks her fragile chest...
Her pale cheeks
are flushed...
Oh! my life! It's over! Alas! To die!
Goodbye to our dreams of love.
Goodbye, life in a dream.

They held onto each other as though they would crumble without the other. At times the music brought tears to their eyes. After hours of clinging to each other, the hardest thing Nora ever had to do was moving one foot off the bed and putting it on the floor, and then the other, and take that first step away from Sammie in order to prepare for her trip home early the next morning. She was completely numb. Her feet were moving but she didn't know how. She watched her hands pack her bags. Neither of them could eat dinner that night.

This return trip for Nora was horribly difficult. She was going home to stay with her parents and start her school year. She would have to wait for two agonizing weeks until they received word from the doctor as to Sammie's condition. Sammie was still hopeful. Nora wanted to be.

She asked him point blank, "If you show improvement, you'll stay to keep recovering?"

"Yes," he answered.

"And if you're the same and show no signs of improvement?"

"We'll have to consult the doctor on that one," he replied.

"I'm sorry to be asking so many questions...What if you're worse?"

Silence.

"I think we should take our direction from the doctor. If he gives me days or weeks to live, I'd like to be at home with you. I don't want to die here."

It was incredibly poignant for both of them to speak so freely of his death and next steps.

Sammie said, "This is what 'chicken-coop-pinky-swear-married every minute of every day' looks like for us."

Their closeness was beautiful, and they could feel it.

14

Keep Right On to the End of the Road

The next morning, Nora was up early and ready to go. She just sat on her bed and watched Sammie sleep by the open window. She gazed out at Mount Baker and thought the phrase that she'd heard so often at Ray Brook with a southern twang, "There's God up in them there hills," and she had a very keen sense of God's hand on Sammie, their future, the here, and the hereafter. She often waffled between expecting a miracle and accepting that he was dying, hope for recovery and hope for a painless death. *There was already a chill in the night air. Maybe the cooler air would provide the miracle they were praying for?* thought Nora.

She placed her hand on his arm. "I need to go now."

He looked at her and held her hand. "I know what I did wrong," he said.

"What's that?"

"I didn't want to have TB, so I let myself forget that I had a disease, and I overdid. I'm so sorry."

Nora just listened. "In all of the plans to get married and buying the farm, I let myself forget too," responded Nora.

They shed so many tears together in that moment. They weren't allowed to kiss for fear that Nora would become ill herself.

Tears filled Nora's eyes, "Samuel Dewey Telford, in the event that this is the last time we see each other…" she could barely get the words out. "I want you to know that even though my body will be in White Creek, I'll be right here with you in spirit. Remember, I love you and everyone back home loves you and, one day, we will see you again in heaven."

They were both crying. Tears dripped from his eyes and onto his pillow. He gave her hand a squeeze. Though it was forbidden, she gave his forehead a long kiss.

They spent another moment in silence, then the nurse came in and spoke quietly, "Nora, if you're going to catch the morning train, you better skedaddle. We'll take good care of Sammie and call you if we need anything."

She had an assistant take Nora's bags and flag a car for her. And Nora squeezed his hand and held back her tears until she got out into the hallway where she audibly burst into tears. For a moment, everyone in the hall froze and looked. She didn't care, the emotions came pouring out. She walked to the elevator weeping. The elevator doors opened, and she got in with a few people and sobbed and blew her nose loudly in her kerchief. People tried to console her, but she couldn't speak, she just nodded and cried. She let it out all the way down in the elevator and all the way out to the car that had been flagged for her. The assistant, not unfamiliar with seeing these tears, put her bags in the car and told the driver to get her to the train station quickly. Tears helped free Nora. She welcomed them and, for the first time in her life, didn't try to hide them or stifle them.

Finally, at the train station, the only words the driver said were, "This one's on the house, ma'am."

On the train ride home, Nora decided to write down all she was grateful for. She needed every tool she could use to battle what she knew could surely become a black mood or ennui. So many things came naturally to Nora as she was smart and a hard worker. But saying what could be a final goodbye before their first anniversary was more than Nora could handle on her own. She could hear her mother's words, *when life feels broken, take something else that's broken and fix it.* Nora thought about projects around her school building that needed fixing. She would start there. She would add "Gratitudes" to her morning routine for her 13 students. Then she would get at some of her mending.

Her face was hot. *How awful to live so close to death,* she thought. And then her thoughts began to wander. *This wasn't supposed to happen to Sammie. Tragedy doesn't strike someone like him. He bounces back when hard times knock him down. We love each other. We work too hard and go to church and stay out of trouble to have this happening to us.* She fought hard against throwing herself a pity party, but she felt as though she deserved one. Her thoughts were racing, and her emotions were following. Many miles clickety-clacked by. *No. Enough of this foolishness. I need to keep busy and plan for school.*

But soon her thoughts wandered again. *Why is this happening to me? It seems like yesterday that I was at Mrs. Hovey's House with the girls and chatting about boys with my whole life ahead of me, and now I'll soon be a widower. Where's God in all of my God-honoring, hard-working plans? How could He let all of this shit happen to me?"* Now she was good and angry and stewed in her anger for a good bit. *If only I had kept a better eye on how hard he was working, I could have made sure that he didn't overdo. If only I hadn't gotten caught up in our wedding planning and farm and house preparations.* Nora flipped through her magazines and saw an article about the popular Sir Harry Lauder, his popular song lyrics read,

Ev'ry road thro' life is a long, long road,
Fill'd with joys and sorrows too,
As you journey on how your heart will yearn
For the things most dear to you.
With wealth and love 'tis so,
But onward we must go.

Keep right on to the end of the road,
Keep right on to the end,
Tho' the way be long, let your heart be strong,
Keep right on round the bend.
Tho' you're tired and weary still journey on,
Till you come to your happy abode,
Where all the love you've been dreaming of
Will be there at the end of the road.

She was emotionally spent. *Sir Harry can kiss my hairy ass.*

Nora remembered that train ride home as the most tumultuous and emotionally excruciating hours of her life; trying to reconcile her gut level human emotions with her calmer, more rational, "pull yourself up by your bootstraps" side all while speeding away from the love of her life whom she might never see again. She realized that she both hated yet needed God at the same time, and God was just going to have to be cool with it until further notice. Her only escape was the new novel by Thomas Mann, called Magic Mountain. The recent novel was set in a sanitarium called Berkoff; a combination hospital, luxury health spa, and winter sports resort located high in the Swiss

Alps. Nora was intrigued by the similarities between her Ray Brook Hospital experience with Hans visiting his tubercular cousin at Magic Mountain. In both places, there was little regard for time, which was drastically different from the outside world. In the novel, they called people driven by time, 'flatlanders.' Nora knew she was going back to the land of flatlanders, and she was going to have to make the best of it.

As Nora started in teaching, she prayed for Sammie every day. Some of her prayers started with, "Dear God, you know I hate you right now, but..." She asked the family to pray for the miracle Sammie needed and wanted... they all wanted. She asked the church prayer meeting to pray for a miracle because she didn't know if God was hearing her prayers. She was being consumed by excruciating pain and her only escape was her Magic Mountain. She tried reading the Bible, but the words rang hollow.

While just about all of White Creek was praying for a miracle, Sammie, unfortunately, took a sharp turn for the worse. Dr. King from the Trudeau San came every day for a week to examine him. Sammie became incredibly weak. Nora feared that something was wrong and couldn't eat, as her stomach was in knots. Dr. King didn't wait the full 2 weeks with his update.

"Nora, I'm sorry to say that Sammie doesn't have months, he has weeks to live. He wants to make the trip home and be there when his time comes."

Nora was frozen.

"Thank you, doctor. I know you did everything you could. It helps hearing it from you. I'll be there in the morning."

She felt hollow and like she would topple over. But there were things that had to be done. She drove to Pa Telford's to deliver the news to him and Will. They brought her over to her parents and she told the rest of the family the news they had all feared.

They called Florence over and discussed Sammie's plan of action in the event that things turned south for him. Nora was so happy that Sammie had a plan in place. There was no guessing as to what he wanted. Nora just had to make it happen and bring him back to White Creek where Florence would take care of him. Florence had already agreed to keep him comfortable. Nora would stay there as well and share a room with Julia and go back and forth to school from there, which was actually more convenient for her. The weight of the world was on Nora's shoulders, but she could actually feel the love from her family and that they were sharing her burden. They were sharing each other's burdens. There were no two ways to look at it. Sammie was coming home to die. Henry didn't have words. He just held Nora and gently kissed the top of her head.

They needed to get going. Ma got busy brewing coffee and putting sandwiches together. Seth sat with Will and Pa Telford. They didn't deal with emotions very well. Seth could really be a brick in times of crisis and Ida's heart was softened as she overheard the kind words he was saying to them. Ray drove Florence and Nora all night and they arrived at Ray Brook Saturday morning. Their eyes filled with tears when they saw their frail Sammie in his wheel chair. The nurses and aids helped them get Sammie into the car.

As the nurses said their farewells, you could feel the love and appreciation in the air. The nurses truly cared about their patients, and Sammie was no exception.

Nora and Sammie both gave a tearful, “Thank you so much. We appreciate all you did.”

Nora realized that leaving Ray Brook and going back home was another step toward his death and she was shaking. Ray managed to get the car moving without being rude. It felt good to be going home, but they feared that Sammie may not make it. He was in much worse shape than they imagined. They had never seen him so gaunt and lifeless. Before they got far, they were stopped by a customs officer, searching with mirrors under the mud guards for contraband liquor. “Oh heavens,” said Florence to the officer, “you’re wasting your time on this car,” knowing full well that Sammie was given 2 bottles of whiskey in case he started coughing on the trip home.

Nora felt helpless. The rugged Adirondack terrain that Nora first saw as beautiful now seemed so unforgiving. She tried to keep Sammie propped up and comfortable with pillows so he could sleep but she couldn’t seem to do anything for Sammie to help relieve his angst. Sammie sensed Nora’s frustration.

“You know, Nora,” he said with a raspy voice, “do you think you could take over writing my diary? My hands are just too shaky now.”

And so, from that day on, it was Nora’s handwriting filling in Sammie’s diaries. Dr. King thought that maybe Sammie had two weeks to live. They needed to make many stops on the way for Sammie’s benefit. It was no use trying to keep him sitting up, so they laid him down with his head on Nora’s lap. That was a sweet time for both of them. She kept a cold cloth on his forehead and stroked his hair.

Finally, an exhausted and silent Ray reached Herb and Florence’s front porch. Julia watched as Herb came out and carried Sammie up to his room.

"You look skinny," said Julia.

"I guess I was pretty fat before," said Sammie.

"Julia, why don't you run in and put the tea pot on?" said Florence.

Julia was happy to have her aunt and uncle live with her. But she didn't fully understand the gravity of the situation even though she went through the same thing watching her Grandma Telford die.

Julia understood that her Uncle Sammie was very sick, but she couldn't comprehend exactly how sick even though she knew that he could die. Her main concern was that she was put in charge of Sammie's dishes. His dishes had to be washed separately from the rest in different water and in a different dish pan. His glass had to be kept separate, marked with a small piece of adhesive tape at the bottom. She had marked each piece of his silver by tying a piece of string around the handle to identify it as his and his only.

Nora felt guilty letting Florence take over Sammie's care, but she was completely spent after the trip and was feeling quite fragile considering the living nightmare she was in. Sammie, though seemingly out of it much of the time, was concerned about her. He was ready to die. He had accepted it and even welcomed it. He disliked having to be looked after. Florence pointed out all that he had accomplished in his 26 years, and he was grateful for all that God had allowed in his life. He was content. His last concern was making sure Nora knew that she would be okay and that she could still build a good name for herself.

September turned into October but with some welcomed cooler air. Nora's birthday came and Julia prepared a little Happy 22 surprise party. Nora learned to appreciate the help that poured in from everyone. Meals were organized and dropped off regularly. Some ladies came by and kept house once per week. Men came by and spoke with Herb about his field work and sometimes helped out.

Nora wrote in Sammie's diary, "Brother Will came and brought me drinking tubes and set up a radio for me. Stayed all day in bed." Nora never skipped a day of writing in the diary. "Ray brought up a scale for me. 125#." Bedridden Sammie told Nora who had visited him each day and she jotted it down in his diary. It was almost the end of October. Nora was confused by how well Sammie was hanging on.

She reported to Sammie, "You've lasted one month past your 'due date.'"

She turned to Florence, "Is this a sign that he could still come back from this?" she asked Florence.

"Only the good Lord knows, dear. It doesn't look like it right now, but only the good Lord knows."

As cool October turned to cold November, bitter winds came, and Sammie's window remained open. He prayed, *God, I can smell the corn and I hear Herb and his hired hands harvesting. Please protect them from the cutter knives. I wish I could be out there even for just one more day. But I'm glad I'm comfortable here in bed. Thank you for Florence and Nora. And Julia for making me laugh. I know I am well-taken care of. Please ease my Nora's pain. I don't want her to hurt. Please make my death quick.*

Sammie had lasted a month longer than expected and Nora rekindled her hope for Sammie's recovery. She started to envision him back on his feet and returning to their farm. She fantasized about his recovery and having children with him. She *needed* him to get better. Her life, and their good name depended on it. She felt that that was what God wanted but somehow God wasn't able enough to make it happen. *The right thing is supposed to happen when you pray. I'll never have children. Why would God punish me so? Have I done something wrong?* Sammie could tell that Nora was holding out for a miracle and he would stay with her as long as he could. He wasn't going to give up the ghost as long as she needed him.

Sammie listened to his radio at least 12 hours a day. He listened to President Calvin Coolidge's' speech "Nothing in the world can take the place of Persistence. Talent will not; nothing is more common than unsuccessful men with talent. Genius will not; unrewarded genius is almost a proverb. Education will not; the world is full of educated derelicts. Persistence and determination alone are omnipotent. The slogan 'Press On' has solved and always will solve the problems of the human race." Though he needed to be carried and the trip nearly killed him, he insisted that Henry and Ray take him to Walloomsac to vote for Calvin Coolidge. Every eligible male and female Telford and Andrew voted that night. "Even though we're prospering as a nation, he wants us to save wealth for a rainy day. I think that's smart," said Sammie. He loved listening to his radio though they all thought that the trip to Walloomsac might do him in. Anytime he got out of bed, he had to be carried. He was thrilled to learn the next day that Coolidge won.

November 7 was Sammie and Nora's first Anniversary. It was a somber day. Not much attention was paid but Nora brought a cake up to Sammie. He smiled and Nora fed him a little bite.

"Happy Anniversary," she said. "What a year we've had, eh?"

Nora started crying and feeling sorry for herself. She had had a bad day at school on top of everything. Sammie motioned for her to come lie with him. It took tremendous energy for him to speak.

"I'm here with you now. And I'll be with you even after I'm gone."

Nora understood. She just cried. Sammie coughed a bit, and she gave him some whiskey. Henry and Ray brought up some flowers and ice cream on behalf of the Grange. The ice cream helped Sammie's sore throat some.

November turned to December and Rachel Boot's father offered to get the Christmas tree for Nora's evening exercises. The students decorated it and Nora let Rachel put the star on the top of the tree sitting on her father's shoulders. Everyone told her that they missed Sammie Claus. They didn't realize how bad off he was. Nora received many nice gifts and hugs that night from her students and parents. She was truly appreciated. She was grateful for her work to help take her mind off Sammie's illness. She had to separate Sammie from his TB. TB wasn't only robbing Sammie of his life, but hers as well. She hated TB to her core, but she loved Sammie more deeply.

On Christmas Eve, Nora did some Christmas shopping and bought presents for her family, Herb, Florence, and Julia plus a special present that was from Sammie for Julia. Henry bought some fish from King down the Falls and brought it over for all to eat. Seth and Ida came over and cooked it up just right with potatoes and carrots and biscuits with plenty of homemade butter.

"Frank Hewitt died of TB earlier today," said Henry loudly while they were waiting for their peach pie. Silence.

"I'll bring a plate up to Sammie," said Nora. She was proud that he had lasted much longer than the doctor's thought and was still hanging on, though he wasn't able to eat much of anything with his sore throat. Florence asked Julia to fetch a large chunk of ice from the ice house. It pained her to see her brother in such dire straits. She had to constantly separate her loving sister-half from her nurse-half as she laid the ice on his chest to help relieve him of his deep rattling cough.

"Aghhhh," he cried out in pain. It was just too much to bear. He was now hanging on as best he could.

The Tabors sent over a large 50-year-old bottle of their spring mineral water from their spring with instructions to simply wipe him down with it. Nora did so, hoping that *something* would turn things around. She could not bear to lose hope while Sammie was still hanging on. She dampened the cloth with the spring water and then carefully took his arm out from under the blanket, wiped it down and then placed it back under the warm blankets. Then the opposite arm. She dampened the cloth with the magic waters and wiped behind his ears and around his neck.

Sammie, who struggled to stay awake for more than 5 minutes at a time sat up straight and said, "What the hell is that God-awful smell?" and he laid right back down.

Nora was shocked and decided that if he didn't see the value of getting wiped down with what she called the 'rotten egg' water, then she certainly wouldn't torture him with it, blessed as it may be. So, she dumped the awful stuff out.

They each took turns going up to see Sammie for short visits while his radio played Christmas hymns. Florence instructed them to keep their distance, but Ray had a different plan. Sammie had kept scratching at his scruffy facial hair so Ray asked Herb if he could borrow his razor and shaving soap. Herb jumped to it and heated some water and while a radio choir sang Sammie's favorites, Ray whipped up the shaving soap into a good hot lather while Herb sat in the corner and sharpened his straight razor on the leather strop. Ray brushed the thick hot foam onto Sammie's face and neck. The comfort and warmth brought tears to Sammie's eyes. He hadn't shaved for a good month or so and the itch was irritating him. Herb handed him White Crikk's sharpest ever straight blade and Ray carefully started shaving him. He put his hand on his cheek to hold up the skin while he drew the blade down. It made a scratchy sound. Ray scrunched his lips to one side. "

Go like this," and Sammie scrunched his lips to one side as well.

Then the other side. Then chin up which was painful for Sammie with his sore throat. A choir continued over the radio and filled the freezing room with 'Adeste Fideles laeti triumphantes, Venite, venite in Bethlehem.' Ray swished the blade in the hot water and wiped both sides on a towel and continued to touch up Sammie's face.

"Go like this," and Sammie tightened his upper lip over his top teeth.

Ray shaved his sparse mustache.

"Ya know, we could just get the cat in here to lick this cream off your face and you'd have the cleanest shave ever," said Ray.

How poignant that something as ordinary, as quotidian, as shaving could be so beautiful. Ray gently covered Sammie's face with a towel and rubbed it around to get all the shaving cream off and clean him up. Sammie was appreciative.

"Ah! That feels much better," said Sammie gratefully.

"Anything's an improvement on that face," said Ray with a smile. It was the first Sammie had smiled in a long time.

Later, Dr. Shaw came up for a visit, "Do you recognize that stale beer smell?" he asked Florence. "That's the smell of TB."

Dr. Shaw appreciated Florence and took every opportunity to train and encourage her in her medical interests and acknowledged how challenging it must be to be caretaking for her own brother. He tried to distance himself personally from his patients, but Dr. Shaw loved both the Telfords and the Andrews. They were his kind of people. He had been invited to stay for more dinners and pieces of pie than he could count. He especially appreciated what a good chap Sammie had been to him over the years delivering hay for his horses and ice and sawdust to stock his ice house.

The good doctor brought a pint of whiskey for Sammie and joked that he was to go easy on it. He gave Sammie a small shot to take as he noticed a pronounced rattle in his breathing. Sammie did his best to smile, and before he fell back asleep, Sammie asked, "Did I see Mother in here earlier?" There was silence. Nora and Florence watched the doctor take a listen to Sammie's lungs. He asked Florence to help him get Sammie out of bed and onto the scale. Sammie was not too happy to have to get out of bed and shivered in the cold.

"Florence, hurry! I'm freezing!" yelled Sammie.

Everyone was taken aback.

"Come now," said Dr. Shaw, "life is not so short, but there is always time enough for courtesy."

They helped Sammie stand up on the scale. He could barely hold himself up. 110 pounds. Florence wrote it down while Dr. Shaw helped lay Sammie back down and Nora got him an extra blanket and helped him get comfortable. She wiped his mouth clean.

He looked up at Nora and asked, "Why is it so crowded in here?"

Dr. Shaw stood up tall and straightened his back, took a deep breath and thought for a moment. He turned toward the ladies.

"The doctors at Ray Brook are quite intelligent. They know when a patient has two weeks to live sometimes just by the sound of the cough. But our Sammie has carried on for a good three months now. You both are taking very good care of him…maybe too good…" Dr. Shaw paused here. "Sometimes our loved ones needlessly hang on and suffer because they think we need them."

Florence put her arm around Nora. Nora knew what Dr. Shaw meant and his words pierced her heart. Nora was holding onto Sammie even though he was suffering. She had to let Sammie know that she could rely on God to take care of her. He was suffering needlessly on her account. He was so faithful and loyal to stay with her that he was choosing suffering by refusing to die so he could emotionally support her. She knew she had to tell him. It pained her so to see Sammie in such pain. She slipped away to her cot in Julia's room to have a good cry into her pillow.

It was late on this snowy, windy Christmas Eve in White Creek when Nora went to Florence, "I have to have a talk with Sammie, but I'm not sure he can hear me. He's out of it."

Florence paused and said, "Hearing is the last sense to go. If you speak from your heart, he'll hear you."

So, Nora went to Sammie late that night. Nora trusted Florence's words and sat on the bed next to him and took his cold hand. He was dead asleep.

"I'm worried about you, Sammie Dewey Telford. I'm worried that you're hanging on in this freezing room because I need you so desperately, and I do need you. I so want a big miracle to happen for you so we can have our life and our farm back. So we can build our good name together. But I realize that I'm being selfish. You've been so strong for me, and I love being chicken coop pinky swear married to you every day…" She clasped his pinky in hers. "But it's time for me to be strong for you." She could hardly speak through her tears. "I can't bear to see you suffer like this any longer. Let me be brave for you." She choked back her tears. "Don't you keep suffering on account of me. It's okay to let go. You know and I know that I'll be alright. I'll keep doing my best, taking my next right step. I have everyone to take care of me; my family, your family… our family. I still have our family. I'll keep going to church." Sammie 's cold blue hand squeezed hers. She buried her face in his chest and cried. "Merry Christmas."

A few moments later her tears stopped, she breathed a sigh of relief. She knew she did the right thing and she felt free. She threw another blanket over him and fluffed his pillow. And, more importantly, she knew that she had freed Sammie. She slept better than she had in months that night.

15

Love, Here Is My Heart

On Christmas morning, the wind had died down. Herb had gone out and taken care of his cows early in the am. Florence got up to check on Sammie. Julia had her chores to do as well. On a farm, there are no breaks. Milking needs to be done even on Christmas Day. After breakfast, the sun was bright and reflected off the snow. They opened presents downstairs before going up to see Sammie. Nora gave Florence the blanket she had knitted. She gave Herb a nice pair of gloves, and Julia a beautiful dress.

"Aunt Nora! I love it! Thank you so much!" Julia ran to her room to try it on and then modeled it for everyone.

"You must have been good this year for Santa to be so nice to you," responded Florence.

The adults had been doing their best to include Julia in discussions about Sammie, but there were many things that she just couldn't quite comprehend. As children do, she had absorbed the emotional tensions of the adults and the kindness of the dress just brought tears to her eyes. She had been overhearing her parents' conversations about heaven and just needed to know that she was loved and safe.

They decided it was time to go up and see Sammie with their presents.

Florence said, “I was up in the night with Sammie a few times getting that cough and sore throat under control. He’ll be tired this morning so let’s go in quietly.”

Julia said, “Mama, Sammie doesn’t look like Sammie anymore. He’s bony and shaky. I don’t like it.”

“That’s right, dear. He’s not well, but you can always look right straight into his eyes. His eyes never change.”

His window was always open, so they often wore their coats and hats and mittens just like they were getting ready to go outside. When they finally roused him from his sleep, he was confused by having everyone in his room. They needed to remind him that it was Christmas morning as they propped him up with the buckwheat pillows Nora made for him. Julia turned the radio on, and a choir sang, ‘O Little Town of Bethlehem.’

“Merry Christmas,” he said to them all.

Florence was wrapped in her new blanket and Herb in his new gloves. Sammie commented on Julia’s new dress from Santa. She twirled around for him. They each presented their gifts to Sammie. Nora opened them for him: tie clasps, socks, cash, and a knit-cap that she made.

“I need that today,” he said, and Nora pulled it gently down over his ears. “Knitting burns 9 calories per hour,” he said. Apparently, that was something he learned at Ray Brook.

He had no energy and could barely move. He was emaciated. Nora pulled a beautifully wrapped package hidden underneath her coat. “

This one says, ‘to Julia, from Sammie-Claus,’” said Nora.

Julia was so excited. She couldn't believe she was getting yet another present. She savored the moment and slowly opened her present to find the beautiful, glazed porcelain doll she had admired in Lurie's shop window. Sammie had told Nora to buy it even though it was too expensive.

"We walk this earth but once," he said with a raspy whisper, realizing the gravity of his statement.

Julia looked directly into Sammie's eyes, "Thank you, Uncle Sammie. I love you."

"I love you, too," came the reply.

They didn't want to keep Sammie awake much longer. They had all noticed that he had been sleeping a lot. As they all exited, Julia reported that they were going to go sledding out back. Sammie smiled at her. After they left, Nora tidied things up and then stayed a bit to be with Sammie. She adjusted the new hat on his head, wiped his mouth clean, rearranged his pillows again and gave him a kiss on the forehead before she headed downstairs. She looked at him in his complete vulnerability. He relied on someone else for every bodily function. He looked small and disheveled curled up in his bed and she loved him more than ever and was grateful for their beautiful morning together.

As she started to leave, he took her hand and firmly grasped her hand and wouldn't let go. He looked into her eyes. He clearly wanted her to stay. She sat down on the side of the bed. His breathing was belabored, irregular and rattling. For a moment he clasped her pinky finger with his. Then he began coughing. Nora poured him a shot of the whiskey and it spilled when he put his hand up to push it away.

He continued to cough so gruesomely loud that Nora couldn't believe his tired, emaciated body was capable of making such a sound. She took his sputum cup and gave a towel for him to cough into. Blood. She started toward the window to call for Florence, but he just firmly held her hand. They looked at each other with fear in their eyes. They could hear Julia and her parents playing in the snow outside. The deep coughing and rattled breathing persisted producing even more blood. She got tough for him and anchored herself on the side of the bed. Nora looked past the blood into her dear sweet Sammie's eyes. Tears were dripping off her cheeks and their eyes locked; they knew this was his time.

"I've got you," she said.

Nora gave him another towel. Sammie saw that she had blood spatter all over her face. Their eyes remained locked. She silently prayed for the end to come quickly. She knew that he was drowning in his own blood and liquified remains of his infected lungs. She didn't know how long she could bear to watch him suffer. But she stayed right there with him all the same. He couldn't catch his breath through the gurgling. It was horrific. Finally, Nora couldn't take it and started for the window again to call for Florence. Sammie held onto her, and they locked eyes again. He only needed her. More lung-ripping hacks.

"I'm here," she reaffirmed loudly over his coughing. She gripped his hands firmly.

"I love you, Sammie." And just like that, his coughing stopped, and his body sank lifeless onto the bed. The struggle was over, and the light left his eyes. He was gone and Nora sobbed uncontrollably. Time stopped. She held his hand and wept bitterly. She could still feel him in the room.

"I love you, Sammie," she whispered through her tears. She still had hold of his hands. She had no words, just tears. She rubbed the back of his hand.

She was in no hurry to tell the others. She knew that as soon as someone else knew, it would set off a flurry of activity. She just wanted to stay in the quiet with her Sammie. She noticed that she felt relief that his struggle was over. She heard a choir on the radio, 'In the bleak midwinter, Frosty wind made moan, Earth stood hard as iron, Water like a stone, Snow had fallen, Snow on snow on snow, In the bleak midwinter, Long, long ago…' She just sat with her sadness and her Sammie. It was oddly peaceful.

The next she knew, Florence appeared and placed her hand on her shoulder. Nora clasped her hand. Then Florence started quietly and respectfully cleaning up without disturbing Nora. Florence tearfully closed his eyes and then brushed his hair. Nora was glad Ray had shaved him. Florence gave Nora a wash cloth and encouraged her to look in the mirror. Her face and clothes were covered in blood spatter. Her hair needed brushing. Nora stood frozen at the dresser mirror wiped her face clean. Florence encouraged her to put on a new change of clothes and bring her the blood-soaked clothes. She thoroughly cleaned herself up and put on a change of clothes and came back in the room and sat in stunned disbelief next to Sammie's body, her hands helplessly resting on the mattress.

"I don't know what I'm supposed to do," she cried.

"There are no rules and silence is just fine," said Florence. By this point, Sammie had been wiped clean and the bed linens replaced. "This is the first he's been at peace in months," said Florence. That came as a great relief to Nora.

Herb poked his head in and quietly asked if he could bring in Julia to say goodbye. Nora nodded. Julia hesitantly entered the room with her father. It wasn't the first time she had seen a body, but she loved her Uncle Sammie and her tears made all of them cry.

In a house where emotions were often not shown, Florence said, "It's perfectly okay to cry when a loved one passes. You're going to be just fine. Let it out. Uncle Sammie loved you very much but look at him. He's not coughing. His throat isn't sore anymore. He's resting and more comfortable than he's been in a long time."

Herb agreed and Julia appreciated his rare tenderness. Florence encouraged her to touch Sammie's hand. She explained to Julia that Sammie was cold because his soul was no longer in his body.

"He's in heaven now with Grandma Telford, but we can speak to them anytime we like."

"I bet Grandma is happy to have Sammie keep her company," said Julia "I bet they're playing cards."

After a few moments, Florence gently ushered them out and insisted that they all immediately go to the kitchen and wash their hands and face with hot water.

Nora felt completely disoriented.

Herb came and spoke softly, "Will and Pa will be arriving soon and your family as well."

"Thank you." Nora realized how much she needed them all.

Florence spoke softly, "Reverend Manning and Johnnie Baker need to be contacted." Nora tried to assemble her thoughts.

"Could you, please, make those calls for me?" asked Nora.

Florence agreed and asked, "Do you think you might be more comfortable on the couch by the fire?"

It was so hard to leave his side. She stood up and placed his hands on his chest. She played with his hair a bit. She squeezed his hands and slowly walked toward the door. Again, she wondered how her feet were moving. She stood in the doorway and looked back at him for the last time. Florence waited patiently and then both women walked downstairs. Florence encouraged Julia to sit on the couch with Aunt Nora in the parlor and went to the kitchen, started the water for tea, and made her phone calls. Julia let Nora hold her dolly while she sat at her feet and rested her head on her Aunt Nora's knee half-heartedly played her new Lincoln Logs. Herb needed to keep himself occupied so he went out and plowed the road, so the snow wasn't a problem for anyone arriving.

As Nora held the doll and stroked Julia's hair, she realized that she'd never have a child with Sammie. She was completely devastated and amazed at how much emotion burst out of her. So much so that Florence heard her and came from the kitchen to see what was happening. When her tears eased up, she told Florence that she had no words. Just tears.

"Is that okay? I'm just a ball off flesh crying my eyes out."

Florence understood and squeezed her hand. She was like an old sage to Nora and other young ladies in White Creek.

Florence responded, "Words are less needful to sorrow than to joy, Love." And the two of them cried together.

Florence really started to breakdown. She had been strong for both Nora and Sammie for 4 long months. She was physically and emotionally exhausted from caring for him and suddenly it all hit her like a ton of bricks; she had lost her brother and she no longer had to separate her nurse side from her sister side. She could finally let her tears flow. They were sharing a good cry when Julia stood up off the floor and sat on her mother's lap and started crying as well.

"It's sort of like we are crying in a 3-part harmony," said Julia.

"We probably sound better crying together than we would singing together," said Nora.

It was barely noon and Nora had already celebrated Christmas with Herb, Florence and Julia, and then again with Sammie, and then held onto him through his dramatic passing, and now she was back at the Christmas tree. She was experiencing a roller coaster of emotion. Another deep wave of sorrow surged when Ida came into the parlor. As they embraced, Nora felt that her Mama was the sweetest and wisest mother that ever a girl could have.

Ida stroked her hair and kept saying over and over, "You'll be okay dear. I am so sorry, my love. Let it out…" They both wept. Nora was a bit embarrassed to be emoting so publicly. She wasn't used to being the emotional center of attention, but she knew it was necessary because everyone had encouraged her to let it out. Seth, who rarely showed emotion, came over, his eyes swollen with tears, took Nora's face in his hands, and kissed her forehead. Henry and Ray came to her side, and they all comforted each other.

Herb invited Julia to help him bring in some apple tree wood.

"Why are we whispering?" asked Julia.

"I don't know. It just seems like we should be. Anyway, apple tree wood will make the house smell sweet. Perfect for Christmas Day." And with that, Nora realized how it was that life didn't stop when

Sammie did. Life kept moving, and it was already going faster than she could handle. Chores still needed to be done. Florence was baking extra goodies in the kitchen and making phone calls. It was all too much for Nora.

As those who wished went up to pay their respects at a distance. Nora's mother explained to her, "Dear, we all have our daily chores to do, and today and for many days to come, your only chore is to do a good bit of crying. It's the only way we survive. We'll take care of everything else."

Nora found herself filled with gratitude and encouragement for every single person in the room.

"Henry, Sammie could never get over how strong you are. He always said that you were stronger than an ox! And the both of you never EVER turned down an opportunity to help us on the farm. We truly wouldn't have survived if it hadn't been for you and Ray. I don't know how I'll ever repay you."

They could all hear Florence and Ida in the kitchen getting a wonderful lunch ready.

"Something smells good. You got anything good 'round here ta eat?" Seth called out.

"Well, if you get your hands washed up, I just might let you have a crumb or two," Florence retorted. Everyone smiled.

Eventually, everyone served themselves up a plate and sat in the parlor.

Pa Telford stood up, eyes red with tears, "Dear Lord, we do thank you for our 26 years with Sammie. Bless this food. Merry Christmas. Amen."

Everyone was moved by and shocked that he spoke out loud to everyone, let alone say a prayer. The tears and despair eventually turned into storytelling as people started eating. At first, the accounts were of Sammie's dedication to his church and how he led the Epworth meetings, his business acumen, and desire to lead the effort of gathering farmers to work together, and his never-ending support of the Grange. On and on it went as though he could do no wrong.

Then Nora said, "You could also send him to the Crikk Store for just one thing and he'd forget what it was by the time he got there!" And then, when the men joined in, the tales became lighthearted and soon tears and laughter filled the house. Pa Telford even told about the time Sammie farted in church during Aunt Ethel's funeral. Julia was amazed to hear the adults talk about such things.

Ida told the story of the first time that Sammie stayed all night at the house when he and Nora were courting. He slept on the couch, but as a joke, she "bundled" him, nonetheless, sewed him into a big burlap sack, and stitched it tight around his neck so that he could barely move. In the middle of the night, she could hear him hop through the downstairs and out the back door to use the outhouse.

"I don't know how he handled things once he got there!" she said.

Seth told the story of the time that he and Sammie were standing in the back door yard when Henry brought Nora home from school.

"Nora's skirt got caught on the bolt as she jumped off the buckboard. She landed on the ground just fine, but her skirt was almost clear up over her head with her bloomers in full view. Poor Sammie didn't know what to do. Should he help? Should he look away? I don't know who was more embarrassed, Sammie or Nora?" They all laughed.

Nora replied, "Ugh! I guarantee you that I was more embarrassed! That was awful. And you just stood their laughing. Poor Henry didn't know what to do but at least he came around and picked me back up so I could get myself put back together!"

Henry said, "No brother should ever see his sister's bloomers."

Once everyone laughed at his first comment, he joined in with the story of the time they were out fixing fence in the pasture.

"We was taking a lunchtime break and we sat right down under the tree over by the pond. It was me, then Ray, then Sammie. The geese came up out of the water. They were quacking away, and we were throwing them some bread from our lunch. None of us realized that the bull had slowly come up behind us and lined his big old head up with poor Sammie's back and, in a split-second, drove him right along the ground for about 15 feet and then ran away. It's like he was there with us, and then he was gone. Sammie wasn't hurt at all, but you should have seen the look on Sammie's face!"

Ray piped up and said, "You should have seen the look on my face too because I didn't know what the outcome of bull vs. Sammie was going to be!"

Seth added "You don't know the power that a bull has until you've experienced it."

Ida asked, "Is that Mark Twain?"

"No. Mark Twain says 'A man who carries a cat by the tail learns something he can learn in no other way. But my words present the same level of wisdom."

There was a great outpouring of love and understanding for Pa Telford that day.

He was a man of few words, and everyone listened when he spoke. "The funniest thing I've ever seen," he said with a smile, "was the time he found a bee tree over home and wanted to get the honey out, but instead, the bees decided they didn't want him anywhere 'round their honey and stung him but good. I could hardly recognize him because his face was so swollen! He had one bulge on this side of his forehead and his cheek was puffing out on the opposite side. I told him that he needed to wait 'til the weather got colder when the bees were asleep! Ma fixed him an' he was alright."

Ida turned to Florence, "what do you think is the best way to treat bee stings?"

"I just take out the stinger out with my fingernail, wash it up good with soap and water, and them wipe it down with apple cider vinegar. That brings the swelling down and draws out any of the poison from the bees. Baking soda and water made into a paste will do the same thing."

As the stories continued, Florence went over and sat next to her brother Will. He was awfully quiet all afternoon. He was mourning in his own way, so she just sat with him and offered him some cake.

The atmosphere went somber again when the undertaker arrived. Johnnie Baker was a long-time friend of both families. Herb opened the door to welcome him and his assistant. Johnnie was surprised at the level of levity on such a dismal day.

He was greeted by a chorus of "Hello. Merry Christmas. Thank you for coming."

He came in and shook Herb's hand and said, "Hello, Herb, I am sorry for your loss. This is my assistant, LeRoy Anderson, and we're here to take care of everything."

Johnnie graduated from the Hoosick Falls High School the same year as Sammie and now was working with his father as an undertaker up in Cambridge.

Johnnie and LeRoy made their way to Nora and shook her hand, "I am so sorry for your loss," and then gave her a hug. "Sammie was one of those all-around great guys. I gotta tell you, he helped me in math even when I was a jerk in high school. This whole town's gonna miss him."

Nora didn't really know what to say, so she just said, "Thank you."

As Johnnie explained that he and LeRoy were there to take Sammie's body to Cambridge and prepare it for burial, all but Ida, Will and Pa Telford made their way into the kitchen.

"I'm calling it Sammie's body because we know it's not Sammie. We know that Sammie is in heaven and he's not suffering any longer. Our services provide a respectful way to care for his body. As you probably already know, we cannot have an open casket due to the tuberculosis. However, would you like us to have his closed casket here on the 28th for afternoon and evening calling hours right here in the parlor, and then again on the 29th for morning calling hours?"

"I don't think we need the casket for calling hours," said Nora. Ida was amazed at Nora's strength and put her arm around her.

"The casket will be at the cemetery for the graveside funeral service on January 1, but after everyone leaves, since we can't put the body in the frozen ground, we will store the body back at our Ice House. This information can be disturbing to some people. Are you aware of how bodies and burials are handled during the winter?" Ida, Will, and Pa Telford shook their heads no.

"Yes, I am. And thank you for going over everything," replied Nora. "I'm glad that you worked out all of those details with Florence."

"Come the end of March, or sometime thereabouts, when the ground is thawed enough, we'll give you a call and arrange a time for you and maybe some of your good family here, to come up and have a quiet, respectful time to actually put his body in the ground. Now, you can do as much or as little as you want on that day. Some people have their Reverend come and, sometimes, families don't even come at all." None of this was news to Nora, but she was very appreciative to have it all explained by Johnnie Baker, the undertaker.

Johnnie went on to explain, "Due to the nature of TB, his body is still very contagious, and we have certain procedures we need to follow to remove it as soon as possible. We will first put the body in a post mortem bag. Do we have your permission to go up and prepare him for the trip up to Cambridge?" Nora nodded her head and a few more tears fell. "You may wish to join the others in the kitchen for a cup of tea as we will be just a while," he added.

Nora did as he said and moved into the kitchen where Florence and the others were talking and had a cup to tea and pie ready for her. She couldn't eat. She just sipped her tea. They all tried their best to keep conversations going but there were awkward silences as you could hear the bed being moved, the clank of the stretcher, the zip of the body bag and the muffled voices of Johnnie and LeRoy in the bedroom above.

They soon came down the stairs with Sammie's body on the stretcher. Pa and Will got up to help. Everyone else was completely still. There were no words to describe the deep solemnity that accompanied the moving Sammie's body. Sheer somber respect. They wheeled him through the parlor and the grisly silence was deafening.

You could hear the squeak of the wheels turning on the rug and the men whispering directions to each other as Pa and Will joined them on either end of the stretcher. Herb opened the front door for them, and a blast of cold air rushed into the house. Everyone listened in complete silence as the stretcher rolled out onto the porch. Nora didn't watch but the sounds of it all played like a movie in her head. The snow was too deep and the path Herb had shoveled too narrow to roll the stretcher, so the men simply collapsed the wheels of the stretcher and lifted it up over the 2 ½ feet of snow to the awaiting hearse. The back was opened. They slid the stretcher into the back as gently as possible. The large tail gate of the hearse slammed shut, the men solemnly shook each other's hands, and they watched them drive off. The silence was too much. The men came back in, and Florence gathered everyone's attention offering to warm up their tea. Julia went around with the kettle and Florence whispered to the men to all wash their hands thoroughly.

The men spoke softly about it being chore time. Nora said her goodbyes to each of the men, and they hugged her. She could feel more tears coming on. She was grateful not only for her family but also that she was able to allow their love into her heart. Without them, she would never have made it through the day. As the men left, Leah and Verna showed up with all kinds of food and the women sat and talked some more.

Though Nora hadn't slept in the same bed with Sammie for about 9 months, that night, her little cot in Julia's room felt very small and very lonesome. She recounted the emotional swings of the day: Christmas joy, eternal love, fear, horror, chaos, great sorrow, deep loss, gratitude, more gratitude, healing, more love, peace. She continued to write in Sammie's diary:

Sammie passed away this morning at 10:45. He knew us to the last. He suffers no more.

Nora tossed and turned all night between periods of sleep and questions running through her mind. Would she even be able to get out of bed. Would she ever stop crying. How could she ever teach again? In the morning, for a split second, she awoke and wondered if his death had been a dream. It had not. She could hear Julia downstairs telling Florence that there was a flock of cardinals outside. Florence rushed to the window.

"Did you know that a flock of cardinals is actually called a 'radiance'? Some people believe that cardinals are a sign that Sammie is here with us. With Nora."

Before Nora got dressed and ate breakfast Julia burst into her room and gave her a hug and told her to watch out the window for the radiance of cardinals. "It's a sign that Sammie is here with us," said Julia. Huge tears rolled down Nora's face as she watched the cardinals play against the backdrop of snow.

Herb was waiting for her to go pick up Seth and head up to Cambridge to make final arrangements. She purchased the casket, $175 and a lot next to his mother at Woodland's Cemetery, $65. They ordered the double headstone and spoke with the engraver. They were home by lunchtime and Florence, Nora, and Julia went down the Falls after a hearty meal and each bought a new coat and hat. Nora gave herself permission to not expect too much from herself and it felt wonderful. She simply relied on Florence to know what the next right step was. When they returned home, Florence sat Nora down so they could work on writing Sammie's obituary. Sometimes, the next right step is easy, but this next step was a difficult one.

Florence advised, "Sometimes, when we're overwhelmed with impossible thought of writing your husband's obituary, we simply use the form that the undertaker left for us." In those days, newspapers took it upon themselves to "fix" or expand submitted obituaries. Several of the obituaries added their own flare such as *White Creek has lost another of its cherished sons. Beloved, Samuel Telford, loved by all who knew him, succumbed to a long illness on December 25, 1924. Though he had been ill for some time, it still came as a shock by those who knew him…*

Her closest friends knew that Nora needed them now more than ever and they created an informal schedule to make sure that someone was with her all the time. The following day, Verna Lowe came over to help her wash and fold Sammie's clothes and select an outfit for him to be buried in. The air was smokey and it smelled terrible when she arrived. Herb had built a big bonfire in the back and was burning Sammie's blood-stained linens, pajamas, pillows, Nora's bloody clothes and the curtains and carpet from his room. Verna went inside and gave Nora a hug.

Florence said to Nora, "I have to go to a delivery over in Quaker-hood. Shall I bring Julia with me?"

"Oh, please no. I need her here with me. She can keep me and Verna company." For a young lady, Julia had a knack for knowing when to disappear when the conversation became too adult.

Verna had no experience comforting a young widow, so she just decided to be her flexible friend ready for whatever state she was in. *How awkwardly horrid the first days after your young husband dies must be*. She was pleasantly surprised to find Nora up and around. As they worked together gathering up Sammie's things, Nora had moments when she spoke through tears as various things triggered tender memories. Verna cried right along with her. They selected his burial clothes and shoes and socks.

"I think we need to bring his wedding ring, cuff links, tie and tie clasp, and belt," said Nora. On the drive up to the undertaker, Nora started shaking her head. "I also brought a pair of Sammie's underwear. Clearly, he won't need underwear, but it seems so wrong to let him spend eternity without it. I've never had to think such morbid things through before, but he doesn't need a belt because his suit jacket will cover his waistline and it's not like his pants will fall down because he's lying down."

Verna said, "I think you're doing great. My mother suggested you a have a small box for Sammie's gold tie clasps, extra cuff links, maybe the broken watch fob? At some point you might consider taking those to the jewelers to have something memorable made that you could wear.

"A locket would be nice. But I'm not ready for a trip to the jewelers just yet," said Nora. Verna stayed with Nora through dinner.

After dinner, Florence said, "I have an idea. Julia, why don't you mop and scrub down Sammie's old room? We need to make it Nora's new room. If we clean it in the morning, Herb can paint and paper it in the afternoon." All of this clearly came as news to Herb. "Nora, tomorrow I'll give you money to go to the Falls for paint, paper, linens, pillows, and curtains. Pick out a rug while you're at it."

Nora said, "Oh my, that actually sounds fun. Can you come along with me, Verna?" And the next day was planned.

Florence and Julia stayed home to clean and prepare the house for Calling Hours. Nora had been graciously sharing a room with Julia for the last 4 months and Florence wanted to give her a new space to call her own. She and Julia rearranged the bedroom so that it felt different than the way it was laid out before. But the biggest change came from closing the window and letting the heat from the kitchen woodstove rise up through the vent that had been closed for the last 4 months. Nora and Verna had a splendid time together; however, word of Sammie's death spread quickly, and Nora noticed that wherever she went, people made her feel uncomfortable with their pointing and whispering, so she decided that home was the best place to be.

They came home for lunch and Nora and Verna volunteered to paint while Herb did the papering. They put on Sammie's radio and a choir was singing Christmas carols and Nora started crying while she painted. What had been Sammie's room was now being sanitized away. All she could smell was the Clorox Julia used to mop the floor and paint fumes. The windows were bare. It was the first time she had ever been in that room when it was warm. The ceiling and walls were all getting painted or papered. Already, Sammie's story was less tangible and more a part of her memory. In a few hours, the painting and papering was done.

Julia said, "Aunt Nora, you and I will go down and fix dinner while Mother and Father and Verna set everything up. Then you'll have a nice surprise after dinner." Everyone thought that was a good idea and they made it happen. Herb rolled out the new rug. They flipped the mattress and moved the bed to the far wall and the dresser by the window. Herb even had time to paint the headboard and dresser. They brought up a chair from downstairs. Verna hung the new curtains while Florence made up the bed with fresh new linens and pillows and Herb dusted everything.

Herb said, "It looks great if I do say so myself!"

They all went down for dinner, and they skipped dessert so they could show Nora her new room. Julia made her walk up the stairs blindfolded, and they all stood in the doorway with her as Julia removed the blindfold. Nora burst into tears. Happy tears. Bittersweet tears.

Julia said, "See, we moved the bed over here and I love your new blanket. Look at your curtains! The rug is so soft."

Herb said, "It sounds to me like Julia can't wait to get you out of her room!" Eventually, Florence invited everyone to go down and have dessert. She sat on the bed with Nora.

"Dear, no one gets over death like they get over a cold. You'll be baffled by how often you're moved to tears for months and months, if not years. No need to apologize for them or hide them. You'll eventually move through your grief, but you'll always carry Sammie with you forever." With that, Florence handed Nora a little gift. As she opened it, more tears. She gave Florence a hug. It was a new 1925 diary just for Nora.

Before Nora knew it, it was the afternoon for Calling Hours. Florence and Julia had the house spick and span. It almost felt like being backstage on opening night. Many of the women from town had already dropped off baked goods and little sandwiches. Women flooded the kitchen with so much food that they had to stack boxes on boxes on boxes and they even had to store some cakes upstairs in Nora's bedroom. Nora's job was to look pretty, receive condolences, and let Florence know if she needed a break or not. Henry, Ray, Seth and Ida stood on one side of Nora and Pa and Will, Florence, Herb, and Julia on the other side. The kitchen was being run by Aunt Maggie, Ma Telford's sister, and a platoon of Nora's friends. There was coffee and tea and hot or cold apple cider for everyone.

Nora never remembered seeing Pa Telford at church, but he said, "Reverend Manning, before folks start coming, would you say a prayer for the whole family?" And they all bowed their heads. Everyone was in their places when the cars started rolling in. Nora just kept taking the next right step.

Crikkers never disappoint when it comes to these times. It seemed to Nora like the entire town showed up in full force and not with just their sincere condolences and Sammie stories, but they also brought flowers, gifts of cash, salt pork, canned meat, strawberry preserves, maple syrup, milk, eggs, and fresh bread. That was the one thing they didn't plan for; a place to put all the items people brought. So, Nora received the gifts and put them on the chair behind her and Julia ran everything up the stairs into Aunt Nora's new room.

Sammie and Nora were both beloved figures in town and everyone felt for Nora and the Telford and Andrew families. Plenty of relatives from both sides traveled from as far as Niagara Falls and Philadelphia. Nora was concerned about Will.

"Will, come and stand next to me and help me with your relatives' names," she said. Thomas and Anna Moses came through and didn't have to speak any words. Anna gave Nora's hand an extra squeeze after they hugged, and she gave her a small, embroidered project she'd been working on. May Nichols came down from Greenwich to share her condolences and recalled how impressed she was with Sammie. Fremont paid his respects along with his mother and two brothers. Just about everyone from Post's Corners came through including Dr. Shaw. Nora had no idea how many people Sammie knew! Well into the evening, Ida gazed at her daughter in the receiving line and just cried for her.

The older boys and girls kept the children occupied with games. The school board members and all of her students and their parents came through. Nora was eternally grateful for all of the heartfelt condolences. She received each one of them. There were times when Nora's eyes were dry and other times when the tears wouldn't stop. It was exhausting and wonderful all at the same time.

Eventually, the crowd dwindled down and the Telfords all needed their sleep because they had to do it all over again the next morning after barn chores. Nora went up to bed and found that there was barely any path for her to walk through all of the gifts. Her heart swelled again. Truly, a magnificent showing of love and support from the Crikkers. The morning calling hours went off without a hitch and Nora experienced complete emotional and physical exhaustion afterwards. She took a long nap in the afternoon and was grateful that the next day had no services. Tomorrow was December 31,1924.

16

Second Nora of 1925

It was New Year's Day, 1925; the day of the funeral. Nora awoke and couldn't believe that one week had passed since Sammie died. The hours seemed to drag each day, yet the days seemed to fly by. At the beginning, she didn't know how she would be able to get through one day, let alone one week, yet here she was.

At breakfast, she said, "Florence, I can't begin to thank you enough…and Julia, you have been my Guardian Angel."

She was grateful that all of the arrangements and calling hours and service planning had kept her occupied. It was time to get dressed. The funeral service was here at the house and then a short burial service at the cemetery. She had lost weight and still could not bring herself to eat very much. Verna showed up to accompany her to the funeral.

Henry, Ray, and Herb had the cars all washed and they loaded everyone up to go to the church for the funeral. It was packed. Standing room only. Rev. Manning was particularly heartfelt and encouraging. He loved Sammie and was impressed with how well he led the Epworth meetings with Nora. Ida was happy to see that her ground pine garlands were still looking beautiful as ever. Nora noticed that there was a large Christmas tree again this year and they had to cut the branches in the back so that Marilyn could slide in behind it again. Nora went with what the organist had recommended: Amazing

Grace, It Is Well With My Soul, and I Need Thee Every Hour. During the service, Nora kept dabbing her tears but not far into the sermon, the little Tuttle boy started grunting filling his diaper. At first everyone ignored it, but during the prayer, he was having such a time that it became humorous and eventually hilarious. Such a somber time needed some catharsis.

That's just the kind of thing Sammie would have loved, thought Nora.

It was then time to drive directly up to Woodland Cemetery for the burial. It was plenty cold, but just about everyone drove up. Johnny Baker had carried up the casket as well as all the flowers, a grave blanket of pine boughs and holly branches, wreathes and bouquets. Nora selected a double headstone engraved so that both Sammie's name and her name appeared together forever in stone. That is where she wanted to be buried one day. Ma Telford was buried on the other side of Sammie. Rev. Manning spoke a few words and closed in prayer. Nora noticed a radiance of cardinals flitted in the little pine tree nearby. Nora was holding back the tears. No one wanted to move. The cold felt brutal. Pa Telford started singing the Doxology and everyone joined in. There was silence. Nora pulled a rose out of out of one of the arrangements, placed it on the casket and patted it. Then she headed back to the car with Verna and everyone else slowly exited amidst stories of Sammie and how badly they felt for Nora.

Nora didn't know how she was moving and greatly disliked being the center of attention. Even though it was cold, she asked Verna for a moment alone in the car. She needed to weep. She needed to stop her heart from racing so. Her heart was pounding in her head. Verna guarded the car so that no one passing by would try to console her. She could hear the muffled wails coming from Nora. Nora was always surprised by how many tears she had. When she thought she had no more tears left, another wave would come with another memory. They were married just a year, but they built their entire life in that time.

January 1, 1925

Sammie was laid to rest today. I paid Will $8 for my share of the pillow with "Sammie" embroidered on it. Big funeral. Happy New Year, Sammie.

Nora could clearly feel the love and support from all who attended. She needed every ounce of it. She was blest to have married such a wonderful man with such a beautiful family in such a supportive town. The events of the last week had kept her busy. She feared things were just going to get tougher now that the funeral was over. She would have to adjust to life without Sammie and that wasn't going to be easy. She also felt that she could know no other love like Sammie's. She was exhausted. That afternoon after all the family had gone home after a long lunch. She found one of Sammie's sweaters that still smelled like him and took a nap with it. She felt as though she could have slept all evening and all night, but she got up and prepared herself some dinner from all of the food that had been dropped off.

The following day, Mr. Stewart called to say he would stop by with life insurance documents for Nora to sign in two days. He expressed his deepest condolences and said he would have a check to her as soon as possible after she signed the paperwork. Henry and Ray took Nora up to the cemetery to take pictures of all the flowers. Nora looked about and took a refreshing deep breath.

Ray didn't really know what to say. "He has a good view from up here." Nora agreed. It was an absolutely beautiful cemetery and the hillside view from Sammie's grave was breathtaking. He and his mother are probably talking all day long and pointing all the houses they know down in town. While she was there, she stopped at the office and paid $15 to the grave diggers for the actual burial they would do in the spring.

Nora was given the first week of January off from the school administration for bereavement and she needed it. Sammie's absence was hitting her more deeply now. She had never been so low and depressed. Ida invited her over for lunch and asked her to pick up some things at the Crikk store. Nora knew that the shopping items were just a ruse to get her out of the house. Both her Mama and Papa, Henry and Ray had lunch with her. The last time it was just the four of them seemed like ages ago and it was good for Nora to hear farm talk and not have her pain be the center of conversation. She agreed to come over on Friday to help do the evening chores. They had a pleasant time until the boys left to do chores.

"I'm just going to go back to Florence's and wash my hair and go to bed," said Nora flatly after a spell.

"Well just a minute, dear. It just so happens that I have water heated. Why don't you let me wash your hair," said Ida.

Nora smiled ever so slightly.

"Come," said Mama, "set yourself down here. Seth, go and get the nice foot stool for her." Without hesitation or fuss, Seth went and got some extra towels and had Nora put her feet up on the foot stool.

"Lay your head back here dear," and Nora leaned back with her head over the large porcelain basin. It made Nora feel safe like a little girl again as Ida poured the water out of the wide-mouth porcelain pitcher that she only used on special occasions.

"We haven't done this in a long time!" said Ida. Seth made sure the water was just the right temperature. Nora was glad the water pouring over her head and hair was hiding her tears and washing them away. It felt so comforting. Nora felt like she was in heaven with Sammie as Ida lathered the soap in her hair and massaged her scalp.

"This is that willow tree soap I made. Remember?" said Seth.

"I remember that the house was hotter than it's ever been," said Ida.

Papa put the radio on. Her parent's kindness brought more tears to her eyes. After a good rinse, Ida wrapped Nora's hair in her nicest towel.

"Father, go and stoke the fire so she can sit in front of it and dry her hair. She can't go outside with a wet head; she'll catch her death of cold. I'll make us some tea." And the three of them sat in front of the fireplace drinking tea and noting how wonderful it was to see so many people over the last week. Ida noted who got fat and Seth noted who was driving the nicest cars, but they all noticed how much love they felt from everyone. Nora brushed her hair as they chit-chatted, and she was comforted even if just for a moment.

Nora agreed to help Mama the next forenoon dyeing some faded sweaters and then she brought lunch over to Pa Telfords and spent the afternoon with him and Will, Fremont, and Aunt Maggie.

"How's the car running?" asked Pa.

"Just fine," said Nora. "I try to drive it as little as possible. I know how much Sammie liked to keep it protected."

They talked about some of their relatives Nora didn't know who came to the funeral, and they helped her piece together which cousins belonged with which Aunts and Uncles.

"I'm not even sure how we're related to some of them folks," said Will. They had all kinds of stories for her.

Fremont threw in a couple of war stories as Sergeant in the Army and said, "I don't know that I've ever seen so many people at a funeral."

She helped Aunt Maggie tidy up a bit and she could feel that they all shared a heavy sadness from Sammie's absence. Eventually, it was chore time and she said, "I'll let you all get about your business," and Will went out to help her start the car.

"Be careful on the roads," Will said.

Nora did her best to stay busy and do the next right thing, so she decided to take Verna's advice and took Sammie's tie clasps, cuff links, and a few other gold items and asked the jeweler in Hoosick Falls if there was enough there to make a piece of jewelry. It turned out that she really didn't like any of the suggestions until the jeweler had a different idea. He showed her a beautifully ornate locket with a clock inside it. The only problem was that the back panel was missing, and the chain latch was broken. If she would like it, he could create a new back panel from Sammie's tie clasps, and she'd have a real piece of fine jewelry.

"How much will that cost me?" she asked.

"Let's just say that it will be 2 hours of labor and the original locket is on the house." Nora deeply appreciated the generosity, and they had a deal. He would send word when it was complete.

On her way to the car, she stepped into the Life Insurance storefront and said to the lady at the desk, "I received a phone call from... Oh dear, now I can't remember who. I'm Nora Telford, and I need to fill out paperwork to make a claim on my husband's life insurance policy."

The lady was taken aback. *This young 22-year-old girl had already lost a husband? Poor thing.*

"What's your husband's name?" she asked. "Samuel Dewey Telford."

"Oh yes. I read about that in the paper. I'm so sorry for your loss." She put out a document and Nora signed it.

"That's it. You should receive a check soon." Nora added,

"Tell Mr. what's his name that I thought I'd save him a trip."

The lady at the desk gave a puzzling look, but just added, "We'll take care of everything." Nora continued about her day.

No matter what happens in life, farm work continues. All life goes on. Chores need to be done. Teeth need to be brushed. Nora spent some time alone reading, but stayed true to her word and went over to the farm and did what she could feeding the animals for Henry and Ray. Florence encouraged Nora to take a long walk with Julia. Nora didn't feel much like doing much of anything. She did continue to keep a daily diary which she had never done before. It was something that made her feel like Sammie was still a part of her. He was always so faithful to keep his daily diary. She spoke to him often throughout the day. Nora could tell that she was feeling worse after her week off rather than better. Time wasn't healing her wounds. She had imagined herself bouncing back and somehow moving on, but that was just not the case. She was moving about but her malaise felt as though her soul was gone.

She heard a knock at the door. It was Mr. Stewart.

"I have the life insurance papers for you to sign.

"Oh, I already signed them in town."

"Hmmm, I don't think so, I've had Sammie's file in my brief case since he passed. Where did you sign them?"

"At the Prudential Office."

"Oh, that's why; I'm with Metropolitan. Sammie opened up a new policy with us. Maybe you signed a canceled policy? This policy is all paid up and ready to go."

"I thought that Prudential Lady looked a bit confused," said Nora.

Nora signed the document and would wait for a check to see which insurance policy was real.

Nora felt like an empty shell on her first day back to school, but her appetite had returned a bit and she drove herself to school with Julia at her side. It was bitter cold, and she arrived early to get the fire roaring. Julia was a true help. Nora had no idea how she was going to face her students. On her desk was a pile of cards made by each of the students the previous Friday. Her eyes welled. Julia came to her side, laid her head on her shoulder, and knew not to say anything. Nora read the cards as the fire crackled in the stove.

The first student to arrive was Rachel Boot.

"Good morning, Mrs. Telford."

"Good morning, Rachel. How are you today?" replied Nora.

"I'm fine, thank you. Do we still call you Mrs. Telford?" she asked innocently.

Nora felt like she was struck by a lightning bolt.

"That will be just fine," responded Nora. The rest of the students filed in, and Julia helped the little ones get their boots and coats off. When it was time to call school Nora rang the bell and took roll call and the morning routine had started. They all stood for the pledge to the flag without being asked.

"I pledge allegiance to my Flag and to the Republic for which it stands, one nation, indivisible, with liberty and justice for all."

And just like that, the day had begun. She realized that she was up and dressed and warm and was responsible for a roomful of children. The students all knew about Sammie's death. They loved him. They were on their best behavior for the morning, but as lunch time approached, they became children again and Nora found she was easily annoyed and lacked the energy to address kids being kids. She cracked down stricter than usual, and you could feel the tension in the room. Julia and the other older students worked hard to keep the littles on task.

Julia had shot up to 6' tall at this point. Not so little anymore. Julia was a Godsend for Nora. Everyone forgot she was only 12 and treated her like she was older because she conducted herself like a mature young lady. Until recently, she and Nora had shared a room, they lived in the same house, they rode to and from school together. Julia was her niece and student; the two got to know each other extremely well and relied on each other. Nora was often quiet, but if she were to share anything, it was usually with her pal, Julia. The day moved slowly for Nora. She felt a bit like a mannequin, she was just taking up space. Even though she felt hollow, she just kept being where she was supposed to be. She ate dinner with Herb, Florence, and Julia. She was quiet and spoke barely enough to be polite. She retired early and for weeks all she would write in her diary each day was,

Lonesome day without Sammie.

The second day back to school, news came that Mrs. Cody and Mrs. Brady died in the night. Nora asked Julia to lead her students in prayer for the Cody and Brady families that they would be surrounded by loved ones. Edward and Rachel were absent.

We have a higher power who is closer to us than breathing and nearer than hands and feet

~Lord, Alfred Tennyson

Later that week, there was so much snow and blowing cold. Nora tried to walk to school but it was no use. She came back to Florence's and called the superintendent and canceled school for the day. Nora felt as though that was the best decision, besides, she had the sniffles and a cough herself. She still would proctor and grade Regents Exams on Saturday up in Cambridge at the Union School. It was a good day to do some reading. She paid Florence for December's room and board and phone. That week, her diaries looked like this:

"All shall be well, and all shall be well, and all manner of things shall be well, for there is a force of love moving through the universe that holds us fast and will never let us go..."

~Julian of Norwich

Thought of Sammie all day when alone.

God only knows how I miss Sammie.

Lonesome day without Sammie.

How I miss Sammie.

"Nora, your sister Sarah's on the phone. It sounds important," called Florence. Nora came to the phone. Sarah was talking uncontrollably, and Nora calmed her down.

"There's been an accident. Howard got a drunk on last night, worse than usual, and he beat little Andrew unconscious. I couldn't stop him. It's my fault; I couldn't keep Andrew quiet," she said, justifying his actions. Andrew had been bloodied and knocked unconscious.

"Get in your car and drive over here now," said Nora.

"I can't do that," said Sarah. "He doesn't like me to drive the car."

"Florence needs to look at Andrew."

Eventually, that made sense to Sarah, so she brought Andrew over.

The first thing Nora and Florence noticed were the bruises on Sarah's face and how she could barely walk. Andrew was speaking incoherently, and Florence immediately rang up Dr. Shaw. They laid Andrew down on the couch, got them both a cold compress and made Sarah a cup of tea. As they spoke, Nora recalled that Sarah's husband Howard hadn't been in a good mood recently and recounted that he seemed gruff when they came through the receiving line for Sammie's Calling Hours. Apparently, he didn't just get lit and tip the bottle every now and again, but he went over the edge with the rams and, this time, beat Andrew severely in a drunken tirade.

"Am I a bad wife?" asked Sarah.

"This is not at all what a marriage is. Wasn't he going to the bands?" said Nora.

Sarah was terrified but had always been taught that women were to stay dutiful to their families including their husbands. She'd been taught if there was something wrong in a marriage that the wife was at fault and deserved any punishment she got. She wasn't a good enough wife. She was at fault for saying the wrong things, for not being able to keep Andrew quiet enough.

"This is not your fault!" said Nora.

Nora had been raised the same way as Sarah, but experiencing such a thing firsthand gave her room to see how small and judgmental she had been. Seeing her clever Andrew conscious but unresponsive moved her to take action. She didn't care if the Biddie Bunch gossiped about her being a liberated woman or not. She sent word to Mama and Papa that Sarah and Andrew needed to stay with them for a while and that Henry and Ray might have to protect them from Howard. Dr. Shaw came over and examined both Sarah and Andrew. He gave them both medicine for pain and inflammation. He offered hope that perhaps there was swelling in Andrew's brain and that his speech may return after the swelling subsided. He arranged for them to see a doctor in Troy the next morning and Nora and Florence delivered them to a waiting Mama and Papa Andrew.

It was a particularly harsh winter. Bitter cold, snowy, and windy. Brutal. After Andrew and Sarah's beatings, Nora was frozen numb inside and out and her tears stopped. She was completely numb. Her sorrow had turned into anger which quickly turned into bitterness. *How could God allow such tragedies?* She was locked in what she felt was a justifiable prison of pity which she couldn't and wouldn't escape from. Knowing Howard drank so much that he was far too off the track to maintain any common sense that he beat her sister and beloved Andrew locked her into her bitterness. She was dead inside.

Julia came in and handed Nora her mail delivery.

"A letter all the way from France?"

Nora took the letter. At last, some relief. Some comfort. She knew it was from Bernadette and this was the first letter in a while.

My Dear Norrie,

I am sending all my love to you in this little letter all the way from Paris. I was much saddened to hear of your Sammie's passing and my heart is broken for you. I can't imagine such a thing happening. But knowing your true form, you will be strong as ever in no time. Our sweet friend Leah is quite worried about you. Her concern has crossed the ocean for you.

"Si può andare avanti dopo che si è stanchi," that is my gift for you today. It's a French saying that mean, "one may go a long way after one is tired." Keep that saying with you as my gift. I know you must be exhausted in every way, but I know you can move through each day one moment at a time. And then enjoy as much rest as you can, just like our dear Sammie and his friends on the cure porches at Ray Brook Hospital. Resting your body and soul is important. We walk this earth but once so please take care of yourself and EAT for goodness' sake.

How I long for our simple days together at Mrs. Hovey's when you would unlock the door for me at 1:00 am and we'd talk all night. Dearest Norrie, do you need a complete change? Come join me in Paris! Truly! Come share my flat with me. It's not much more than a pied-à-terre but you can help me take care of my dear sweet Claire. I sent you our picture. She is the love of my life. Her father abandoned us not long ago and has not returned. But Claire and I are more than fine. We are happy without him. Come. Come and begin again here in Paris. You will be like one of your beautiful flowers transplanted from your country to my city. Write back soon. Better yet, just buy a ticket and board the next steamship. Claire and I will be waiting at the dock along with your new life. Come.

Your friend for life,

Bernadette

Nora held the letter to her chest and dreamed of her old self that seemed so far away and impossible to reconnect with. For the first time in her life, she allowed her mind to escape past the borders of White Creek. In her mind's eye she could see herself waving goodbye to her family and leaving her sorrow and heaviness behind. She boarded a train to New York City where she would wait to board a steamship. She loved the feeling of anonymity in the big apple where she could do anything she wanted. She dreamed of walking and shopping and indulging her guilty pleasure of buying all of the latest Good Housekeeping, McCall's and Gibson Girl magazines and sitting all day at a café indulging in pastries while she waited for her steamship to come in. She would make her escape and walk about the deck daily without speaking to anyone and then retire to her cabin alone with the finest chocolates. Magically, after the two-week journey, she would emerge as a new Nora, ready to take on the new world with Bernadette and baby Claire. She would become the finest English teacher in all of Paris. They would share their small flat until they could afford a sprawling new one in a building with an elevator with a view of Paris that would one day be featured in the very magazines she was reading.

As she sorted through some of Sammie's things, she found one of the publications that came home from Ray Brook with Sammie. At the bottom of a little encouragement card written by consumptives for consumptives was a quote by Robert Frost, "The best way out is always through." She would have to come back to that another day. She had a moment of clarity. Escaping wasn't the answer. She realized that she was stuck in bitterness and didn't see a way forward, the worst place to be. She was trapped in a prison of despair, the unbearable pain of grieving Sammie's loss and Andrew's beating.

She set Bernadette's letter down on her bedstand. She would read it once a day for weeks and dreamed often of escaping. However, she knew in her heart of hearts, that White Creek was her home. No matter how tough and impossible and bitter her circumstances became, she belonged here. White Creek was a part of her; was a part of Sammie, and leaving meant that she was abandoning that good name that she and Sammie worked toward. Right now, however, the fantasy of abandoning herself brought her relief from the energy it took to keep putting one foot in front of the other. With a couple train rides and a relaxing trip on a steamship, she could be gone forever, leaving her pain, anguish, and good name behind.

17

The Bells of St. Mary's

A couple of weeks passed, and Florence asked Nora to run some errands in Hoosick Falls so she drove down and picked up the few items on Florence's list when she heard the noon bells at St. Mary's and felt inexplicably drawn to go there. *Maybe it's an auto-suggestion.* She knew her soul was locked up and the idea of peace and quiet in the sanctuary seemed to make her feel freer. She walked down the street and opened the huge wooden door and walked inside the church. She loved the high ceiling and the beautiful windows. Silence. The noise inside her head ceased for a moment. She just sat in a pew taking in the beauty when a nun quietly came and sat next to her.

"Hello, child. I'm Sister Mary Pat. How may I help you?"

Nora liked her immediately.

"I just needed some quiet," she responded solemnly.

"Is the world getting too noisy for you?"

Nora looked at her with eyes that said, *Sister, you don't know the half of it.*

"Dear, why don't you come with me, and we can have a chat?" and Sister Mary Pat held out her arm for Nora to take and she escorted Nora to a perfect little chapel in the corner of the building.

"Why don't you tell me about some of the noise you've been experiencing."

Nora told her about Sammie; how they fell in love and bought a farm and then Sammie got tuberculosis again, and he died a horrible death in her arms.

"He was a good God-fearing man from a good family. Farmers worked outside and didn't get TB. And now, Little Andrew was beat senseless by his own father who took to the bottle. It's too much to take in. I know I sound like such a cribber. But it's so unfair. It's really unfair!" Nora said angrily.

"I feel like I have cried too many tears already. Now I'm just stuck in misery. Oh, I don't know what I feel."

"That's quite understandable. The Genesis story starts with a great void, and the Creator just started adding things to it until a complete world was made. It sounds like your whole world has been taken. You're stuck in the void. Little by little, pieces of a new world for you will come into place. I can't imagine going through what you've endured."

"Tears seem so far away from me now. I couldn't cry if I tried… and I've cried so many tears already," said Nora.

"There's no statute of limitations on tears. In fact, I pray you have more. Tears are the only way through your grief. You need to ask God for the gift of tears. And when He gives them to you, lean into them and don't ever shut them off."

Nora sighed and rested her head on Sister Mary Pat's shoulder.

The understanding nun placed her hand on Nora's forehead and prayed, "Loving, Precious Father, you know Nora and you know the pain and despair her soul is in. Warm her heart, Lord Jesus, and restore her beautiful soul with the gift of tears."

And just like that, Nora sensed a supernatural warmth welling up from within her. God was flooding her soul with love, peace, comfort, understanding, and healing. Her imprisoned spirit was broken open and God poured Himself in. A wave of mourning and tears overflowed from her.

"It's so unfair!" she wailed.

"I know, dear. Let it out," encouraged Sister Mary Pat.

And Nora let it out but good, and it felt necessary and wonderful. She continued to let the wailing come. So much so that it brought tears to Sister Mary Pat's eyes. This was God's Spirit moving through her, and there were no words for the pain and misery she was in, so she just wailed with sounds that didn't make any sense.

"Don't stop, dear. Just let it flow. God wants to take this pain from you."

After a good ten minutes, Nora quieted down, breathed deeply, and her trembling came to a stop.

After several moments of silence, Sister Mary Pat said, "Gee Willikers, that was a good one!" They both burst into laughter.

Sister Mary Pat spoke softly. "You are exactly right; life is downright unfair. It's like when you're playing cards and you're dealt a bad hand. You don't quit. You can't ask for a redeal. You play the cards you were dealt. God loves us dearly, but He doesn't play favorites. I often ask myself the same thing. Why does God allow the most upright families with good names to experience so much pain and suffering while the family down the road, that lies, drinks, steals, runs around, and is wanted by the law, is healthier than anyone else in town, doesn't run into hard times, and certainly isn't affected by death or sorrow like you've been. Oh, how I do wonder! Because it's not fair. But it's not that God is unfair. It's that the world we live in is unfair. It's just a fact. It rains on the just and the unjust. The sooner I can accept that, I may not like it, but at least I can move through that 'unfair' anger because *you do matter* to God. I can guarantee you one thing. You will know God more because of your suffering. You will experience more of His love because of these awful things that have happened."

Nora listened and took her words to heart.

"What if I'm not sure I want any more of God's love?" asked Nora seriously.

"It's too late; you've already got it. God already loves you more than you can comprehend as I just witnessed. Dear, I'm so sorry! I'm running my mouth too much for you to enjoy your silence, but once I leave you be, silence will allow you to hear God. All that's gone on with Sammie, Sarah, and Andrew… all those noisy things are too loud for you to hear the still small voice of God speaking from within. But enough of me jawing the afternoon away. I'll leave you to light candles for Sammie, and pray for Sarah, and Andrew."

"But, Sister, none of them is Catholic and I'm not Catholic," replied Nora.

"Oh, Nora, we're way past having to be Catholic. Don't tell Father Williamson I told you that. God will listen to you. Pray. If anything, the candles smell really nice. Imagine your prayers floating up to God's ear with the smoke from your candle."

"Sister, may I share some terrible thoughts I have," continued Nora.

"I'm all ears," said Sister Mary Pat.

"I just want to scream at God. I just want to cry out and scream and demand answers about why I'm in such a state. I even want to tell God that I'm mad at Him and I blame Him."

"Oh, my dear Nora, that's beautiful." Nora was taken aback.

"The Bible has a whole book called Lamentations that is filled with the cries and songs of lament from God's people. Did you know that we are to exhaust ourselves crying out to God? He is moved not only by our joys, but also by our tears and sorrow. You can discover that a heart filled with honesty and sorrow can open the door directly to God's heart in a beautiful way. You certainly won't find any answers at the bottom of a bottle or in a romance novel. Listen to me, with the way I've been yammering on. Maybe I should be the one preaching the homily this Sunday!" Sister Mary Pat said with a wink.

Nora smiled.

"I'll leave you be, darling. But you, Nora, you're suffering something terrible. But sometimes, the heaviest burdens we carry are the thoughts in our own head. Helen Keller once said, 'Although the world is full of suffering, it's also full of overcoming it.' You're an overcomer and a sweetheart. Come and see me anytime. Our doors are always open."

And with that, Sister Mary Pat stood up, held her arms open wide for a hug, and then off she went.

She turned back and yelled, "Don't judge what you want to tell God. Just get it out. Yell it out! He will hear you… and if Father asks me who that is screamin' up in the sanctuary, I'll just say, 'O that's my friend, Nora. Don't pay her any mind. She's just yellin' at God.'"

Nora felt welcomed and stayed for a good long time. More than an hour. She knelt down on the kneeler and lit candles. This was all quite different than her Baptist upbringing. When her knees got tired, she sat on a bench and really poured out her angry heart to God. She started with a whisper. Once she even laid down on the bench and was talking out loud. In her mind, she was yelling at God telling him how unfair He was. She told him he was making lots of mistakes. Letting Sammie die was a big mistake. She was yelling now. She could do a better job than He was doing. She emptied out her heart and all the nasty gook that came with it. And she could honestly feel her wall of bitterness come down. She had to yell at God to his face, not through a wall. That actually felt good. She had many moments of clarity.

She imagined what her mama must have gone through losing First Nora at two years old. She empathized with her and was encouraged that mama was able to move through her grief. She knew that women before her had survived terrible grief. She knew that women after her would move through sorrow and losses that were much more tragic and public than hers and she felt connected to their resilience. She could tell that there was a disconnection between what she knew in her head and what she felt in her heart. She had always assumed that bad things happened to bad or foolish people. Not true. She now understood that pain was pain and grief was grief whether it involved poor decisions or not. She could feel a deep vein of judgment leave her.

That afternoon, Mama called her over to visit and have tea.

"Nora, I never told you the end of your great-great-Uncle Charlie's murder."

"Oh my. There's more?"

"Yes. After all the years of being a notoriously bad neighbor, in the end, Uncle Charlie got shot right in front of his two sons. They were young men at the time. One of the boys left home and became a drunk and no one in the family knows much about him after that. But the other son wouldn't let his life be ruined by his father's tragedy. He moved to a nice town, had a family, and worked to build a church. He was a good businessman and raised so much money for the church that they engraved his name on the church bell. Dear, there's one of two roads you can go down after a tragedy—"

"Mama. Do you think I'm going to start drinking?" asked Nora.

"No dear, but I think you could become ensconced in an impossible black mood, and no one would blame you. But a black mood keeps you from living out your purpose in life. It could ruin your life. After I lost my first Nora, I had a terrible time."

Nora heard what her Mama was saying and shed tears with her Mama. Nora told her Mama about her experience at St. Mary's with Sister Mary Pat. They hugged when it was time to go.

Ida had a pile of mending she had finally completed for Florence and asked Nora if she could bring it back to the her along with a juicy pot roast and vegetables for their dinner. Nora put on oven mitts and held the Dutch Oven by the handles. Mama piled the mending on top of it. Nora secured the pile of clothes with her chin.

"Not only will they receive their clothes mended, clean and folded, but warm as well," said Mama. "Do you need me to help you get that into the car?"

"I can get it," said Nora.

Nora walked slowly across the icy driveway toward her car. Her mind was on her St. Mary's experience and Sister Mary Pat and wondered if she still had the gift of tears. She was almost to the car when her feet went out from under her and down she went. As she lay on her back, she was surprised that she wasn't hurt. Her heavy coat had protected her from the hot liquid of the roast which was next to her with carrots and potatoes and onions strewn about with the mending. She waited for someone to come to her rescue, but no one saw her. *I guess it's just me and God.* She started to get up but thought better of it. For some reason it felt good just to lie there and be still, in the middle of the driveway, on the ice, on her back, with oven mitts on.

After several moments, her gift of tears returned. *God, I can't do this alone. How much longer is my hell going to last? When will this torture end?* And after a moment, up on the corn house roof, she heard a squeak. The wind had changed direction and the weathervane pointed to the north. She looked up and noticed something she had never noticed before in her 20 years of living at that house. In between the S and the N (the South and North) axis was simple metal scrolling that held the weathervane together. But from the correct angle it looked like SσσN; SooN. Did God Himself just answer her? Would her torture, her hell, end *soon*? Was she crazy? Or was this a real sign from God that he was listening, even though no one else was? It sure felt like God to her. She ran inside and beckoned her Mama to come to the back door and look. *Maybe God thinks I matter after all.*

Mama came to the door. "Why did you throw my mending and dinner all over the drive?"

Nora showed her the SσσN. Was it a miracle? She knew that it felt like a miracle from God just for her. She was becoming quite introspective and decided that she should hold nothing back from God. She admitted that she often looked at others as lazy and felt that they just needed to pull themselves up by their bootstraps. But after all she had been through, she now realized that pulling herself up by the bootstraps was "easier said than done." For where she was, she couldn't even find her boots, let alone the bootstraps. She knew that Divine intervention was going to be needed for the place she was in. For the first time in her life, she felt powerless over her circumstances. She now needed help, which was new to this self-sufficient White Crikker.

She understood why people left White Creek rather than rebuild. It was too hard without a support system. The lure of escape is too strong. She remembered Sammie showing her 'the Notch,' high up on the mountain in Pumpkin Hook where eagles lived. It was a place that felt magical to Sammie. It's where Sammie felt close to God. He felt that God had put that amazing place right in White Creek on purpose to show the Crikkers that He was close by and loved them and blessed the land there.

The Notch always made her feel lighter. What was it Ma Telford would call it? A *thin* place. Especially popular with the Telford ancestors from Ireland, a thin place was where there was only a thin veil between earth and heaven. Where one could easily connect with God. The notch was a *thin* place for Sammie and now for Nora. In one of the church hymns Nora remembered singing about *raising an Ebenezer*, a pile of stones to mark where God did amazing things for people. People would gather at these sorts of thin places as ports in a storm and would take pause there to experience life in God's presence; his tangible peace and protection. *Had Sammie been trying to take his thin Notch experience and bring it home with him so he could live close to God every moment of the day? Even during his mundane chores?*

Her healing continued to be a challenge. A harsh winter of death fell on White Creek just as Nora, herself, was at times, still soul-frozen and dead inside. She received word that her student pal, Little Rachel Boot died from pneumonia. With every one of the 19 deaths that winter, especially the children and her relatives, Nora relived her anguish of losing Sammie and the pain of Andrew's physical abuse. She sorely missed Sammie and their life together. She found that she could choose to lean into gratitude and God's grace or let anger and bitterness consume her. It was a real struggle. She seriously wondered if it was worth going on. She felt as though her life was ruined. Nora noted every death in her diary.

Sammie Telford died of TB
Mary Brady
Mrs. Cody
Mrs. Thomas O'Brien
Miss Mary Bowker
Uncle John Leet
Uncle George Parsons
Little Rachel Boot 11
Mrs. Charles Kenyon 81
Albert Harrington
John Peacock
Odette Dundas
James Bennette of Bennette and Sisson
Mr. Charles Harrington died of pneumonia
Charles W. Pratt died of heart trouble
Olin Huntington
Mrs. Ambrose Green
Nellie Houlihan's little boy was drowned in Bennington
James Lake

Nora knew that if it weren't for her family and having to teach school, she would have died of a broken heart. Thank goodness for her students and the hours that it required to prepare and teach. She did enjoy teaching and kept them on a strict routine of reading aloud each morning and delegating the older students to help with the younger. Though she dreaded the start of each day and would much rather stay in bed, deep down, she knew that there was a kind of magic in having a daily routine. Routine was somehow saving her and getting her out of bed.

There was no quick fix. At times, her soul was as frozen as Wolfrum's pond. But she persisted in bringing her anguish to God rather than holding it in. Emotionally, she couldn't handle Valentine's Day, so she canceled it at school. Under any other circumstances, she would have students make cards for each other to practice their writing, but she managed to keep everyone busy and just ignored Valentine's Day. The students made no mention of it, so she didn't. She just made sure that they got some extra play time at the end of the day.

Leah and Mason sat next to Nora at church one blustery cold Sunday in the middle of February right after the news of Rachel Boot's passing. Afterwards, Leah took Nora aside. It was the kind of talk where two women in church sit very close together off to the side and everyone knew not to disturb them.

"You don't look good, Norrie. Don't get me wrong, Florence is the bee's knees, but do you think sleeping in the bed where Sammie passed is the best thing for you?"

They both teared up and just sat in silence together holding hands.

Leah continued, "I heard through the grapevine that Verna's mother is looking to rent out a room. Maybe that's something to consider?"

Of course, Nora and Verna were the best of friends. Nora instantly had split feelings about the idea. On one hand, the idea of another move just deflated her. She was already consumed with exhaustion. In the last 12 months, she had gotten married, moved on and off the Nichol's property, moved to Florence's and helped nurse Sammie through TB until his death while teaching school. The thought of moving yet again just exhausted her. Although Leah's suggestion brought her a sense of hope, she would have to leave the timing up in the air for now.

"I can't even begin to think of a move. It takes everything I have to make it through the day. I can barely manage my teaching."

Nora coughed a bit into a tissue and Leah handed her a butter-scotch candy.

"You won't have to lift a finger. I'll pack you up. I know Henry and Ray and Mason would move you and you wouldn't even have to be there. I can make all the arrangements for you," encouraged Leah. "You just give me the word and I'm on it." Nora nodded gratefully.

Mama served Sunday dinner with everything made special just for her. It was nice to hear some other voices in her head other than her own for a change. She laughed as the boys caught her up on all that was going on at the farm.

Henry said, "Ray was trying to help a cow that had fallen in the feed trough. He got her out and then he fell face first in the manure. He still stinks!"

Ida shared all the news she learned from bumping into the other mothers in town. "John is leaving Mary and moving in with Muriel! Can you imagine?"

Nora had some tidbits herself.

"I can't say who's having a baby, but a little bird told me that we just might want to check with the Hendersons before we get rid of that little bed in the attic!" It was amazing how much school kids shared with their teacher!

"The Thomas boys are calling it quits on their farm. They'll be having an auction soon," said Seth. "Life certainly keeps moving on!"

"Henry got a lot of manure on him, too," added Ray, failing to add any interest to the conversation.

"I can see myself teaching and growing old with a garden and some cats." Nora's words just popped out of her mouth during dessert. Everyone fell silent.

Mama chimed in, "Oh dear, it's much too soon to be making plans like that! You'll find your way. When God closes a door on one of His children, he always opens a window."

"That's dumb," said Henry flatly. "I can't imagine God wanting His children to be crawling through windows when there's a perfectly good door right there. The door was shut. Just open it again! That's what a door does. It opens and shuts. That's it's job."

Everyone burst into laughter. Such wisdom from Henry! Ray patted Henry's shoulder.

"Maybe iron ore can be educated into gold after all!" Seth said.

Nora couldn't remember when she last laughed out loud. It felt good.

Late that night, Mama called Nora with the doctor's report on Andrew. Sarah had taken Andrew to Troy to see the doctor on Saturday.

After his beating, Andrew was still not right in the head. He wasn't speaking. He was just making slurred sounds. Sarah was in a devastated panic. He could understand some things, but Sarah wanted to know if there was any medicine that would help. The doctor didn't offer much hope. He told her that Andrew's condition was permanent. His brain had been permanently injured from the beating. The entire family was bereft. Part of Nora's grief had been that she might never have a child. Nora went from laughing out loud at dinner to a free fall into a dark despair. *The hits just keep coming.*

That evening, Nora fell quite ill. Her persistent cough turned into a deep dry cough. Her throat was raw. She had a fever.

"You, young lady, aren't going anywhere." And just like that, Florence ordered Nora to take the entire week off due to illness. Florence even called the school administrator herself and told him that Nora would need one full week to recover.

He said, "Why don't you have her call in 3 days to give me an update." But there was no arguing with Florence,

"I think we should save the money of the phone call because she's not going to be better by Wednesday." And just like that, Nora had a solid week to recover.

She was relieved not to have to get up the next morning in the windy cold. She slept when she wasn't coughing. Florence made up the best concoctions she knew for a sore throat and deep cough and fever. She learned about some new brews from Sammie's time of being sick. They tasted horrible but Nora knew to take her medicine and follow instructions. Her fever rose steadily for 3 days. Florence was fearful and became convinced that after nursing Sammie through TB, that she recognized the same cough in Nora.

"Julia, I don't want you visiting in Aunt Nora's room anymore. She needs her rest. I'll bring her food and tea to her." Heartbroken, she relayed her fears to Dr. Shaw.

Word spread that Nora was very sick with a cough and fever, and everyone in town began to assume the worst, that Nora had TB. It made sense since she was so close to Sammie. Her fever was over 100 and refusing to break. Herb and Florence thought it. Nora's Mama and Papa feared it. Pa Telford refused to let such thoughts be voiced in his presence. Nora even wondered if she had TB. Her cough was horrid. She rarely got sick, but contracting TB did make sense. She did her best to be careful with Sammie, but she still spent a lot of time in the room with him. She did kiss his forehead. She was covered with his blood on the day he died.

Florence kept her cough at bay with special teas and chicken broth. Nora's fever persisted through Thursday. Verna and Leah came to see her, but Florence allowed no visitors in her room. Julia brought home cards from school that all the students made. People started keeping the Andrew and Telford families at arm's length. Dr. Shaw appeared. Word of his visit spread all over the Crikk. She still had a fever over 100 and was taking all kinds of concoctions to relieve the coughing. She was exhausted from coughing.

"Given her recent contact with TB, if her fever doesn't break by Sunday, we need to get her to Dr. Irish," warned Dr. Shaw. "This could be very serious." Florence's mind ran wild with "what ifs." *What if Nora has TB? What if she has to go to Ray Brook? What if she dies? What if it's too much for Julia to take in?* She stopped herself. *"What if" thinking is just a useless rabbit hole.*

A disheveled Nora appeared in the kitchen at lunch time.

“I think I’m hungry,” she said.

Florence sent her back up to bed and then took her temperature. It was down to 99. She called for Julia to bring up a tray of water, tea, a sandwich, an orange, and custard. Nora ate all of it. By Sunday she was feeling a bit better although she still looked awful. While she lay in bed all week, she had considered many “what ifs” as well. She came to believe that the wrong mindset could completely throw you off course.

Late Sunday afternoon a nor’easter came through. This was the kind of storm that school children and teachers pray for, as it usually cancels school. It was late in the day and lasted a full day. School was canceled on both Monday and Tuesday. Nora was grateful for the extra 2 days to recover. During that time, she had lots of unplanned time for introspection.

She realized that part of what was making her exhausted was that she was clinging to her bitterness and not bringing her lament to God. Choosing to have a hard heart is like placing an anchor around your neck and it was dragging her down. Horrible things had happened. She felt justifiably angry from her losses and ill health. She was drowning. Clutching her pain wasn’t doing her or anyone else any good. She had to surrender it. She remembered Rev. Manning’s wisdom from the pulpit, “Anger is an acid that can do much more harm to the vessel in which it’s stored than anything on which it is poured.” Nora had been storing a lot of acidic anger inside that was preventing her healing. As soon as she poured it out, it filled right back up again. Her emotions had been on a see-saw for months, but her nor’easter quiet time seemed to take hold. She felt that Sammie was right there nodding his head as if to say, “Yes, Nora, you’re on the right track!” She could hear him say, “Despair uses up more ergs than a positive attitude.” She saw herself release that anchor of bitterness and replace it with the life preserver of gratitude. She instantly felt lighter. She started rising up from the deep murky water. She was filled with gratitude for having known Sammie. She pictured Sammie saying, "Thank you for being my partner through the best and worst years of my life. I can't imagine going through the last 4 years without you." She could feel that her head was above water. She had been rescued. She could breathe. And she consciously continued to work every morning to get to that good breathing place.

On Wednesday, there were a few pieces of mail for her. Sammie's Life Insurance check from Metropolitan had arrived. It brought tears to Nora's eyes like a giant love letter from Sammie. These were tears of gratitude. Not tears of pity or sorrow. It wasn't about money; it was about the fullness of having known Sammie. Nora could feel a difference in her tears. Sammie was always faithful to pay up his life insurance premiums, which was an investment in her, even when she thought the money could be spent better elsewhere.

She was ever so grateful for her Sammie. Florence noticed a change in her countenance. Life slowly started picking up energy for her. A week later, she received yet another life insurance check, but this one was from Prudential. She was in disbelief. Had a mistake been made? And then she figured out what had happened; Sammie had taken out his new policy and forgotten to cancel the old policy as she had reminded him. Again, not because she felt grateful that she had more money, *well, maybe a little*, but because it felt like a miracle. And these miracles kept her feeling close to God. She could get so mad at Sammie for forgetting things. She always saw his forgetfulness as something quite negative and a character flaw that she needed to fix. Now, she was willing to take a step back and have a broader view of others' "faults." This "fault" of Sammie's actually turned out to be a huge positive even after his death. *Perhaps I'm not the best one to play God.*

Nora began getting up very early and walking to and from school every day. When asked why, she said, "An early morning walk is a blessing for the whole day." She started breathing more deeply. And she felt that the bitter darkness inside her was oozing out of her along with her grief with every step. People moved from pitying her to admiring her dedication to walking.

She made arrangements to rent that room and move into Verna Lowe's house the 1st of March. She cried as she told Florence that she would be moving out. Florence knew the day would come. They both knew that her leaving was like the end of a wonderful and monumental, brutal and bittersweet chapter in their lives. Nora was eternally grateful to Florence. She paid her well for her exceptional servant heartedness wisdom, and strength.

Leah stayed true to her word and packed up Nora's things. Henry, Ray, and Mason were able to move Nora's things just fine.

"To think," said Nora, "it wasn't even a year ago that it would have taken a full week to move everything Sammie and I had. Now it all fits in one car. Thank God for the things I don't own!" Henry and Ray were so grateful to have their Nora back in good spirits. After they unloaded Nora's things, she felt as though an impossible weight was lifted from her.

She wrote in her diary that night, "Be of good cheer."

On March 4, Calvin Coolidge was inaugurated and after school, Nora brought a meal over to Rachel Boot's mother. She knew that the pain lasted long after the funeral and stopped in to have a cup of tea.

Nora knew pain and suffering and knew that there was life afterwards. She was still finding it, but she had hope for the first in a long time. She made arrangements to watch the other Boot children on that Saturday so Mrs. Boot could take a drive and be alone. Nora realized that helping the bereaved fulfilled a purpose deep within her.

"Norrie," said Verna, "I've got an idea for you."

Nora gave her a curious stare.

"We're going to give you an invisible transformation."

Again, another bewildered look. Verna got her to catch the trolley not knowing where they were headed. They jumped off near Lurie's in Hoosick Falls and Verna bought them both fancy new union suits and bloomers.

"You won't believe how wonderful it feels to have all new under-clothes. It's like walking around town with a huge secret." The girls laughed through lunch and even splurged on dessert. Nora had lost so much weight. They walked slowly through town, arm in arm leaning into each other. Nora told her of the things she had experienced since the funeral. They caught the trolley back home. Nora could feel hope blossoming in her heart.

Each Sunday after church, she went up to the cemetery to water the wreath or bring a new plant for the Sammie's headstone. She would talk to Sammie as if they were having a lazy Sunday afternoon together. There were still always tears, but she never failed to see anything other than the beauty of what they had together.

Henry and Ray were glad to see that Nora started attending Grange meetings with them again. Nora had been fairly secluded, so she was seeing many of her friends and acquaintances for the first since the funeral. People didn't seem to know what to say and often said the wrong thing by going back into the worst parts of her grief. Nora overcame her shyness and transformed the awkward conversations into moments of expressed gratitude.

"Melody, so good to see you! Thank you so much for coming to Sammie's funeral. I could really feel your support. TB was awful and Sammie's no longer suffering. He's in a better place now. How are the kids?"

She was taking her life back. Elizabeth Cottrell was at the Grange meeting. Neither Henry nor Elizabeth cared much for the degree team, at least, not when they could disappear together.

Ray thought he might check on them, but Nora just suggested with a smile, "just let them be. They'll show up when it's time to go. The art of being wise is the art of knowing what to overlook."

Prayer meeting became a large part of reconnecting with church. The older ladies welcomed her with open arms. The Biddie Bunch esteemed Nora for how she came through her grief and was in church so faithfully. Even though they had their differences, they had nothing but love for Nora and they worked well together on church projects. Nora could feel that Sammie was still a part of her building a good name.

On Saturday, in the forenoon, Verna and Nora hiked up into the hollow to find arbutus and made wreathes and brought them to the cemetery. Now that it was Spring, the ground was thawed enough to dig Sammie's grave. It was poignant but not overly sorrowful for Nora. She firmly believed that if anyone could make it to heaven, it would be Sammie, and that his body was just that, a body. Her heart would forever be connected to Sammie's soul and didn't care much that the ground had been too frozen to actually bury Sammie's body that winter. She knew that he would be kept frozen in his casket in a special "dead house" behind the undertaker's house. It all sounded rather morbid, but she had grown up with such things.

There was no special service, just Verna and Nora standing by the casket. She rested her hand on the casket and sighed deeply. *Well, Sammie we certainly made a go of it together here in White Crikk.* She smiled. Verna was in tears. *Thank God that you are not suffering any longer. I want you to know that I'm a thorough mess because of you, and you know how much I hate a mess. I am eternally grateful God chose me to be by your side for the last 4 years. I can't imagine that God wanted you to go through TB alone.* Verna handed her a large bouquet of flowers to lay atop the casket as the men slowly and respectfully lowered it into the ground.

Seeing the casket brought up more emotions than Nora expected, and remembering Sister Mary Pat's words, she just let the tears flow even though reticence was the norm of the day. Her tears had more to do with the complete beauty of their relationship than sorrow. The gravediggers asked Nora if she wanted to toss the first handful of dirt onto the casket. She wasn't prepared for that. She asked Verna to take a handful of dirt too and they would both do it together. It felt oddly symbolic that she was putting Sammie to rest when her heart was healing and moving from one tender chapter in her life to another. The men finished covering the grave, neatly raked the dirt, then left quietly. Verna and Nora laid their sweet smelling wreathes over the bare dirt and placed new flower pots on either side of the headstone. It was sobering to see her name and birthdate engraved in the headstone.

"We walk this earth but once," she said, "so we better do our best."

Mama Andrew had a hot dinner waiting for them back home. Before they sat down to eat, Nora hugged Andrew and let her tears flow. He knew and understood her but had lost all verbal abilities. It was a terrible sad story and Nora knew that he would spend the rest of his life in this state. Nora was learning to accept that deep sadness a part of life as much as happiness and that, at some level, she had always judged people harshly for having sadness and trauma in their lives. She had a new respect for sadness and terrible circumstances whether brought on by poor decisions or otherwise. Nora announced that she was ready to give away Sammie's clothes. And asked everyone who they thought was built like him. The clear winner was King, the fishmonger. Nora would leave a few boxes of Sammie's clothes on his doorstep. She felt good about it.

But Nora held back a few items. She gave Sammie's favorite sweater and pocket watch to Will and reminded him how much he meant to Sammie. He gave her a hug. And she gave Sammie's overcoat and radio to Pa Telford.

"Sammie said it was the warmest coat on the planet and everyone knew how much he loved his radio. It helped him stay connected with the world even when he was leaving it."

Pa's eyes filled with tears, and he gave Nora a grateful hug.

Henry and Ray had helped so much in every way that she wondered how she could repay them. She chose to leave cash under their pillows. They knew it was her way of showing Sammie's endless gratitude for them.

April 24, 1925 was the annual Arbor Day Frankfort Roast at Jermain Hall, which Nora helped arrange. She learned that helping in the kitchen was always the best way to help the time go by. It kept her mind occupied and it gave those she was helping something to talk about. Nora realized that she had had her entire life planned out with Sammie: marriage, farm, children, building a good name, growing old together. She didn't just lose Sammie; she lost her whole life plan. She started courting Sammie right out of high school. She didn't know who she was without Sammie. She realized that it was time for her to build her own life now. Mr. Perry came through the line at the Frankfort Roast, and he asked her if she would be having a garden this Spring? He would be happy to prepare it for her. She paused for a moment to think. *Even though it's a lot of work, I do love having a garden, and the way she and Sammie combined notes on planting it worked very well.*

Her reply, "Well, only if you'll let me bake you a pie. I think Mason and Leah will let me have a garden back at the farm."

She was pleased when Administrator Walt Hunt stopped by the school asked her to keep her school building again for another year. After the hardest year of her life, she received that as an accomplishment. She took her Kodak camera out of her desk and took pictures that day until the film ran out. She took her film to the drug store along with all the undeveloped films she had rolling around on her dresser. She had not had the time nor the will to gather up those films. She didn't even know where some of them came from. She imagined that some of the undeveloped roles were two years old. She hoped they were still good. She stopped at Lurie's and bought two large maroon photo albums and couldn't wait for her 10 rolls of photos to be developed and returned in the mail.

On May 25, it would have been Sammie's 27th birthday. She was teaching when Verna came running into the school. At first, she thought there was an emergency, but she saw that she was carrying mail. All of her developed photos including two mystery rolls film that she suspected had been taken by Sammie.

"Oh, my lands!" she said.

Her students were more eager than she was to see the photographs, which they considered modern technology. Mrs. Telford had them sit in a circle as she instructed students how to hold the photographs from the edges. She and Verna and all of her students sat on the floor and passed the photos around. There were photos of Sammie from Ray Brook, wedding photos, photos from the Nichol's property, photos of their animals, photos of Andrew from before his head injury, and, best of all, photos of Sammie that Nora had taken on their Sunday afternoon drives. In that moment, as Nora told the stories behind the photos, often with tears in her eyes, she and her students knew that they had formed a special bond. *What a gift on Sammie's birthday!*

Julia said, "Momma always says that we often receive a special blessing on the birthday of our deceased loved ones." Nora just smiled with happy tears.

Nora said, "Verna, you're going to have to help me get these photos into my new photo albums this weekend."

Once every photo had been viewed and returned, she felt blessed beyond measure and needed to pass that blessing along. Nora had students pack up their books early and declared May 25 as forever 'Kick the Can Day'. The students erupted with joy and Nora and Verna both went out and played kick the can with her students for the rest of the afternoon. They worked up a good sweat and then collapsed in the shade to enjoy the breeze. Nora got a bucket and ladle and grabbed onto the pitcher pump handle to work the water up from the school's cistern. As the students took turns taking a refreshing drink of cool water, Nora knew that she was in the exact right place. No question. Verna could see it also. Her students were lying in the shade, using each other as pillows, and running out the clock at the end of the school day. One of the little girls rested her head on Julia's lap. One of the boys asked Mrs. Telford to dump water over his overheated head. Nora smiled and dipped a ladle full of water. He put his head down and closed his eyes and waited for the cool water on his head. But Nora, to the surprise of all, dumped the entire bucket of water over him. Kick the Can day had now become Water Fight Day! The parents were quite confused as they collected their soaking wet children.

On that hot Memorial Day Weekend, Nora, Henry, Ray, and many others were baptized at the White Creek swimmin' hole and officially joined the White Creek Baptist Church. Spirituality, for Nora wasn't a cure for her pain, but it was a way to reconnect with herself and everyone else she loved. She realized that she was responsible for her own health, but she wasn't to blame for Sammie's illness, nor was he. Nora was baptized to show that she had made her peace with God, Henry and Ray joined the church because they thought it made their dating resume look better. Henry invited Elizabeth to church that day, and Ray invited his new sweetheart, Etta. Sarah was there with Howard and Andrew and her new baby. Not much is known about Howard attending the bands, but Sarah and Howard did attend the Embury Methodist Church regularly.

There was always a big church picnic after a baptism with swimming and games. There was an exceptional turnout for this church picnic. At first, Nora thought it was a show of solidarity for all she had been through. But she quickly realized that the numbers were out of proportion with lots of young men. The boys were just there to see the well-endowed Nellie Zehr get baptized so they could see her come up out of the water in a wet baptismal robe, which were just the old choir robes repurposed. *I will never understand boys and boobs. Whatever it is, poor Sammie certainly got the raw end of the deal with my flat chest!*

Henry gave Nora a hug and said, "It's good to see you back to your old self."

Nora thought for a bit. She was happy with her *new* self.

Papa Seth made a rare church appearance and helped celebrate with a bushel basket of popcorn on the cob to share. He brought his wire basket popper for those who wanted to shell their popcorn. Others made a large tin foil pouch and put the whole cob inside it. All you needed was an opening in the pouch for a stick to shake it. Nora had gathered newspapers and showed the kids how to make cone cups for the popcorn. It was the perfect after-swimming snack.

"Homegrown popcorn with homemade butter on a beautiful day. Life doesn't get better this," he said.

Back at the farm, springtime meant plowing and planting. Nora understood how much work farming was and she wanted to help. When it was time to plant potatoes, she put herself to work cutting up all the seed potatoes so the boys could plant them. She then went over to Pa Telford's to do the same. She and Fremont stood at the kitchen sink and cut an acre's worth of seed potatoes.

"What do you get out of church?" he asked her.

"Well, that's a good question. I wonder myself sometimes."

"So why do you go when there are so many other things you could be doing?"

"I find that I like doing repetitive things. While my hands and feet are busy, I find that my mind is free to hear from God. Walking, laundry, dishes, knitting, cutting seed potatoes, and going to church… all repetitive things that bring me peace even though they would be tedious to some, but you know how much I need peace! You probably experience the same thing when you're outdoors going back and forth over a field you're planting or when you milk cows every day or when you go out into the woods to gather running ground pine for the church decorating at Christmas time."

Nora got a call from the jeweler that her locket was ready. She and Verna went down to the Falls immediately to pick it up. Nora loved it. It was so much more beautiful than she imagined. Verna helped her put it on. She was now able to keep Sammie's memory with her wherever she went.

After prayer meeting one night, the ladies in the Missionary Society asked Nora if she would help them organize a Pound Party for Rev. Manning. He wasn't paid very much, so every June, the congregation showed their appreciation by throwing a party bringing all types of "food by the pound" to give to his family. Nora found that her eye for detail helped her organize an event just as easy as she could whip up an apple pie. She could feel herself taking the next right step.

One success led to another. Her head wasn't just above water, but her soul was water skiing! She was then asked to keep the books for the Cambridge Fair with committee meetings over in Gannon's Grove and met many fine people. It was the perfect thing to keep her busy during the summer months. Her last entry in her diary was in August: *Delivered the books to the Fair Committee.*

Nora kept serving the White Creek community that she loved so much and wherever else she was needed. She continued to be-at-the-ready to assist Florence with births and various nursing duties. She helped her Papa and Pa Telford with anything she could handle on the farm from running errands to nursing baby animals and feeding the livestock. She gave up on wearing a dress while she did her chores and wore pants while she worked, to which the Biddle Bunch gave the nod of approval. She loved investing in her students in her little one-room school house. There was no denying it; she was woven into the fabric of the town for good and people continued to admire her courage and grit.

She found herself singing Sir Harry Lauder's Keep Right On to the End of the Road as her song of inspiration. She experienced her version of Americanism through her White Creek friends, neighbors, and even strangers who were always ready to lend a hand. Nora's doorstep became a favorite place for people to drop encouraging surprises for her; a basket of fruit from one family, a roasted chicken and potatoes from another, and on and on the list went for months and months. Nora learned that accepting help graciously with a Thank You note built a good name for someone just as much as helping others herself. True connection was key. You build a good name by taking care of yourself, taking the next right step, and playing the cards life dealt you. *You change the world by making your bed.* Life wasn't looking like she once thought it would, but she was enjoying the ride she was on, nonetheless.

Nora realized that serving others kept her humble and was constantly baking for fundraisers at Jermain Hall. She organized a baby shower for Leah and Mason at the Jermain Hall. She invited Sister Mary Pat and Anna Robertson to attend. Mason and Leah were excellent tenants and Nora was truly happy for them. Nora's joy had returned with her acceptance of Sammie's passing. She was grateful that she was able to be with Sammie through his illness and death.

People still walked up to her and asked how she was doing.

"I am grateful that God chose me to be Sammie's partner through TB. Can you imagine if he had to go through all of that alone?" she would ask people.

Epilogue

You may be asking, *how can this book be written by Nora's grandson if she never had children with Sammie?* Part of Nora's response to her terrible grief was to fit all of her photos into those two large maroon photo albums which she kept with Sammie's diaries. She started keeping her own diary in 1925 which helped greatly in her healing and it also let's us know how life-after-Sammie unfolded for her. She continued to teach and go to church and bake pies for Jermain Hall social events. One afternoon in 1927, about two years after Sammie's death, Fremont Meerwarth arrived at Nora's school house and tied his horse to the old hitching post. The children were all playing outside, and Nora was sitting in the doorway.

"What's the news?" asked Nora.

And in front of all the children playing in the yard, he replied, "Well the only news I have is an invitation. I'm wondering if you're free this Friday to go see that new war picture. It's a 'talkie' playing over in Bennington."

The children, even the boys, all got quiet and ran over to see what she would say.

"Well, even though your presence here as a single man could make the Board send me down the road, I think Friday might work out just fine."

The children cheered with joy, and she and Fremont laughed.

Nora added, "But you'll have to play Kick the Can until the bell rings."

The children screamed with delight. Fremont agreed and played fiercely. And that, they say, is how the rest of the story goes. Nora knew she was wise to ignore the disapproving looks of the biddies who thought that 2 years was much too short a time for her to grieve Sammie's death. *There will always be naysayers who don't have anything better to do. They're just looking for ways to find fault with others to make themselves feel better. They should be pitied that their lives are so empty.* When someone dies, their spouse's mourning is so intense, that they're often ready to move on long before anyone else is.

Nora and Fremont continued courting and eventually fell in love. A year later, they were married. She found out later that when Sammie was very sick, he told Pa and Will to make sure Nora got married again. Fremont was their first choice. They encouraged him to ask Nora out on a date. Fremont Meerwarth, the young farmer from State Line Road in White Creek and Sergeant of the 310 Infantry whose stepfather sold the farm out from under him while he was away at war, was playing the cards life had dealt him. He and Nora found out that they made an excellent pair. They had each been building a good name for themselves as individuals, and now they were building a good name for themselves as a family.

Mason and Leah moved to a farm down the road in White Creek and Nora and Fremont built their life together back on the Nichol's property and ran their own farm, raised three beautiful children, and even expanded the farm to include two additional smaller farms, one to the east and one to the west, (one for each son) and they built a good name for themselves right there in Post Corners in the middle of White Creek for the rest of their lives.

Anna Marie Robertson, known now as Grandma Moses, eventually started creating magical paintings of local landscapes and events at age 77. She became world renown for her artwork; some of which featured scenes of bucolic White Creek, Eagle Bridge, and Hoosick Falls. Fremont's brother, my uncle Peter Meerwarth (my namesake) had a daughter who was an art major in college and Grandma Nora made the connection so that she could study art with Grandma Moses.

Henry and Elizabeth were married and lived up on Lincoln Hill Road. The story in our family that was that Nora had to call before she stopped by to visit because she once brought food to them, and they were having sex in the living room while she was ringing their doorbell.

Andrew Evers never did recover. He lived to be an old man, but his life was incredibly difficult, and Nora continued to keep her eye on him.

I had the privilege of knowing Second Nora Jane Andrew Telford Meerwarth, my grandmother. I was very dedicated to her. Through the diaries, my family's stories, and the stories of other Crikkers, and the firsthand accounts from Julia Niles Rae and Elizabeth Howard, I was able to piece together the stories in this book.

My dad, Fremont Meerwarth, Jr. took over the farm on the Nichol's property before I was born. I grew up there and the tillable land had been expanded to 250 acres and the barn to hold 80 cows.

Mr. Perry still came to plow, disc, and drag grandma's garden every spring and every spring she baked him a "thank you" pie. It wasn't the same Mr. Perry but his son who carried the love and support for a fellow Crikker. Crikkers like to show their support. Talk about it? Not so much.

I once asked her, "Why does Mr. Perry plow your garden when my dad had tractors and a plow?"

She smiled and said, "It's a story that goes back a long way."

It's definitely a White Crikk thing. She no longer needed the help that she did in 1924, but the Perry family had her back right up until she died. White Crikk is like that. Americanism at its best.

Grandpa Fremont died in 1969 when I was 3 years old. He and Nora were married over 40 years. I never got the chance to get to know him very well, but my father had infinite love and respect for him and told me stories that could fill a whole book (and many of those stories not fit for print!). My father visited him on his death bed, and thought he was talking incoherently in his sleep. But he listened closer, and his dying father was praying for the all of the farmers in the area. He knew where their fields were too wet and what problems they had, and he prayed for them by name. The Greatest Generation kept to themselves often and valued their privacy always.

Nora said, "You didn't know that your father prayed like that, did you? He wasn't one for church, but he prayed often for the farmers in White Creek."

My dad, a church man himself, was impressed. Grandma took care of Grandpa until the end. He developed emphysema from smoking, his death certificate read that he died of tuberculosis just like Sammie.

Grandma Nora outlived Fremont by 25 years. She kept herself busy with gardening, keeping her three-acre lawn mowed, and by taking care of people who needed her help medically. She delivered babies and tended to the sick who had no one to watch over them. Some of them younger than her! I remember that she took care of Miss Alice Ashton, who had been the "stern" school nurse when I was little. She had had one of her legs removed. I went to Miss Ashton's house one time to get a ride home from Cambridge with Grandma. And there was Miss Ashton and my Grandma on the front porch laughing hysterically in a very non-school-nurse kind of way.

While Grandma finished up some things, Miss Ashton turned to me and said, "You know, your grandmom is a very special lady, don't you?"

I smiled and agreed. There was no disagreeing with Alice Ashton anyway! I found out later that Grandma worked for $2/hour taking care of people for 15 years and saved just about all of that money, and by the time she died, had quite a little nest egg.

Grandma Nora was a big fan of house magazines and always had a fantasy of having her house featured in a magazine. In 1978, her house and barns were selected to be the setting for a Hallmark Card Commercial. All of White Creek was abuzz with the news that day! She loved entertaining the cast and crew and baked apple pies for them before they left. They needed an old farm truck to be parked next to the house. Grandma's Buick didn't qualify, so Julia loaned her old green farm truck to be used in the commercial. There was a trained Hollywood dogs that was scripted to run through the shot at one point in the commercial. It was quite a cold day and she refused to even step out of their warmed Hollywood crate, so Julia brought her old barn dog who behaved perfectly and was the dog they used in the commercial.

Grandma took great care of her house and barns set perfectly among the fields and hills and woods and streams of White Creek. In 1993, my wife and I had our outdoor wedding reception there complete with wild flowers planted along the field and dancing on the big barn floor. That property continues to be a "thin place" that represents love and acceptance and safety for me.

As a teen, I walked into Grandma's house one afternoon, to find a table full of ladies, all Grandma's age, laughing like there was no tomorrow.

"Come in and let me introduce you, Peter!"

It was the girls from Mrs. Hovey's house at Oneonta Normal. They had planned a road trip reunion meeting up with some of their "Hovey Housemates" from some 50 years earlier. Leah Harrington was there, and I did see those two maroon photo albums out on the table. I never heard my grandmother laugh so hard as she did that day!

Julia told me that when her mother passed, she had been in the hospital for some time with an infection in her leg. When the doctor told her that she was ready to go home, she got so excited that she died of a heart attack! Julia loved her mother, Florence, dearly, but she had to admit the story of her death was humorous. The road they lived in on is now called Niles Road. Julia Niles Rae passed away at age 97 in 2008. I stood and sang AMAZING GRACE at her graveside service in White Creek. I saw Rachel Boot's gravestone there and heard many stories about how tough and resilient Julia had been her whole life. She had married older in life, continued to milk a few cows and goats by hand, and took in four unruly brothers who were in foster care. One of them was at her funeral and spoke about how much she meant to him. Before she passed, however, she took the time to write out her life story, and that document provided many of the details in this book.

Not that long ago, around 2015, my dad (Fremont Meerwarth, Jr. 1935-2018) and I were playing cards at the Nichol's property where he lived his whole life. He told me that he had done some figuring and that there had been a Fremont Meerwarth farmin' it in White Creek for over a hundred years starting with his father born in 1895. He was very proud of that. After I read the diaries, I realized that Sammie's impossible promise to Nora of one hundred years of building a good name in White Creek actually was kept. Not like he thought it would, but it happened, nonetheless. There are still Meerwarths in White Creek building a good name for themselves today. White Creek, especially our little hamlet of Post Corners, is full of people making good names for themselves as teachers, farmers, artists, and all sorts of hard-working professions.

In Grandma's final days, I was helping her in the garden. We had just finished planting snap dragons and as she was teaching my young nephew how to plant broccoli with some well-aged fertilizer I got from the barnyard. The three of us planted 2 long rows of broccoli, (we let my nephew put a scoop of poop under each one) and she pointed out the bed of catnip at the end of the row and she called her kitties to give them some. Cabbage and Swiss chard would be planted next. As I read about companion gardening now, I realize that her garden had always been planted strategically.

Some of the ground needed breaking up and I was surprised at how vigorously Grandma could hoe the garden at 92! The next day, she was cleaning her basement. While she moved the refrigerator to clean behind it, she suddenly felt quite ill. She climbed two flights of stairs up to her bedroom. When she didn't feel any better, she called for my sister to come get her, clean her up, put on a change of clothes, and take her to the hospital. You have to dress up to go to the hospital, apparently. She had had a heart attack and lost 75% of the use of her heart. During that last week of her life, her three children, ten grandchildren, and fourteen great-grandchildren all got to come and play one last hand of cards with her before she passed in her sleep surrounded by a roomful of her family.

Grandma died in June of 1995 and her garden was in full swing. Each of her kids and grandkids came in the cool of the summer evenings and weeded and hoed and harvested the garden as needed. Before we left each night with a bushel basket full of delicious veggies for our families, we would pause to tell Grandma stories. I remember one night when my sister and my cousin, Jean, who has since passed from cancer, sat and talked for an hour about how we were dealing with life and how great it was that a 92-year-old woman would still be feeding her family even after she was gone.

I like to think that the spirits of the saints are still with us. I often look at the portrait of Grandma Nora and Grandpa Fremont that's hanging in my house, and I think that they're with me and they know that I'm writing this book. I think Sammie is happy that someone has been reading his diaries. I picture our loved ones who have passed forming a choir of saints, a band of encouragers prompting us with songs and messages from God's loving heart to ours.

It's 2023, a century after Sammie and Nora's wedding. I visited Sammie Telford's grave at Woodlands Cemetery up in Cambridge. I found their double headstone; one side for him 1898 - 1924 and next to his name was Nora Jane Andrew Telford. October 1, 1902 -. Clearly, in 1924, Nora could see being buried nowhere else but with him. Her name was etched in stone next to Sammie's in Cambridge and in White Creek next to Fremont's. After reading the diaries, I felt as though their relationship needed to be commemorated in stone, so I had her death date, June 12, 1995, engraved on their shared headstone. It felt like a small way to acknowledge and bring closure to their story that had been forgotten by so many.

The road that the Andrew Family lived on is now officially named Andrew Road and it intersects with Telford Road. Ray married his sweetie named Etta and built a house at the end of Andrew Road. I can imagine that our houses and our towns somehow "remember" the things that went on for centuries and the memories come out in different ways. Remember young May Nichols who lost her husband in the Great War? A house close to hers in the tiny town of Greenwich was later rented by composer Walter Kent in the 1940s. He composed I'll Be Home For Christmas. Bing Crosby recorded it, and it became a Top Ten hit. It was written to honor soldiers who desperately wanted to be home for Christmas, "if only in their dreams."

I can imagine the stunning Adirondack Mountain pines soaking up the joys and sorrows of all those who breathed in their air and cured there. In the 1940s, Bella Bartok, though sick with leukemia, isolated himself in Saranac Lake as doctor's thought that he was suffering from TB. He found a new kind of creative energy there and wrote his final orchestral works there including the viola concerto, which was finished by his son in 1990. The first 35 seconds of that piece of music bring me to tears. I believe it is truly inspired by the smell of the pines that absorbed the excruciating pain and despair as well as joy and relief of those who cured in Saranac Lake. Bartok wasn't a terribly religious man, but he was a nature lover and didn't ever hesitate to mention the miraculous order of nature with great reverence. There is God in them there hills.

My wife and I held our outdoor wedding reception at Grandma Nora's house on the 4th of July. I painted the five barns with a fresh coat of red paint to spruce things up. Friends planted wild flowers along the field and around the barns. We cut the cake in what used to be the old ice house and Grandma sat and twirled her locket as she watched us dancing on the barn floor.

Grandma's three children were born in the Cambridge hospital. I was born there and so were our boys. And before we ever knew anything about Samuel Telford, call it auto-suggestion if you will, we had a beautiful bouncing baby boy and named him Sammy.

As a little kid I was having breakfast with Grandma, and I asked if I could see the locket she was wearing. She saw no harm in that and handed it to me. It was much heavier than I expected. While she finished her coffee, I carefully opened it up and saw the clock with a picture of Grandpa Fremont that was cut to fit into the inside cover. Upon further inspection, I found another miniscule latch that opened the back of the locket. From there, I could see the inner workings of the clock and the picture of a different man placed into the back cover.

"Who's that?" I asked.

"Who's who?" she said. She pretended not to know. She didn't even look. She simply said nothing and gently took the locket from me and told me to go play, and I never thought about it again until I read the diaries.

Grandma relayed her few dying wishes to her only daughter, Jane. She told her what dress she wanted to be buried in and that she didn't want to wear underwear for all of eternity (but not to tell anyone). She wanted to be buried next to Fremont in the Center White Creek Cemetery and most of all, she made Aunt Jane promise that she would be buried wearing her treasured locket close to her heart. And Nora's good name was celebrated just as she wished and just as was promised.

Made in the USA
Middletown, DE
04 January 2024

46934614R00166